THE LIFE OF ANCIENT JAPAN

Author of
Mirror, Sword and Jewel
A Study of Japanese Characteristics
[Japan Library Classic Paperbacks, 1997]

THE LIFE OF ANCIENT JAPAN

*Selected Contemporary Texts
Illustrating Social Life and Ideals
Before the Era of Seclusion*

*Edited
with 34 Plates and Introduction*
BY
KURT SINGER

JAPAN
LIBRARY

THE LIFE OF ANCIENT JAPAN
SELECTED CONTEMPORARY TEXTS
ILLUSTRATING SOCIAL LIFE AND IDEALS
BEFORE THE ERA OF SECLUSION

First published in 1939 by
Iwanami Shoten, Tokyo-Kanda

This edition first published 2002 by
JAPAN LIBRARY

*Japan Library is an imprint of Curzon Press Ltd
51A George Street, Richmond, Surrey TW9 1HJ*

British Library Cataloguing in Publication Data
A CIP catalogue entry for this book
is available from the British Library

ISBN 1-903350-01-8

Printed and bound in England by Cromwell Press Ltd, Trowbridge, Wilts.

TABLE OF CONTENTS

Introduction, by Kurt Singer 1

A PROLOGUE

Love Songs From the Ancient Records (Kojiki)
The Wooing of a God 19
Divine Estrangement and Reconciliation 21

YAMATO PERIOD (x—a. d. 592)

Archaic Rule and Conflict (Nihongi)
A Sage Emperor (Nintoku Tennō) 27
An Ordeal 31
Two Sisters 33
A Song-contest 37
Emperor and Local Chiefs 41

ASUKA AND NARA PERIODS (a. d. 592–794)

From the Chronicles of Japan (Nihongi)
New and Old Cults and Gods
  1. Devotion and Demise of Empress Suiko 49
  2. Rain-making: Rites and Results 52
  3. Divine Inspiration 53
Administration and Etiquette under Temmu Tennō ... 56
New Year Festivities 63
Illness and Death of An Emperor 65
The End of A Conspiracy 71
Slaves 73
Flood and Relief 74

CONTENTS

Imperial Edicts of Late Nara Period

1. Discovery of Copper in Eastern Japan 75
2. Ceremony and Music 76
3. Discovery of Gold in Eastern Japan 77
4. On the Death of a Minister 78

HEIAN PERIOD (A. D. 794-1185)

A Governor Travels (From Tosa Diary)

1. The Departure 81
2. Delay 83

Servant Quarter's Tales (From Ochikubo Monogatari)

1. Preparations for a Third Night 86
2. Vengeance 90

A Lady-In-Waiting (From Makura no Soshi)

1. Arrival at Court 96
2. Holiday-Problems 97
3. Table Manners 100
4. Annoying Things 101

The House Beautiful (From Genji Monogatari)

1. On Ladies 105
2. The Festival of Red Leaves 112
3. "Chinese Banquet" 115
4. An Imperial Companion 117
5. Brothers and Sisters, and a Cherry-tree 121

Pages From Murasaki Shikibu's Diary

1. At the Mansion of the Prime Minister 127
2. A State Banquet and its End 129
3. The Queen and her Ladies-in-Waiting.......... 133

A Voyage and A Dream (From Sarashina Diary)

1. A Small Girl Starts for the Capital 135
2. The Widow 141

vi

CONTENTS

KAMAKURA PERIOD (A. D. 1185-1392)

ROMANCE AND CHIVALRY (FROM HEIKE MONOGATARI)
1. Early Dancing Girls 147
2. Autumn Leaves : A Boy Emperor and his Servants... 151
3. The Death of a Poet-Warrior 152
4. An Amazon 154
5. The Beginning of the Final Fight 157

THIS WORLD OF CALAMITIES (FROM HŌJŌKI)
Fire, Famine, Plague and Earthquake........................ 162

AN AESTHETE-RECLUSE (FROM TSUREDZUREGUSA)
The Right Life 171
On Taste 171
Going to the Country Side 172
Sensibility 173
Scene at a Country Temple 173
A Glimpse.. 174
On Accomplishments 174
On Marriage 175

A WORLD OUT OF JOINT
Nijō Gawara no Rakushu 177

ASHIKAGA AND MOMOYAMA PERIODS (A. D. 1392-1568)

THE ACTOR AND HIS PUBLIC (KWANZE SEAMI)
1. On Patrons 181
2. Further Advice to Actors 184

THE CULT OF TEA (SEN RIKYŪ) 186

AN EPILOGUE

DELIVERY (FROM SHUNKWAN)..................................... 193

CONTENTS

SEVEN APPENDICES:
LAWS, RULES AND CUSTOMS

I: THE LAWS OF PRINCE SHŌTOKU 197
II: THE TAIKWA REFORM 203
 1. An Edict against Unlawful Appropriations 203
 2. The Great Edict of A. D. 646 204
 3. Miscellaneous Regulations (of Kōtoku Tennō) 209
III: LAWS CONCERNING MONKS AND NUNS 217
 (FROM THE YŌRŌ-CODE)
IV: THE HŌJŌ-CODE OF JUDICATURE 223
V: THE ASHIKAGA CODE (KEMMU SHIKIMOKU) 256
VI: FEUDAL LAW AND ADMINISTRATION IN SOUTH KYŪSHŪ 265
VII: SOME NOTES ON EARLY JAPANESE MARRIAGE INSTITUTIONS, BY KURT SINGER 279

INTRODUCTION

THERE is scarcely a country, Greece and Italy excepted, on which a greater number of books continues to be written, year by year, than the bow-shaped series of volcanic islands, emerald forests and garden-like fields that faces the eastern edge of the Eurasian continent. If in spite of this, Japan has retained the reputation of being inscrutable, elusive, and even mysterious, the reason ought to be sought in the very nature of this nation rather than in the geographic peculiarities of its environment. For all great nations seem to have wandered and warred till they found a soil congenial to their most profound aspirations, only the weaker tribes being obliged to live where others allowed, and to conform to the dictates of environment. There have been many island states in the history of our globe, from the Greek archipelago, Crete and Sicily to Britain, Ireland, Madagascar and Tahiti, but none of them, not even England, developed and refined that sense of shyness and reserve, that tendency to hide from profane looks and draw fences around themselves which has characterized the Japanese from their earliest days. These qualities may have been strengthened by an atmosphere which seems to delight in enveloping things and men with a humid, though faintly lustrous veil of clouds, mist, and rains. But these external stimuli must have met with similarly directed inclinations of a race of conquerors, essentially aristocratically minded, and therefore opposed to easy familiarity; small groups of warriors perpetually endangered by foreign invasions, actual and potential, and even more by the disruptive forces of their own ambitious kith and kin. These people were scattered over a number of islands, every one of which is

INTRODUCTION

again divided by mountain ranges into a set of island-like districts, and they lived and enjoyed a perilous existence which made them stronger and still more secretive.

Traits and tendencies of this order are in the strictest sense ultimate data of sociological analysis. It has been a far-reaching error of nineteenth century science to believe that any organic structure, in the realm of nature as of social life, could be explained by pointing to those external conditions under which it has grown or decayed. For, if these conditions have been able to strengthen or to limit a specific form of life, the reason must be sought not only in the character of its environment, but also in its own tendencies and structural peculiarities, its entelechy as we may call it with Goethe. The student of social history has to respect these phenomena as religiously as the student of physics has learned, by a long and laborious process, to respect the data of the senses. But even if the sociologist gives up any attempt to transcend the limits set to his enquiry, his field remains appalling—the vast domain stretching between the innermost sphere where a nation wishes to converse with its own gods and demons, undisturbed by intruders not sharing their spiritual life, and the promiscuous and ambiguous surface of everyday life open to all. Much has been done in this intermediate sphere since the first Europeans came to Japan, but still more remains, and in no province of research more than that of social history.

The purpose of the present book is to facilitate these studies, by presenting a co-ordinated number of texts dating from the epochs in which the foundations of Japanese civiization were laid.

It is only seldom observed that knowledge of social and economic conditions and processes is much more difficult to convey than that of literary, artistic, religious or political subjects. The history of poetry, music, sculpture or philosophy, of empires and churches, deal with works, ideas, and deeds which are easily conceived as a whole and which have a strong hold on the imagination of the reader, even infusing him with some feeling of its nature before the task of the writer has begun. It is different with the topics of social sciences. Here, the student has to build up his picture out of a vast mass of small details, handed down in documents and reports, the selection of which has been largely determined not by their intrinsic value but by accidental causes at work throughout the vicissitudes of history. Usually, these sources speak with an uncertain voice, and many of their best teachings are to be gained only by applying indirect methods. Moreover, even if they should allow the creation of something resembling a miniature or a fresco painting, the reader has a right to remain unsatisfied until this picture is shown not only in its static aspects, but in motion. This motion is again of a kind less easy to realize than that of state actions and great spiritual movements, being necessarily slow, ambiguous, complex and elusive. Such difficulties, inherent in the subject matter, should account for the fact that the art of the social and economic historian has been so slow to develop and that masterpieces are still extremely rare: if the names of A. de Tocqueville, Fustel de Coulanges, Sir Henry Maine, Jakob Burckhardt, Sir William Ashley, and Georg Friedrich Knapp are told, very few can be added to the list of classical authors in this domain. It must even be recorded that social science, in progressing along the lines followed during the last generations, is apt to withdraw from, rather than move nearer to the approach made by these classics. Many additions have been made to unwieldy masses of materials unearthed, or discovered in archives, and classified; but

INTRODUCTION

there has been no corresponding growth of synoptic vision and power of plastic representation. Perhaps these dangers are especially great in a country like Japan where the later stages of Buddhist and Confucian traditions have for centuries weakened that sense of the symbolic, which enables men to grasp " the many in the one and the one in the many," and where native scholarship has been for a long time identical with an accumulation of knowledge similar to that of the great polyhistors and antiquarians of the 17th and 18th century in Europe.

Where science fails, however, a more powerful charm may come to aid : poetry and art. Instead, therefore, of giving a colourless or oversimplified summary of general or cultural histories of Japan which are easily accessible to every Western reader and which ought to be consulted by him wherever our texts are compelled to leave blank areas, this introductory volume prefers to present a selection of pages taken from the classical literature of Japan, which accompanied by a number of legal texts and some pictorial illustrations may better aid in giving a living picture of what Japan has been and of the aspirations of her formative epochs.

These fifty odd pieces were selected not for their aesthetic value but in view of the sociological information that they may be able to convey, if it is allowable to define that word in such a way as to include the whole range of studies on Man and the forms of his social existence in all their national and temporal varieties. Some of these pages are chosen as they throw light on ways in which the Japanese in remoter periods felt, thought and behaved. Some may illuminate details of social organization, economic conditions and administration. The most beautiful however may be taken as definitive formulations of standards and norms, moral, religious, aesthetic and sentimental; expressions of the innermost life of a nation which give significance to its existence and justify its greatest aspirations. These standards have not varied since they were first established down to the present day, although the life which has produced them and which has been again moulded and remoulded by them, has sometimes taken a subterranean course, for shorter or longer periods of disorientation.

As in Europe, it is a common characteristic of classical literature in Japan that it depicts not ordinary but festive life, not the dreary sequence of everyday existence of the average man but the culminating events of days of unusual greatness, beauty and tension. It reveals little, if anything, of the methods of life and ways of thinking of peasants and artisans, pedlars and slaves, save only to set off the character and attitudes of the classes who ruled and also set the standards of spiritual life. Such a limitation is perhaps of less consequence in Japan than in most Western countries, ancient and modern. For nowhere have the manners and ideas, the forms of expression and adornment, originally restricted to the highest strata of society—come to be those of men and women living in the most humble stations. The rigours of a social hierarchy, attributing to each his manner of life, his outlook, his privileges and his burdens with the precision of a geometric pattern, have as their counter-part a homogeneity of civilization, attained not by dragging the sublime and the exquisite to the level of the obvious and the commonplace, but permeating even the everyday existence of ordinary men with some of the distinctive qualities of a society of court ladies guided by the most fastidious of tastes and capable of producing prose works which have not lost one grain of their freshness and charm after nine centuries, and of warriors trained in the paradoxes of an agnostic mysticism. Relics and traces of this cultural unity are even to-day omnipresent where the corroding influences of Western civilization have not been permitted to reduce the existence of the urban masses to a state of confusion verging on intellectual and aesthetic anarchy.

*　　*　　*

This small anthology breaks off before the Tokugawa age, which corresponds to the Modern Period in Western history not only chronologically but also in a sociological sense. For a student eager to distinguish between organic forms and conventional masks, or between tectonic elements and subsidiary constructions will easily observe that the apparently " feudal " society of the 17th, 18th and early 19th centuries was in Japan, as in Europe, essentially not feudal but rational, centralised and paternal, co-ordinating a strong bureaucracy with the beginnings of capitalistic transformation. The greatness of the Tokugawa State was to establish a frame-work with a remarkable degree of stability for a civilization with subtle qualities, but all the essential elements of this civilization had been created before that time. While the Modern Period in Europe, thanks to the Renaissance in Italy, France and England and to the late but, as we think, still more incisive epoch of German " Rebirth " in the age of Goethe, produced the greatest assembly of men of genius of modern Europe, the function of the Tokugawa age was not to create but to re-arrange, not to invent but to adapt, not to conquer but to administer. This work of order and proportion, utilization and refinement should not be underrated. It may even come to be considered as a prototype, if ever the West should decide

INTRODUCTION

in the near or remote future to eliminate the elements of unrest and instability, of danger and risk from its social life to the degree that was realized in Japan in the peace and seclusion of the Tokugawa Benevolent Despotism. This is not the place to discuss the question whether Western nations will ever come to such a decision, running contrary, as it seems, to the main current of their history; a history beginning with the ancient and mediaeval cities when they drove out lords and governors not chosen by the free will of the citizens, and leading finally, through a series of similar struggles and fights for emancipation, to the various forms of mass-rule of today. On the other hand, it is, according to an observation of that great sociologist Max Weber, a history in which from the beginning of Western nations and in contrast to the social history of the Mediterranean city-states of the Antiquity, the desire for peace and industrial work seems to have furnished these struggles with their dominant note, leading up (or downward, as some would say) to the ideal of a thoroughly stable state of security and order resembling the organization of the bee hive and the ant hill. The French encyclopedists and their f iends, Diderot as well as Abbé Galiani, were perhaps the first to feel the coming of such ideals and tendencies to power, and they did not fail to remark that this would mean an approximation to Eastern Asiatic forms of living. The interest of Leibniz in things Chinese is well known[1], and Hegel speaks of the organization of government and society in China with a warm note of sympathy, rare in his works. It may be that these tendencies will

[1]. I understand that there is a learned work of Professor Gorai on this problem, of which a translation would certainly be welcome, as well as of that of Professor Goto on the influence of China upon the thought of French encyclopedists. The latter, although originally written in French, is not now accessible to European readers.

INTRODUCTION

find a ready echo in many Western countries in a near future, and that the experiment of the Tokugawa will gain new admirers, who have never been lacking since the days of Engelbert Kaempfer. However, it also should not be forgotten that the age of Iyeyasu and his followers was built on moral and intellectual foundations laid in former ages—an heritage that gave charm, significance and a redeeming grace to a system resembling in fact a human ant hill, sacrificing the individuals to the necessities of a well-ordered group life. And it is this very heritage, the product of the Nara, Heian, Kamakura and Muromachi periods, from the 7th till the 16th centuries, which constitutes, in the eyes of the present writer, the main contribution of Japan to the common fund of human civilization in poetry, art, meditation and all the higher forms of social intercourse and personal refinement.

No reader familiar with the works of European Antiquity and of the Middle Ages can fail to be impressed by the fact (though curiously enough it seems never to have given due weight in books on Japan) that the novels and diaries, the shrine architecture and the mythological traditions, the short and long poems and the texts of the Nō plays, the Shintō rituals (noritō) and the Heike Tales present less difficulty to his understanding than most of the works of the later phases of Japanese history. It is as if those earlier productions were children of a world which was, and is, our own world, separated from our sphere of life by differences which can easily be accounted for by the interplay of well-known geographical and historical factors, but not essentially strange, singular or odd. The realm of the " japonaiserie," the quaint and the all-too-conventional, begins after the passing of the watershed that separates classical and Tokugawa Japan. The best specimens of old Japanese poetry,

INTRODUCTION

to give only one instance, keep a fair balance between the word and the silence which surrounds a poem—an island embedded in an ocean of that which cannot enter human language. It is in the haiku peculiar to the taste of the last centuries that this equilibrium is broken, that the words are used, not on account of their instrinsic value, but as mere stepping stones to the imagination of the hearer, that rhythm is lost and the demarcation line between the poem and riddle is often effaced. It is only during these last centuries that the cult of the simple, the unconventional, the detached, which was the soul of the tea ceremony as understood by its first great masters, has degenerated into a conventional set of rules, the search for curios and an occasion for display. The novels and the plays of the Tokugawa period may offer to the historian a mine of precious information on the customs of the age and an easy playground for non-artistic desires, sentimental, erotic, or intellectual. Scarcely any other type of books affords so many opportunities for weeping, excitement, and curiosity—arranged, it is often argued, with a masterful technique of composition; though I doubt whether this term can be applied where the author seems to have little else in mind than to keep an unruly public interested by all possible means; for these are mostly works of entertainment for those classes which the Shogunate tried to compensate for their political subjection by affording them easy and copious sources of rather elementary pleasures. Where something further and better has crept into these productions, thanks to the nobler instincts of writers and their public, it is the heritage of the Nō and of earlier heroic tales and ballads and it is in fact to the credit of the nation that such a large space was accorded to these ingredients. The townspeople of the Tokugawa period offer the singular spectacle of a growing class of tradesmen

INTRODUCTION

and menials imbued with a decidedly non-bourgeois spirit, especially in Yedo, the residential city of the Shōgun, where even the ordinary citizen tended to rival his feudal masters in prowess, generosity and lavishness, and to resemble, if need be, rather a Don Quixote than a Sancho Panza.

It seems that these observations do not apply without great reservations to Ōsaka, the most flourishing trade centre also of that epoch, a city enjoying a higher degree of self-government than most of the other cities but scarcely determined to use these privileges in the sense in which the European "burghers" jealously guarded and enlarged them by persistent struggles. They relied not on money and mercenary soldiers but gained freedom and power in the only way in which it can be built up, retained and deserved, namely, by equipping armies of well-disciplined men from their own ranks. The Ōsaka merchants, as an interesting page cited in Professor Skene Smith's "Tokugawa-Japan" shows, preferred to follow the opposite way, and to evade even the peaceful exercise of their civic rights to participate in municipal government (which entailed loss of money and time) by living in rented houses and forfeiting thereby their municipal rights. Is it pure accident that this town was the birth-place not only of the most extravagant gourmandise, but also the bunraku (puppet theatre), in which the great episodes of chivalry were transformed into exquisite ornamental displays of colour and movement, handled with uncanny skill and accompanied by the most heart-breaking lamentations, sung on a high-pitch by over-pathetic ballad singers?

I have dwelt on the fundamental differences of the two great divisions of Japanese history at such length, not only because the Japan which the West came to know first was that of late Tokugawa age, and the impressions then gained

INTRODUCTION

have misled foreigners to take the singularities and limitations of that period as characteristic of Japanese civilization in general—but also because this identification seems to underlie the still prevalent view of many Japanese of the recent generations, that this civilization is a dead thing, labelled "feudal" and therefore alien to any real living interest of contemporary men and women. This view seems to me historically wrong, and morally misleading. It serves to foster the idea that the Japanese of to-day and to-morrow are faced with the alternatives, either of becoming satisfied with the traditional forms of thought and sentiment, mores and manners, codified during the last three hundred years, or of turning their back on the whole of their past as something of only antiquarian or emotional interest. This alternative which is a pseudo-antithesis, has already been overcome in the field of politics by the Meiji Restoration. A similar movement directed towards the revival of a past more remote, but also richer in human values, has led to the revivification of the poetry of the Nara period, handed down in the oldest anthology of Japanese poetry, the Manyōshū, against those schools that believe the later collections to hold in them the quintessence of Japanese poetry. The fact that during the last years, the Nō has apparently begun to regain the central place which it is destined to hold in the spiritual culture of the country, may be taken as a similar symptom, but there still seems a long way to travel until the real proportions and values of the Japanese past have been realized. It is easy to understand that young Japanese still find Balzac more nutritive than Bakin, Shakespeare rather than Chikamatsu and Goethe than Bashō, and it is certainly not to be expected or hoped, that the passionate desire to assimilate as much of the best of Western culture as the potentialities of their souls allow, should be allowed to cool. But the equipoise of their souls will remain disturbed until they realize what hidden treasures in their own tradition are still awaiting rediscovery or rebirth; and that the works of their classic age, with their unique blending of " Ursprünglichkeit " and " Vornehmheit ", (the " primitive " and the " distinguished " are the nearest English terms, but there seem to be no clear and direct equivalents) will have to serve as beacons in every new adventure in spiritual seafaring. They indicate the best of which the Japanese soul has proved to be capable, and her essential and unique note in the chorus of nations.

If too much temerity should be ascribed to a foreign author speaking with such a determination on matters which the nation must decide for itself, it may be permissible to reply that some objects require to be seen from a great distance, and they are certainly not the smallest and least important. Perhaps this short and incomplete anthology, assembling lens-like, many rays as in a burning-point, may serve to strengthen and to clarify a movement already well under way, but sometimes apt to lose its true bearings; the movement of the Japanese mind swinging, often vehemently, from one extreme to the other, establishing equilibrium by alternative displacements of centres of gravity—a way not so irrational as dogmatic believers in abstract principles are inclined to think, for it is exactly the way in which man walks.

* * *

The main purpose of the present volume is introductory. No selection of this kind if confined to moderate dimensions can be exhaustive, and an element or arbitrariness necessarily enters any choice between texts of such varied significance. But the editor entertains some hope that the book

INTRODUCTION

will be helpful both to the general reader who wishes to know more of the actual life of those epochs which have produced poems, novels, paintings and works of decorative arts that appear so charming to many refined minds of the West; and to the student of social and economic history who wishes to see the shadowy classifications of social science taking on flesh and blood, and to realize those cultural values and achievements which alone justify those labours, worries and sufferings of peoples, which form the main theme of the sociologist's studies.

The book includes only passages taken from works that have already found adequate English translators. The more exacting reader is therefore enabled without difficulty to fit every fragment in which he is interested back into its original context. The very few explanatory notes added are mostly from the pen of the translators themselves; the standard works of James Murdoch, Sir George Sansom, Professor Anesaki, Professor Honjō, Ass.-Prof. Tsuchiya and others are now easily available to English-reading students, and will have to be consulted, chapter by chapter, by any reader with scholarly inclinations.

As there is, to my knowledge, no English anthology of Japanese prose, the book may, until a counterpart to Professor Révon's " Anthologie de la Littérature Japonaise " is published, perhaps be treated as a kind of first approximation to such a volume, the greater number of texts being accessible to readers without specific sociological leanings. Materials of a more technical character have been relegated to a small number of appendices. These will appeal mostly to historians and men of the legal profession, but they ought to convey to the general reader also some important hints about the ways of living and thinking of men known to him from the literary side alone. He must be warned,

INTRODUCTION

however, not to take for granted that every paragraph of these laws and edicts was always strictly enforced. Many of them may have never emerged from, or quickly slided back into, the limbo of pious postulates and dreamy intentions.

Though this is a book of small compass and limited aspirations, it could never have come into existence without the collaboration, assistance and consent of quite a number of persons and institutions, to whom the editor feels it a most agreeable duty to express his gratitude as he takes leave of the work—begun, some years ago, in the meditative solitude of Kamakura, after retiring from his guest-professorship at the Tokio Imperial University, and now concluded in the spare moments of leisure afforded by his new scholastic duties in north-eastern Japan. He feels deeply obliged to Professor K. Doi, Professor R. Fukui and Professor Muraoka, of the Department of Law and Literature of Tohoku Imperial University, who never tired of giving advice, answering questions and putting materials at his disposal; to Professor N. Skene Smith, until recently of the Tokio University of Commerce, in collaboration with whom was begun a series of publications on Japanese economic and social history[1] to which the present volume was intended to serve as a " Prelude," and who kindly undertook to revise the English of this Introduction and of the last Appendix; to the Kokusai Bunka Shinkokai (Society for International Cultural Relations) in Tokio, which relieved the publisher from the burden of financing the illustrations, and which

1. Some of these volumes are now being published in the Transactions of the Asiatic Society of Japan. The reader may find the answer to many questions suggested by the present volume in the translation of Mr. Tsuchiya's Outline of Japanese Economic History, edited there with illustrations and notes by this writer, and also in Professor Skene Smith's Tokugawa Japan of which the first volume has just been published in that series.

INTRODUCTION

also lent technical help at various occasions; to many authors and publishers who readily gave permission to include passages still under copyright (their names being indicated at the end of every passage) ; and to the owners of paintings reproduced in the illustrations (the names of which are given in the List of Plates).

The problems of selecting and reproducing pictorial evidence of an age which is mainly portrayed on scrolls and folding screens owned by private collectors of fastidious taste, were especially great. They would never have been solved if Professor Fukui had not come to my succour in the most amiable manner, directing my attention to rare works in which I might find what I had been seeking from an angle quite alien to his own studies ; putting at my disposal his precious collection of original photographs and the technical facilities of his Seminary ; and allowing me to include in the text of my List of Plates some data based on his unquestioned authority in the History of Japanese Art.

But the Editor alone has been responsible for the final decision as to which pictures were to be included in this small gallery of scenes showing types of persons in every station and walk of life ; and in making this decision he had in some cases to sacrifice purely artistic criteria for significant traits of a more material order. For such is the fate of the sociologist. If this should seem a crime against the Spirit of Art, the Editor hopes he has made atonement by reproducing (for the first time in a book accessible to the public) some of the freest creations of the Japanese mind : the bold variations of Sōtatsu on themes of the old Ise Monogatari, made on the threshold of a later bleaker world, the Tokugawa Age. They recall the innermost life of Ancient Japan with a magica command and simple grandeur reminiscent,

INTRODUCTION

as no other work of Japanese art or literature, of Shakespeare's sovereign power in evoking the soul and spirit of a Past that through his Vision has become timeless.

* * *

Not the least obligation the Editor has to acknowledge is to the Japanese houses in which he has lived during a number of years and which have taught him more of the style and spirit of Japanese life than books or social experiences :—austere and graceful, unadorned and refined, inviting to that meditation from which action springs and to which it returns in equal serenity after victory or defeat ; all-open to air and wind, and yet hermetically centered in its own silent life ; opposing to storms and shocks only its flexibility, disdaining too much precaution against the manifold dangers of this fleeting world of dream and death ; ready to emerge from every night of terrors unchanged in virginal freshness : an abode for poet-warriors and wandering hermits of cloud-like spirit and heart indomitable.

K. S.

A PROLOGUE

LOVE SONGS FROM THE ANCIENT RECORDS

I

The Wooing of a God

THIS Deity-of-Eight-Thousand-Spears,[1] when he went forth to woo the Princess of Nuna-kaha in the land of Koshi,[2] on arriving at the house of the Princess of Nunakaha sang, saying:

> (I) *His Augustness the Deity-of-Eight*
> *Thousand-Spears, having been unable to*
> *find a spouse in the Land of the Eight*
> *Islands, and having heard that in the*
> *far-off Land of Koshi there is a wise*
> *maiden, having heard that there is a*
> *beauteous maiden, I am standing (here)*
> *to truly woo her, I am going backwards*
> *and forwards to woo her. Without having*
> *yet untied even the cord of my sword,*
> *without having yet untied even my veil,*
> *I push back the plank-door shut by the*
> *maiden; while I am standing (here), I*
> *pull it forward. While I am standing*
> *(here), the nuye sings upon the green*
> *mountain, and (the voice of) the true*
> *bird of the moor, the pheasant, resounds;*

1. The Great God of Izumo, commonly called Ōkuni-nushi, Great-Land-Master.—Ed.
2. In north-west Japan.—Ed.

LOVE SONGS FROM THE ANCIENT RECORDS

*the bird of the yard, the cock, crows.
Oh! the pity that (the) birds should sing!
Oh! these birds! Would that I could beat
them till they were sick! Oh! swiftly-
flying heaven racing messenger, the
tradition of the thing, too, this!*

Then the Princess of Nuna-kaha, without opening the door, sang from the inside saying:—

*Thine Augustness the Deity-of-Eight-
Thousand-Spears! Being a maiden like
a drooping plant, my heart is just a
bird on a sand-bank by the shore; it
will now indeed be a dotterel. Afterwards it will be a gentle bird; so as
for thy life, do not deign to die. Oh!
swiftly-flying heaven racing messenger!
the tradition of the thing, too, this!*

(Second Song of the Princess)

*When the sun shall hide behind the
green mountains, in the night (black
as) the true jewels of the moor will I
come forth. Coming radiant with smiles
like the morning sun, (thine) arms
white as rope of paper-mulberry-bark
shall softly pat (my) breast soft as
the melting snow; and patting (each
other) interlaced, stretching out and
pillowing (ourselves) on (each other's)
jewel-arms,—true jewel-arms—and with
outstretched legs, will we sleep. So
speak not too lovingly, Thine Augustness*

> *the Deity-of-Eight-Thousand-Spears! The tradition of the thing, too, this!*

Quamobrem ea nocte non coierunt, sed sequentis diei nocte auguste coierunt.

II

Divine Estrangement and Reconciliation

AGAIN this Deity's Chief Empress, Her Augustness the Forward-Princess, was very jealous. So the Deity her husband, being distressed, was about to go up from Izumo to the Land of Yamato; and as he stood attired, with one august hand on the saddle of his august horse and one august foot in the august stirrup, he sang, saying:

> *When I take and attire myself so carefully in my august garments black as the true jewels of the moor, and, like the birds of the offing, look at my breast,—though I raise my fins, (I say that) these are not good, and cast them off on the waves on the beach. When I take and attire myself so carefully in my august garments green as the kingfisher, and, like the birds of the offing, look at my breast,—though I raise my fins, (I say that) these, too, are not good, and cast them off on the beach. When I take and attire myself so carefully in my raiment dyed in the sap of the dye-tree, the pounded madder sought in the mountain fields, and, like the birds of the offing,*

> *look at my breast,—though I raise my*
> *fins, (I say that) they are good. My*
> *dear younger sister, Thine Augustness!*
> *Though thou say that thou will not*
> *weep,—if like the flocking birds, I*
> *flock and depart, if, like led birds,*
> *I am led away and depart, thou wilt*
> *hang down thy head like a single eulalia*
> *upon the mountain and thy weeping shall*
> *indeed rise as the mist of the morning*
> *shower. Thine Augustness (my) spouse*
> *like the young herbs! The tradition of*
> *the thing, too, this!"*

Then his Empress, taking a great august liquor-cup, and drawing near and offering it to him, sang, saying :—

> *Oh! Thine Augustness the Deity-of-Eight*
> *Thousand-Spears! (Thou), my (dear)*
> *Master-of-the Great Land indeed, being a*
> *man, probably has on the various island-*
> *headlands that thou seest, and on every*
> *beach-headland that thou lookest, a wife*
> *like the young herbs. But as for me,*
> *alas! being a woman, I have no man except*
> *thee; I have no spouse except thee. Be-*
> *neath the fluttering of the ornamented*
> *fence, beneath the rustling of the cloth*
> *coverlet, (thine) arms white as rope of*
> *paper-mulberry bark softly patting (my)*
> *breast soft as the melting snow, and*
> *patting (each other) interlaced, stretch-*
> *ing out and pillowing (ourselves) on*
> *(each other's arms),—true jewel-arms, and*

DIVINE ESTRANGEMENT AND RECONCILIATION

*with out-stretched legs, will we sleep.
Lift up the luxuriant august liquor!*

She having thus sung, they at once pledged (each other) by the cup with (their hands) on (each other's) necks, and are at rest till the present time. These are called divine words.

From: "Kojiki," or "Records of Ancient Matters" (712 A. D.). Translation by Professor Basil Hall Chamberlain. Transactions of the Asiatic Society of Japan, Supplement to Vol. X (1882). Second Edition, J. L. Thompson & Co. (Retail) Ltd., Kobe, 1932.

YAMATO PERIOD
(X—A. D. 592)

ARCHAIC RULE AND CONFLICT
Chronicles of Japan (Nihongi)
A Sage Emperor (Nintoku Tennō)

[A. D. 319[1]]

7TH year, Summer, 4th month, 1st day. The Emperor was on his tower, and looking far and wide, saw smoke arising plentifully. On this day he addressed the Empress saying :—" We are now prosperous. What can there be to grieve for?" The Empress answered and said :— " What dost thou mean by prosperity?" The Emperor said :—" It is doubtless when the smoke fills the land, and the people freely attain to wealth." The Empress went on to say :—" The Palace enclosure is crumbling down, and there are no means of repairing it ; the buildings are dilapidated so that the coverlets are exposed. Can this be called prosperity?" The Emperor said :—" When Heaven establishes a Prince, it is for the sake of the people. The Prince must therefore make the people the foundation. For this reason the wise sovereigns of antiquity, if a single one of their subjects was cold and starving, cast the responsibility on themselves. Now the people's prosperity is none other than Our prosperity. There is no such thing as the people's being prosperous and yet the Prince in poverty."[2]

Autumn, 8th month, 9th day. For the Imperial Prince

---

1. The dates put here in brackets are based on official chronology. According to Professor Wedemeyer, Nintoku Tennō reigned in the first half of the 5th century.—Ed.

2. This whole episode is the composition of some one well acquainted with Chinese literature. The sentiments are throughout characteristically Chinese, and in several cases whole sentences are copied verbatim from Chinese works.—A.

Ohine Izaho-wake there was established the Mibu Be,[1] and again for the Empress there was established the Katsuraki Be.[2]

9th month. The provinces, without exception, petitioned, saying :—" Three years have now elasped since forced labour was altogether remitted. The Palace buildings have therefore become decayed, and the Treasury empty. The black-headed people have now abundance, and remnants are not picked up. Therefore in the villages there are no men without wives or women without husbands, in the houses there is store of spare provisions. If at such a time there was no payment of taxes with which to repair the Palace buildings, we fear that we should incur guilt in the sight of Heaven." The Emperor, however, continued to be patient, and would not grant their petition.

[A. D. 322]

10th year, Winter, 10th month. Forced labour for the building of a Palace was imposed for the first time. Hereupon the people, without superintendence, supporting the aged and leading by the hand the young, transported timber, carried baskets[3] on their backs, and worked their hardest without distinction of night or day, vying with one another in the construction. In this manner, ere long the Palace buildings were every one completed. Therefore up to the present day he is styled the Sage Emperor.

1. This Be is also called the Nibu Be. There are several places in Japan of this name. It was originally the group of peasants whose duty it was to provide wet nurses, etc., for infant princes.—A.

2. The Kojiki says that these two Be were instituted as " miodai " of the Prince and the Empress, i.e. in order to perpetuate their memory, the Be in such cases taking the name of the person or of his or her residence. The last explanation might apply to the Empress, but it is not clear how the name of Mibu could perpetuate the memory of this Prince.—A.

3. Of earth.—A.

A SAGE EMPEROR

[A. D. 323]

11th year, Summer, 4th month, 16th day. The Emperor commanded his ministers, saying :—" Viewing this land, the moors and marshes extend far and wide, and the cultivated fields are few and rare. Moreover, the river waters spread out to each side, so that the lower streams flow sluggishly. Should there happen to be continuous rains, the tide from the sea flows up against them so that one may ride in boats through the villages: and the highways, too, are covered with mud. Therefore do ye Our ministers examine this together, and having ascertained the source of the divergence, make a channel for them to the sea, and, staying the contrary flow (of the tide), preserve the fields and houses."

Winter, 10th month. The plain north of the Palace was excavated, and the water from the south diverted into the Western Sea. Therefore that water was called by the name Hori-ye.[1]

Moreover, in order to prevent the overflowing of the Northern river the Mamuta embankment was constructed which gave way and could not be stopped up. Then the Emperor had a dream in which he was admonished by a God, saying :—" There is a man of Musashi named Koha-kubi[2] and a man of Kahachi named Koromo no ko,[3] the Muraji of Mamuta. Let these two men be sacrificed to the River-God, and thou wilt surely be enabled to close the gaps." So he sought for these two men, and having found them, sacrificed them to the River-God. Hereupon Koha-Kubi wept and lamented, and plunging into the

1. Excavated estuary, or canal.—A.
2. Strong-neck.—A.
3. Garment-child. These are personal names. Such names are in the original put after titles, but I have reversed this order in accordance with European practice.—A.

water, died. So that embankment was completed. Koromo no ko, however, took two whole calabashes, and standing over the water which could not be dammed, plunged the two calabashes into the mid-stream and prayed, saying :—" O thou River-God, who hast sent the curse (to remove which) I have now come hither as a sacrifice. If thou dost persist in thy desire to have me, sink these calabashes and let them not rise to the surface. Then shall I know that thou art a true God, and will enter the water of my own accord. But if thou canst not sink the calabashes, I shall, of course, know that thou art a false God, for whom, why should I spend my life in vain?" Hereupon a whirlwind arose suddenly which drew with it the calabashes and tried to submerge them into the water. But the calabashes, dancing on the waves, would not sink, and floated far away over the wide waters. In this way that embankment was completed, although Koromo no ko did not die. Accordingly Koromo no ko's cleverness saved his life. Therefore the men of that time gave a name to these two places, calling them "Kohakubi's Gap" and Koromo no ko's Gap."

This year men of Silla[1] came to the Court with tribute, and were made to labour at this public work.

[A. D. 324]

12th year, Autumn, 7th month, 3rd day. The Land of Koryö sent tribute of iron shields and iron targets.

Winter, 10th month. The Great Canal was dug in the district of Kurikuma in Yamashiro for the irrigation of ricefields. By this means the peasants of that district had always years of abundance.

---

1. A kingdom in South-Eastern Korea, usually hostile to Japan.—Ed.

[A. D. 325]

13th year, Autumn, 9th month. Now for the first time official granaries were established at Mamuta. The Usume[1] Be was accordingly instituted.

Winter, 10th month. The Pond of Wani[2] was made. In the same month the Yokono Embankment was constructed.

[A. D. 326]

14the year, Winter, 11th month. A bridge was made at the Wikahi ferry. It was this place which was called Wo-bashi.[3] In this year a highway was constructed and laid down within the capital from the South Gate extending in a straight line as far as the village of Tajihi. Moreover, a great canal was dug in Konku[4] by which the water of the Ishikaha River was brought to irrigate the four waste plains of Upper Suzuka and Lower Suzuka, Upper Toyora and Lower Toyora. By bringing these into cultivation there were gained more than 40,000 K'iüng[5] of rice-land. Therefore the peasants of those places enjoyed abundance, and there was no longer the plague of bad years.

An Ordeal

[A. D. 415]

4th year, Autumn, 9th month, 9th day. The Emperor[6] made a decree, saying :—" In most ancient times, good government consisted in the subjects having each one his

---

1. According to Aston : millers. In fact : rice-hullers.—Ed.
2. In Kahachi.—A.
3. In Kahachi.—A.
4. In Kahachi.—A.
5. A Chinese measure of land equal to 100 mo, or more than fifteen English acres. This exact number of K'iüng occurs in a Chinese book of the Han period as the extent of land reclaimed by a similar operation.—A.
6. Ingiō-Tennō. He reigned according to Wedemeyer 438-454.—Ed.

ARCHAIC RULE AND CONFLICT

proper place, and in names[1] being correct. It is now four years since we entered on the auspicious office. Superiors and inferiors dispute with one another: the hundred surnames[2] are not at peace. Some by mischance lose their proper surnames; others purposely lay claim to high family. This is perhaps the reason why good government is not attained to. Deficient in wisdom although we are, how can we omit to rectify these irregularities? Let the Ministers take counsel, and inform me of their determination." All the Ministers said:—"If your Majesty, restoring that which is lost and correcting that which is perverted, will thus determine Houses and surnames, your servants will stake their lives in recommending the adoption of such a measure."

28th day. The Emperor made a decree, saying:—" The ministers, functionaries, and the Miyakko[3] of the various provinces each and all describe themselves, some as descendants of Emperors, others attributing to their races a miraculous origin, and saying that their ancestors came down from Heaven.[4] However, since the three Powers of Nature[5] assumed distinct forms,[6] many tens of thousands of years have elasped, so that single Houses have multiplied and have formed anew ten thousand surnames of doubtful authenticity. Therefore let the people of the various Houses and

---

1. Literally surnames and personal names. What is really meant is titles. There were no proper surnames at this time.—A.
2. The word for "hundred surnames" is hiyakusho: which is also used for the nation generally, and in later times Japan for the peasantry. Here its original meaning must be kept in view.—A.
3. Miyakko: a kind of high local officials, originally probably bondmen of the Imperial clan, compared by Wedemeyer to the "pueri regis" of the Franks.—Ed.
4. The "Sei-shi-roku" contains numerous instances of this.—A.
5. Heaven, Earth, and Man.—A.
6. Since the creation, as we would say.—A.

surnames wash themselves and practise abstinence, and let them, each one calling the Gods to witness, plunge their hands in boiling water." The caldrons of the ordeal by boiling water were therefore placed on the "Evil Door of Words" spur of the Amagashi Hill. Everybody was told to go thither, saying :—" He who tells the truth will be uninjured ; he who is false will assuredly suffer harm."

This is called Kuka-tachi. Sometimes mud was put into a caldron and made to boil up. Then the arms were bared, and the boiling mud stirred with them. Sometimes an axe was heated red-hot and placed on the palm of the hand.[1]

Hereupon everyone put on straps of tree-fibre, and coming to the caldrons, plunged their hands in the boiling water, when those who were true remained naturally uninjured, and all those who were false were harmed. Therefore those who had falsified (their titles) were afraid, and slipping away beforehand, did not come forward. From this time forward the Houses and surnames were spontaneously ordered, and there was no longer anyone who falsified them.[2]

Two Sisters

[A. D. 418]

7th year, Winter, 12th month, 1st day. There was a banquet in the New Palace. The Emperor[3] in person played on the lute, and the Empress stood up and danced.

---

1. Ancient Glossary.—Ed.
2. This measure can only have been applicable to a dominant caste. The nation cannot have been all subjected to the ordeal at Amagashi. Doubtless, then as now, the bulk of the people cared little for genealogies, and indeed had none but personal names.—A.
3. Ingiō Tennō.

When the dance was ended, she did not repeat the compliment. At that time it was the custom at a banquet for the Dancer, when the dance was ended, to turn to the person who occupied the highest place, and say, "I offer thee a woman." Now the Emperor said to the Empress:—"Why hast thou failed to say the usual compliment?" The Empress was afraid. She stood up again and danced, and when the dance was over, she said:—"I offer thee a woman." The Emperor forthwith inquired of the Empress, saying:—"Who is the woman whom thou offerest me? I wish to know her name." The Empress could not help herself, and addressed the Emperor, saying:—"It is thy handmaiden's younger sister, whose name is Otohime." Otohime's countenance was of surpassing and peerless beauty. Her brilliant colour shone out through her raiment, so that the men of that time gave her the designation of Sotohori Iratsume.[1] The Emperor's wishes had dwelt upon Sotohori Iratsume, and therefore it was that he insisted on the Empress's offering her to him while the Empress, knowing this, was reluctant to make the compliment. Now the Emperor was delighted, and the very next day he despatched a messenger to summon Otohime. At this time Otohime dwelt with her mother at Sakata in the land of Afumi. But she feared the feelings of the Empress and therefore refused to come. Again seven times she was sent for, and yet she obstinately refused and did not come. Upon this the Emperor was displeased, and again gave command to one of the Toneri,[2] a Nakatomi named Ikatsu no Omi, saying:—"The damsel Otohime, who was given to me by the Empress, has not come although sent

---

1. Clothing-pass-maiden. The "Kojiki" makes her the Emperor's daughter.—A.
2. chamberlain.—A.

for. Do thou go thyself and bring Otohime here with thee, and I will surely reward thee liberally." Hereupon Ikatsu no Omi,[1] having received the Imperial command, withdrew, and having concealed a stock of provisions in his clothing, went to Sakata, where he prostrated himself in Otohime's courtyard, and said :—" By command of the Emperor, I summon thee." Otohime answered and said :— " Far be it from me not to fear the Emperor's command. But I am unwilling to hurt the Empress's feeling. Thy handmaiden will not come, though it should cost her her life to refuse." Then Ikatsu no Omi answered and said :— " As thy servant has received the Emperor's commands, I must bring thee back with me. If I bring thee not back, I shall surely incur punishment. Therefore it is better to die lying prostrate in this courtyard than to return and undergo the extreme penalty." So for seven days he lay prostrate in the courtyard, and although food and drink were offered to him, he refused to taste them, but secretly ate the provisions in his bosom. Hereupon Otohime said :—" By reason of the Empress's jealousy, thy handmaiden has already disobeyed the Emperor's commands. To be the ruin of my Lord, who art his faithful servant, would be another crime on my part." Accordingly she came along with Ikatsu no Omi. When they reached Kasuga in Yamato they had food by the well of Ichihi, Otohime herself gave sake to the Omi, and soothed his spirit. The Omi that same day arrived at the capital, and having lodged Otohime at the house of Akiki, the Atahe of Yamato, made his report to the Emperor. The Emperor was greatly rejoiced. He commended Ikatsu no Omi, and showed him liberal favour. The Empress, however, showed her vex-

---

[1]. As he was Toneri, the Ikatsu no Omi is clearly a mere title, like the no Kami's of recent times.—A.

ation, and Otohime could therefore not approach the interior of the Palace. Accordingly, a separate building was erected for her at Fujihara, and she dwelt there.[1] On the night that the Empress gave birth to the Emperor Ohohatsuse, the Emperor for the first time went to the Fujihara Palace. The Empress hearing this, was angry, and said:— " Many years have passed since I first bound up my hair and became thy companion in the hinder palace. It is too cruel of thee, O Emperor. Wherefore, just on this night when I am in childbirth and hanging between life and death, must thou go to Fujihara?" So she went out, set fire to the parturition house, and was about to kill herself. The Emperor, hearing this was greatly shocked, and said:—" We are wrong." So with explanations he soothed the mind of the Empress.

[A. D. 419]

8th year, Spring, 2nd month. The Emperor went to Fujihara, and secretly observed how matters were with Sotohori Iratsume. That night Sotohori Iratsume was sitting alone, thinking fondly to the Emperor. Unaware of his approach, she made a song, saying:—

> *This is the night*
> *My husband will come.*
> *The little crab—*
> *The spider's action*
> *To-night is manifest.*[2]

The Emperor, when he heard this song, was touched by

1. Hence perhaps the name Soto-wori-hime, or the Lady who lives without, as opposed to Oho-nakatsu-hime, the dame of the Great Interior.—A.

2. It was considered that when a spider clung to one's garments, it was sign that an intimate friend would arrive. Little crab is another name for spider. Sotohori-hime was in after times looked on as the " Muse of poetry." This poem is a regular Tanka, as are the other in this passage.—A.

it, and made a song, saying :—

> *Loosening and removing*
> *The brocade sash*
> *Of small pattern,*
> *Not often have I slept—*
> *But one night only.*

The next morning, the Emperor looked at the cherry flowers besides the well, and made a song, saying :—

> *As one loves the cherry*
> *Sweet of blossom,*
> *Did I love another,*
> *Then her I should not love—*
> *The girl whom I love.*

This came up to the Empress's ear, and she was very wroth. Hereupon Sotohori Iratsume addressed the Emperor, saying :—" Thy handmaiden desires to be always near the Royal Palace, and night and day without ceasing to view the glory of Your Majesty. But the Empress, being thy handmaiden's elder sister, is, on her account, continually resentful towards Your Majesty, and is also vexed because of thy handmaiden. I pray therefore that I may be removed far from the Royal dwelling, and I wish to live at a distance. This might perhaps cause the Empress's jealousy somewhat to abate." The Emperor forthwith built anew a palace in Chinu in Kahachi, and frequently went-a-hunting to the moor of Hine.

A Song-contest

[A. D. 498]

The Emperor Wohatsuse waka-sazaki[1] was the eldest

1. His posthumous name is Buretsu Tennō.—Ed.

son of the Emperor Ohoke. His mother was called the Empress Kasuga no Iratsume. He was made Prince Imperial in the seventh year of the Emperor Ohoke. When he grew to manhood, he was fond of criminal law, and was well versed in the statutes. He would remain in Court until the sun went down, so that hidden wrong was surely penetrated. In deciding cases he attained to the facts.[1] But he worked much evil, and accomplished no good thing. He never omitted to witness in person cruel punishments of all kinds, and the people of the whole land were all in terror of him.

In the 11th year, the 18th month or his reign, the Emperor Ohoke died. The Minister of State Heguri no Matori no Omi usurped the government of the country and tried to reign over Japan. Pretending that it was for the Emperor's eldest son, he built a palace, and ultimately dwelt in it himself. On all occasions he was arrogant, and was utterly devoid of loyal principle. Now the eldest son wished to betroth to himself Kagehime, the daughter of Mononobe no Arakahi no Ohomuraji,[2] and sent a middleman to Kagehime's house to arrange for their union. But Kagehime had already formed an illicit connection with Shibi, son of Matori, the Minister of State. Fearing, however, to offer opposition to the eldest son's proposal, she answered him, saying—" Thy handmaiden wishes to wait upon thee on the street of Tsubaki-ichi." Accordingly the eldest son, in order to go to the place of assignation, sent one of his personal attendants to the house of Oho-

---

1. This description from "When " down to "facts " is taken from the history of the Chinese Emperor Mingti of the Later Han Dynasty.—A.
2. Ōmuraji, leader of the muraji, noble families of divine origin, but not related to the Imperial House; according to Professor Wedemeyer "ein älterer Dienst-und Volksadel" (Japanische Frühgeschichte, Tokio 1930, p. 249).—Ed.

A SONG-CONTEST

omi[1] Heguri to ask for official horses, saying that he did so by command. The Oho-omi mocked him, pretending that he would send them, and said:—" For whom (else) are official horses kept? Of course his orders shall be obeyed." But for a long time he did not send them. The eldest son cherished resentment at this, but controlled himself, and did not let it appear on his countenance. Ultimately he went to the place of assignation, and taking a place among song-makers,[2] took hold of Kagehime's sleeves, and was loitering about unconcernedly, when suddenly Shibi no Omi came, and pushing away the eldest son from Kagehime, got between them. Hereupon the eldest son let go Kagehime's sleeve, and turning round, confronted Shibi no Omi, and addressing him straight in the face, made a song, saying:—

> *Of the briny current,[3]*
> *The breakers as I view,*
> *By the fin of the Tunny*
> *That comes sporting*
> *I see my spouse standing.*

(One book has "harbour" instead of "briny current.")
Shibi Omi answered with a song, saying:—

> *Dost thou tell me, O Prince! to yield to thee*

---

1. Ō-omi, leader of the omi, noble families founded by members of the Imperial House, and therefore superior in rank to the muraji. "Oho-omi is written with the character read in later times Daijin, i.e. Great Minister or Prime Minister" (Aston). There are also omi of another kind, on which see Wedemeyer, l.c. p. 111 no. 241.—Ed.

2. For a penetrating study of song-contests in their relation to marriage-customs in Ancient China and neighbouring countries see: M. Granet, Fêtes et Chansons Anciennes de la Chine, Paris 1919. See also Appendix VII of this book.—Ed.

3. Shibi means tunny-fish. This suggests the introduction of the "briny current" of the first line.—A.

ARCHAIC RULE AND CONFLICT

> *The eight-fold bamboo fence*[1]
> *Of the Omi's child?*

The eldest son made a song, saying:—

> *My great sword*
> *Hung at my girdle I will stand;*
> *Though I may not draw it,*
> *Yet in the last resort*
> *I am resolved to be united to her.*

Shibi no Omi answered with a song, saying:—

> *The great Lord's*
> *Eight-fold retiring fence*
> *He may try to build,*
> *Still for want of strict care,*[2]
> *The retiring-fence is not built.*

The eldest son made a song saying:—

> *The eight-fold fastening fence*
> *Of the Omi's child*
> *Should an earthquake come, shaking,*
> *Reverberating below,*
> *'Twill be a ruined fastening fence.*

(A various version of the first line is " Eight-fold Kara fence.")

The eldest son gave Kagehime a song, saying:—

> *If Kagehime, who comes and stays*
> *At the head of the lute,*[3]

---

1. The fence in this and the following verses is the enclosure of the bridal chamber.—A.
2. For want of strict care is in the original Ama-shimi. This word contains an allusion to the Omi's name Shibi. Mi and bi are often interchanged in Japanese.—A.
3. i.e. on my right hand.—A.

> *Were a jewel,*
> *She would be a white sea-ear[1] pearl—*
> *The pearl that I love.*

Shibi no Omi answered on behalf of Kagehime, and made a song saying:—

> *The great Lord's*
> *Girdle of Japanese loom*
> *Hangs down in a bow[2]*
> *Whosoever it may be—*
> *There is no one (but me) whose love she requites.*

The eldest son then for the first saw that Shibi had already possessed Kagehime, and became conscious of all the disrespect shown him by the father and the son. He blazed out into a great rage, and forthwith, on the same night, proceeded to the house of Ohotomo no Kanamura no Muraji, where he levied troops and concerted his plans. Ohotomo no Muraji waylaid Shibi no Omi with a force of several thousand men. He slew him at Mount Nara.

Emperor and Local Chiefs

[A. D. 534]

Autumn, 7th month, 1st day. The Emperor[3] made a decree, saying:—"The Empress, it is true, is of one body with the Emperor, but their designations, one being outer and the other inner, are quite distinct. Moreover let there be assigned a tract of Miyake land from (the revenue of)

---

1. The sea-ear is in Japanese *ahabi*, which may be intended to suggest *ahazu*, "not to become united to."—A.
2. The sole reason why the second and third lines are introduced is to bring in *tare*, "to hang down." The same word is repeated in the fourth line with the meaning "who," thus producing a wordplay, of which Japanese poets are fond.—A.
3. Ankan Tennō.

which to erect a Pepper[1] Court, so that after generations may hand down its memory." Imperial Commissioners were accordingly appointed to select good rice-land. The Imperial Commissioners, having received this charge, addressed Ajihari (otherwise called Satohi), Ohoshi Kahachi no Atahe,[2] saying :—" Thou shouldst now offer to the Emperor the fat rice-land of Kiji." Ajihari conceived a sudden grudging, and deceived the Imperial Commissioners, saying :—" This rice-land is subject to drought, and hard to irrigate. The surface water percolates readily, so that the expenditure of labour would be enormous, and the harvest very small." The Imperial Commissioners, in accordance with these words, made their report to the Emperor without reserve.

Winter, 10th month, 15th day. The Emperor commanded Kanamura, Ohotomo no Ohomuraji, saying :— " Although we have taken to us four wives there has been up till now no heir. When ten thousand years have passed,[3] Our name will be extinct. What dost thou propose should be done, Our uncle[4] of Ohotomo ? Whenever we think of this, Our anxiety knows no rest."

Kanamura, Ohotomo no Muraji, addressed the Emperor, saying :—" This is also a subject of anxiety to thy servant. It is necessary that all the sovereigns of this country who rule the Empire, whether they have heirs or not, should have something by which they should have a name. I

---

1. The private apartment of the Empress, so called because (1) an Empress of the Han had the walls of her palace smeared with pepper in order to generate warmth, or (2) because she always had a supply of pepper flowers about her, hoping to be fruitful like them.—Giles.
2. Atahe, title of uncertain ethymological origin. See Wedemeyer l.c. p. 111 n. 239.—Ed.
3. i.e. when I am dead.—A.
4. Uncle, like cousin or brother in the mouths of European sovereigns, is only a term of friendly greeting.—A.

pray, therefore, that on behalf of the Empress and thy other consorts Miyake lands may be manifested."

The Emperor commanded, saying:—"Be it so; let them be speedily established." Kanamura, Ohotomo no Ohomuraji, recommended to the Emperor that the Miyake[1] of Oharida with serfs[2] from every province should be granted to Satohime, that the Miyake of Sakurawi (one book says, "And in addition the Miyake of Chinuyama") with serfs from every province should be granted to Kagarihime, and that the Miyake of Naniha with spade-labourers from every district should be granted to Yakahime as an indication to posterity, and an example by which to view the past. The Emperor commanded, saying:—"Let it be done as proposed."

Intercalary 12th month, 4th day. The Emperor made a progress to Mishima. Kanamura, Ohotomo no Ohomuraji, was in attendance.

The Emperor, through Ohotomo no Ohomuraji, made inquiry as to good rice-land of the Agata-nushi[3] Ihi-bo. The Agatanushi Ihi-bo was delighted beyond measure, and with the utmost reverence and loyalty offered as a present Upper Mino and Lower Mino, Upper Kuhabara and Lower Kuhabara, as well as land in Takefu, 40 chō in all. Ohotomo no Ohomuraji, by command of the Emperor, addressed him,[4] saying:—"Of the entire surface of the soil, there is no part which is not a Royal grant in fee; under the wide Heavens there is no place which is not royal territory. The previous Emperors therefore[5] established an illustrious

---

1. Miyake originally granaries, later centers of local administration.—Ed.
2. Tana-be.—A.
3. District-lord.—A. According to Wedemeyer, originally lords of Yamato districts subdued by Jimmu Tennō and his descendants.—Ed.
4. i.e. Ajihari.—A.
5. From this point to the end of the paragraph the text is taken from the monument of a personage of the Liang Dynasty of China.—A.

designation and handed down a vast fame, in magnanimity they were a match with Heaven and Earth : in glory they resembled the sun and moon. They rode afar and dispensed their mollifying influence to a distance ; in breadth it extended beyond the bounds of the capital and cast a bright reflection throughout the boundaries of the land, pervading everywhere without a limit. Above they were the crown of the nine heavens : they passed abroad through all the eight points of the compass : they declared their efficiency by the framing of ceremonial observances : they instituted music,[1] thereby manifesting order. The resulting happiness was complete : there was gladness which tallied with that of past years.[2]

Now thou, Ajihari, being an obscure and insignificant subject of the realm, didst suddenly entertain a grudging as regards the lands of the Crown, and hast lightly disregarded the messenger. It is the Imperial will that thou, Ajihari, shalt henceforth cease to hold office of Local Governor." Hereupon, the Agata-nushi Ihibo's heart was filled with mingled joy and awe. He took his son Toriki and presented him to the Ohomuraji as a servant. Then Ajihari, Ohoshi Kahachi no Atahe, was afraid, and had lasting regret. Prostrating himself on the ground, with the perspiration streaming from him, he addressed the Ohomuraji, saying :—
" I am an ignorant subject, and my crime deserves ten thousand deaths. I pray humbly that I may be allowed to furnish from each district in spring-time five hundred spade-

---

[1]. The importance of music as a means of government is often insisted on in the ancient Chinese literature. The interlinear version has here uta-mai, " song and dancing ", which latter was no doubt included. Ceremony and music are put generally for the pomp and circumstances which are the life of an Imperial Court.—A.

[2]. Here we have the Imperial theory formulated in terms, be it noted, which are borrowed entirely from Chinese writings.—A.

labourers, and in the time of autumn five hundred, for the Emperor's service. My descendants to all ages will pray for their lives in dependence on this, and they will keep it before them for ever as an exemplary punishment."[1] He separately presented to Ohotomo no Ohomuraji six chō of rice-land in Sawida. This seems to have been the origin of the labourers of the Agata of Kahachi being attached to the Miyake of Takefu in Mishima as serfs.

From: Nihongi, Chronicles of Japan from the Earliest Times to A. D. 697, translated from the Original Chinese and Japanese by W. G. Aston. Transactions and Proceedings of the Japan Society London, Supplement I, 2 Vol. London, 1896. Kegan Paul, Trench, Trübner & Co., Ltd.

1. i.e. this will be a perpetual ransom for the lives of my descendants.—A.

ASUKA AND NARA PERIODS

(A. D. 592—794)

NEW AND OLD CULTS AND GODS

1. Devotion and Demise of Empress Suiko

[A.D. 606]

14TH year, Summer, 5th month, 5th day. The Imperial commands were given to Kuratsukuri no Tori, saying :—
"It being my desire to encourage the Inner doctrines, I was about to erect a Buddhist Temple, and for this purpose sought for relics. Then thy grandfather, Shiba Tattō, offered me relics. Moreover there were no monks or nuns in the land. Thereupon thy father, Tasuna, for the sake of the Emperor Tachibana Toyohi, took priestly orders[1] and reverenced the Buddhist law. Also thy aunt Shimame was the first to leave her home and, becoming the forerunner of all nuns, to practice the religion of Shaka. Now, we desired to make a sixteen-foot Buddha, and to that end sought for a good image of Buddha. Thou didst provide a model which met our wishes. Moreover, when the image of Buddha was completed, it could not be brought into the Hall, and none of the workmen could suggest a plan of doing so. They were, therefore, on the point of breaking down the doorway, when thou didst manage to admit it without breaking down the doorway. For all these services of thine, we grant thee the rank of Dainin, and we also bestow on thee twenty chō of water fields[2] in the district of Sakata in the province of Afumi." With the revenue derived from this land, Tori built for the Empress the Temple of Kongō-ji,[3] now known as the nunnery of Sakata in Minabuchi.

1. Lit. left his house.—A.
2. i.e. rice-land.—A.
3. Diamond temple.—A.

NEW AND OLD CULTS AND GODS

Autumn, 7th month. The Empress requested the Prince Imperial[1] to lecture on the Shō-man-giō.[2] He completed his explanation in three days.

In this year the Prince Imperial also lectured on the Hokke-kiō[3] in the Palace of Okamoto. The Empress was greatly pleased, and bestowed on the Prince Imperial one hundred chō of water fields in the Province of Harima. They were therefore added to the Temple of Ikaruga.

[A.D. 607]

15th year, Spring, 2nd month, 9th day. The following edict was made :—" We hear that our Imperial ancestors, in their government of the world, bending lowly under the sky and treading delicately on the ground, paid deep reverence to the Gods of Heaven and Earth. They everywhere dedicated temples to the mountains and rivers, and held mysterious communion with the powers of Nature. Hence the male and female elements became harmoniously developed, and civilizing influences blended together, and now in Our reign, shall there be any remissness in the worship of the Gods of Heaven and Earth? Therefore let our Ministers with their whole hearts do reverence to the Gods of Heaven and Earth."[4]

15th day. The Prince Imperial and the Oho-omi, accompanied by all functionaries, did worship to the Gods of Heaven and Earth.

*　　　*　　　*

1. Shōtoku Taishi.
2. A Sutra or Buddhist Scripture called in Sanskrit the Crīmāladevī-simhanāda.—A.
3. Saddharma-pundarika-sûtra.
4. This edict is pure Chinese, and sounds very strangely from an Empress who was devoted to Buddhism.—A.

[A.D. 628]

36th year, Spring 2nd month, 27th day. The Empress took to her sick bed. 3rd month, 2nd day. There was a total eclipse of the sun.

6th day. The Empress's illness became very grave, and (death) was unmistakably near. So she sent for the Imperial Prince Tamura, and addressed him, saying :—" To ascend to the Celestial Dignity, and therewith to regulate the vast foundation, to direct the manifold machinery of government, and thereby to nourish the people—this is not a matter to be lightly spoken of, but one which demands constant and serious attention. Do thou therefore be careful and observant, and let no hasty words escape thee." On the same day she summoned to her Tamashiro no Ohoye, and instructed him, saying :—" Thy heart is young. Whatever thou may wish, do not utter it in speech, but be sure to await the expression of general opinion, and act accordingly."

7th day. The Empress died at the age of seventy-five. She was temporarily interred in the Southern Court (of the Palace).

Summer, 4th month, 15th day. Hail fell, of the size of peaches.

16th day. Hail fell, of the size of plums. There was a drought, which lasted from spring till summer.

August, 9th month, 20th day. The rites of mourning for the Empress began. At this time all the Ministers each pronounced a funeral eulogy at the shrine of the temporary burial place.

Before this time, the Empress had given her dying injunctions to the Ministers, saying :—" Of late years the five grains have not produced well, and there is great famine among the people. Let there be therefore no costly inter-

NEW AND OLD CULTS AND GODS

ment by raising for me a misasagi,[1] but let me be buried in the misasagi of Prince Takeda.

24th day. The Empress was buried in the misasagi of Prince Takeda.

2. RAIN-MAKING : RITES AND RESULTS

[A.D. 642.]

KOGYOKU Tennō, 1st year, Summer, 6th month. There was a great draught . . . Autumn, 7th month, 25th day. The Ministers conversed with one another, saying :— " In accordance with the teachings of the village hafuri,[2] there have been in some places horses and cattle killed as a sacrifice to the Gods of the various (Shintō) shrines, in others frequent changes of the market places, or prayers to the River-Gods.[3] None of these practices have had hitherto any good result." The Soga no Oho-omi answered and said.—" The Mahayana Sutra ought to be read by way of extract[4] in the temples, our sins repented of, as Buddha

1. Burial mound. See Aston, Nihongi vol. I. p. 135 note 7.
2. Lower Shinto priests.
3. This is an old custom in China. A Chinese book says that in a certain village there is a pond. At this pond there is a stone cow. In years of drought, the peasants kill a cow and, mixing its blood with mud, smear it on the back of the stone cow, with prayers.—The " Kogojiui," an ancient Japanese book, speaks of sacrifices of oxen to the Ohotsuchi (great earth) nushi (master) no Kami. The flesh was eaten by the peasants. —The practice of changing the market place as a means of averting drought is also an old Chinese custom. The present custom of closing the city gates of Sŏul, the capital of Corea, to put a stop to excessive rain, may be compared with it.—A modern commentator denounces both these customs (sacrifice of animals and changing the market-place) as contrary to the spirit of Shintoism.—A.
4. The tendoku is the reading of passages of a book to represent the whole. I have seen a dozen of priests each with a pile of books on his right, of which he took one, read a few words at the beginning, made the pages defile rapidly before him, and then reading a few words at the end, passed it on to a gradually increasing pile on his left. In this way a volume

teaches, and thus with humility rain should be prayed for."

27th day. In the South Court of the Great Temple, the images of Buddha and of the Bosatsu,[1] and the images of the four Heavenly Kings, were magnificently adorned. A multitude of priests, by humble request, read the "Mahāyāna Sutra." On this occasion Soga no Oho-omi held a censer in his hands, and having burnt incense in it, put up a prayer.

28th day. A slight rain fell.

29th day. The prayers for rain being unsuccessful, the reading of the "Sutra" was discontinued.

8th month, 1st day. The Emperor made a progress to the river-source of Minabuchi. Here he knelt down and prayed, worshipping towards the four quarters, and looking up to heaven. Straightway there was thunder and a great rain, which eventually fell for five days, and plentifully bedewed the Empire.

(One writing has :—"For five days there was continuous rain, and the nine grains ripened.")

Hereupon the peasantry throughout the Empire cried with one voice, "Bansai," and said, "An Emperor of exceeding virtue!"

3. DIVINE INSPIRATION

[A. D. 672]

TEMMU Tennō, first year, autumn, 7th month, 23rd day.— Before this time, when the army was at Kanatsunawi,

---

takes only a few seconds to dispose of, and although the Buddhist scriptures are pretty voluminous, an hour or two of this sort of thing makes some impression on them.—A.

1. Boddhisatwa.—A.
2. This is the Chinese as opposed to the Buddhist style which had been without result.—A.

NEW AND OLD CULTS AND GODS

Kome, Takechi no Agata-nushi,[1] Governor of the district of Takechi, suddenly had his mouth closed so that he could not speak. After three days, a divine inspiration came over him, and he said :—" I am the God who dwells in the Shrine of Takechi, and my name is Koto-shiro-nushi no Kami[2]. Again, ' I am the God who dwells in the Shrine of Musa, and my name is Iku-ikadzuchi[2a] no Kami.' This was their revelation :—' Let offerings of horses and weapons of all kinds be made at the misasagi of the Emperor Kamu-yamato-ihare-biko.[3] Further they said :—' We stood in front and rear of the Imperial descendant and escorted him to Fuha, whence we returned. We have now again taken our stand in the midst of the Imperial army for its protection.' Further they said :— ' An army is about to arrive by the Western road. Be on your guard.' " When he had done speaking, he awoke (from his trance). For this reason, therefore, Kome was sent to worship at the Imperial misasagi and to make offerings of horses and weapons. He also made offerings of cloth[4] and worshipped the gods of the Shrines of Takechi and Musa.

After this Karakuni, Iki no Fubito, arrived from Oho-saka. Therefore the people of that day said :—" The words of the instructions of the Gods of the two Shrines are in accordance with the fact."[5]

---

1. Here we have an example of an old territorial noble holding the office implied by his ancestral title.—A.
2. Son of Ōkuni-nushi, father of the wife of Jimmu Tennō.—Ed.
2a. Live-thunder. Another reading is Ikudama, live-jewel. This is not one of the eight thunder-deities enumerated as having been born from the putrefying body of the Goddess Izanami. See Nihongi, Vol. I. p. 30. Kome was apparently inspired by two gods at once.—A.
3. Jimmu Tennō.—A.
4. Nusa or mitegura, now represented by the paper gohei.—A.
5. Referring to the prediction that the Army of the West was approaching.—A.

DIVINE INSPIRATION

Moreover the Goddess of Muraya[1] said by the mouth of a priest :—" An army is now about to arrive by the middle road of my shrine. Therefore let the middle road of my shrine be blocked." Accordingly, not many days after, the army of Kujira, Ihoriwi no Miyakko, arrived by the middle road. The men of that day said :—" So the words of the teaching of the god were right." When the war was over, the Generals reported the monitions of these three gods to the Emperor, who straightway commanded that the three gods should be raised in rank[2] and worshipped accordingly.

From: Nihongi, Chronicles of Japan from the Earliest Times to A. D. 697, translated from the Original Chinese and Japanese by W. G. Aston. Transactions and Proceedings of the Japan Society London, Supplement I, 2 Vol. London, 1896. Kegan Paul, Trench, Trübner & Co., Ltd.

---

1. Named Mifuto hime.—A.
2. There were three classes of shrines, Greater, Middle and Lesser. The Greater Shrines included those from the senior division of the first rank to the senior division of the third rank; the Middle included those from the junior division of the third rank to the junior division of the fourth rank; the Lesser included those from the senior division of the fifth rank to the junior division of the fifth rank. The lands allotted to each shrine and the offerings made to them were regulated accordingly.—A.

ADMINISTRATION AND ETIQUETTE UNDER TEMMU TENNŌ

[A. D. 673]

2ND year, Spring, 1st month, 7th day. The Ministers were entertained at a banquet at which sake was provided.

2nd month, 27th day. The Emperor commanded the functionaries to prepare an arena, in which he assumed the Imperial Dignity at the Palace of Kiyomibara in Asuka. He raised his wife to the rank of Empress-consort.[1] She bore to him His Highness[2] the Imperial Prince Kusakabe. Before this he had taken to him the Empress-consort's elder sister, the Imperial Princess Ohota,[3] and made her his consort. She gave birth to the Imperial Princess Ohoki, and the Imperial Prince Ohotsu. His next consort was the Imperial Princess Ohoye.[4] She gave birth to the Imperial Prince Naga, and the Imperial Prince Yuge. His next consort, the Imperial Princess Nittabe,[5] gave birth to the Imperial Prince Toneri. Moreover the Lady Higami no Iratsume, daughter of the Oho-omi, Fujihara, bore to him the Imperial Princess Tajima. Another lady, named Ihohe no Iratsume, younger sister of Higami no Iratsume, bore to him the Imperial Prince Nittabe. Next the lady[6] Ohonu no Iratsume, daughter of the Oho-omi Soga no Akaye, bore to him one son and two daughters.

    1. Afterwards Jitō Tennō.—A.
    2. Mikoto.—A.
    3. Daughter of Tenchi, therefore his niece.—A.
    4. Another daughter of Tenchi Tennō.—A.
    5. Another daughter of Tenchi Tennō.—A.
    6. In Japanese otoji, in Sinico-Japanese fujin, a term applied to the Imperial concubines of lower rank.—A.

ADMINISTRATION AND ETIQUETTE

The first was called the Imperial Prince Hodzumi; the second was called the Imperial Princess Ki; the third was called the Imperial Princess Tagata. The Emperor before this had taken to him Princess Nukada no Iratsume, daughter of Prince Kagami,[1] who gave birth to the Imperial Princess Towochi. Next he took to him Amako no Iratsume, daughter of Tokuse, Munagata no Kimi, who bore to him His Highness[2] the Imperial Prince Takechi; next a daughter of Ohomaro, Shishibito no Omi, named Kajihime no Iratsume, who bore to him two sons and two daughters. The first was called the Imperial Prince Osakabe; the second was called the Imperial Prince Shiki; the third was called the Imperial Princess Hatsusebe; the fourth was called the Imperial Princess Taki.

29th day. Cap-ranks were conferred on these who had rendered good service, varying according to circumstances.

3rd month, 17th day. The Governor of the province of Bingo caught a white pheasant in the district of Kameshi and sent it as tribute. Accordingly the forced labour due from that district was entirely remitted, and a general amnesty granted throughout the Empire.

In this month scribes were brought together who began to copy out the " Issaikio "[3] in the Temple of Kaharadera.

Summer, 4th month, 14th day. With the view of sending the Imperial Princess Ohoki to attend upon the Shrine of Ama-terasu no Ohokami, she was made to dwell in the Abstinence-palace of Hatsuse. This was that she might

1. These and the following concubines seem to have had no special rank or position.—A.
2. Mikoto.—A.
3. The Buddhist canon or Tripitaka. A copy presented to the Bodleian Library or British Museum by a Japanese nobleman was brought to the British Legation, Tokio, in two carts.—A.

ADMINISTRATION AND ETIQUETTE

first purify herself before she by-and-by approached the place where the Goddess was.

5th month, 1st day. The Emperor gave command to the Ministers of State, the Daibu, as well as to the Omi and Muraji, and also the Tomo no Miyakko, saying:—"Let those who first take service (under Government) be at the outset employed by the Ohotoneri[1]. Afterwards let them be allotted to suitable offices, selection being made according to their capacities. Moreover, let the waiting-women who offer their services be received freely, without respect of married and unmarried, or of old and young. In selecting them for particular duties let the rules of the (female) palace officials be followed."

* * *

[A. D. 675]

4th year. Spring, 1st month, 5th day. A platform was for the first time erected from which to divine by means of the stars.[2]

* * *

id. 2nd month, 9th day. The Emperor gave orders to the provinces of Yamato, Kahachi, Settsu, Yamashiro, Harima, Ahaji, Tamba, Tajima, Afumi, Wakasa, Ise, Mino, and Wohari, saying:—"Seek out in your jurisdiction men and women of the common people who can sing well, and also dwarfs and jugglers,[3] etc., and send them as tribute."

* * *

id. 15th day. The Emperor decreed, saying:—"Let the serfs granted to the various Uji in the year Kinoye

---

1. High Chamberlain.
2. The close association of astronomy and divination may be inferred from this.—A.
3. The word used includes jugglers, acrobats, et hoc genus omne.—A.

ADMINISTRATION AND ETIQUETTE

Ne[1] be henceforward done away with. Moreover, let the mountains, marshes, islands, bays, woods, plains, and artificial ponds granted to Princes of the Blood,[2] to Princes and to Ministers and Temples,[3] be all done away with from first to last."

*　*　*

[A. D. 680]

9th year, Winter, 11th month 7th day. The Emperor issued an edict to the officials, saying : " If any one knows of any means of benefiting the state or of increasing the welfare of the people, let him appear in Court and make a statement in person. If what he says is reasonable, his ideas will be adopted the embodied in regulations."

*　*　*

[A. D. 681]

10th year, Summer, 5th month, 11th day. Worship was paid to the august spirit of the Emperor's grandfather.[4] On this day the Emperor issued a decree, saying :—" The deference paid by public functionaries to the Palace officials[5] is far too great. Sometimes they go to their doors and address their plaints to them, sometimes they pay court to their houses[6] by offerings of presents. If there should be any such cases in future, the offenders will be punished

---

1. The third year of the previous reign, viz. A.D. 664.—A.
2. Including the brothers, sisters, and children of the Emperor; others are simply 王 i.e. kings, by which princes are meant.—A.
3. Temples are Buddhist temples; the word " shrine " is used in this translation for Shintō places of worship.—A.
4. He was not an Emperor, and therefore not included in the general worship paid to the Emperors. Or perhaps with Florenz we should understand by grandfather ancestors generally. The original does not indicate number.—A.
5. Female.—A.
6. i.e. families.—A.

ADMINISTRATION AND ETIQUETTE

according to circumstances."

* * *

10th month 20th day. Silla sent Kim Chhyung-phyöng, an Il-kil-son[1] of Sa-tök, and Kim Tl-syé, of the rank of Tè-nama, to bring tribute, which consisted of such things as gold, silver, copper, iron, brocade, thin silk, deer skins and fine cloth—a certain quantity of each. Separately they brought presents for the Emperor, the Empress-consort, and for the senior Prince of such things as gold, silver, flags of haze[2]-brocade and skins, a certain quantity of each.
[A.D. 682]

11th year, Autumn, 8th month, 22nd day. The Emperor issued an edict (prescribing) the character of ceremonies and[3] language.

He decreed further, saying:—" Let the lineage and character of all candidates for office be always inquired into before a selection is made. None whose lineage is insufficient are eligible for appointment, even although their character, conduct, and capacity may be unexceptionable."

* * *

ib. 9th month, 2nd day. By Imperial command ceremonial kneeling and crawling were both abolished from this time forward, and the ceremonial custom of standing of the Naniha Court[4] was again practised.

* * *

ib. Winter, 11th month, 16th day. The Emperor made

1. Name of rank.—A.
2. The reference is to the rosy colour of the morning hazes.—A.
3. Or of the language to be used on occasions of ceremony.—A.
4. Kōtoku Tennō. The Annals of the Thang dynasty state that it was the custom in Japan for suitors to advance crawling. Standing was the Thang custom.—A.

a decree, saying :—" Hear this, all ye Princes of the Blood, Princes and Ministers, as well as ye common people! In regard to trials for offences against the law, whether within the Palace or in the Court, let examination be made at the place where the offence has been committed as soon as seen or heard of, and let there be no concealment. In the case of grave crimes, let those which should be referred to a superior be so referred, and when arrest is proper let the offender be seized. If any resist and are not arrested, raise the soldiers of the place and arrest them. To those judged deserving of flogging there may be administered not more than a hundred blows, to be determined according to a scale. Moreover, when the facts of a crime are undeniable and the accused falsely states that he is innocent, and does not admit the justice of the charge, but disputes with the prosecutor, let his original offence be superadded to this."

12th month, 3rd day. A decree was issued as follows :— " Let the people of every House[1] each determine who shall be the Senior member of the House, and make report accordingly. Moreover, in cases where there are numerous members of the same House, let them divide and each part determine who shall be its own Senior member, all reporting at the same time to the proper officials, who shall thereupon weigh the facts and deal with the matter. Such official decisions must be accepted. And let no one for trifling reasons hastily include in his House persons who do not belong to it."[2]

[A. D. 683]

12th year, Spring, 1st month, 2nd day. The functionaries paid their respects at Court.

---

1. The Uji or noble families are meant.—A.
2. "Such as relations by the mother's side, or by marriage, or distant relations."—" Shūkai."—A.

ADMINISTRATION AND ETIQUETTE

The Viceroy of Tsukushi, Shima, Tajihi no Mabito, and others presented tribute of a three-legged sparrow.

All from the Princes of the Blood down to the Ministers were invited in front of the Great Hall of Audience and a banquet given them. On this occasion the three-legged sparrow was shown to the Ministers.

18th day. The Emperor issued a decree, saying :—" This is the ordinance of Us, the Emperor Yamato neko, who rules, as a God Incarnate, the great eight regions. Hear it, all ye governors of provinces, Kuni no Miyakko, governors of districts and common people! Ever since we first rose to the vast dignity, there have been auspicious signs from Heaven, not one or two only, but many. Now We learn by tradition that auspicious signs from Heaven come as a response when the principles of administering the Government are in harmony with the laws of Heaven. That they should appear repeatedly every year in this Our reign is, on the one hand, matter for awe, and on the other, matter for rejoicing. Therefore the Princes of the Blood, the Princes, with the Ministers and functionaries, as well as the people of the Empire, join with Us in our joy." Accordingly presents were made to all from the rank of Shōken upwards, each according to his rank, and all crimes were pardoned from capital offences downwards. Moreover all forced labour was remitted to the common people.

On this day there was a performance in the Court of the Woharida dance and of the music of the three countries of Koryö, Pèkché and Silla.

From : Nihongi, Chronicles of Japan from the Earliest Times to A. D. 697, translated from the Original Chinese and Japanese by W. G. Aston. Transactions and Proceedings of the Japan Society London, Supplement I, 2 Vol. London, 1896. Kegan Paul, Trench, Trübner & Co., Ltd.

NEW YEAR FESTIVITIES

[A. D. 686]

Shuchō,[1] 1st year, Spring, 1st month, 2nd day. The Emperor[2] took his place in the Great Hall of Audience and gave a banquet to the Princes and High Officials.

On this day the Emperor decreed, saying :—" We shall now propose conundrums[3] to the Princes and High Officials, and we promise prizes to those who give the right answers."

Upon this the Imperial Prince Takechi gave the right answers to the questions and received a present of 3 suits of Imperial garments of hari-suri,[4] 2 pairs of brocade trousers, with 20 hiki of coarse silk, 50 kin of raw silk, 100 kin of floss silk, and 100 tan of cloth. Prince Ise also gave right answers, and was presented with 3 suits of black Imperial garments, 2 pairs of purple trousers, 7 hiki of coarse silk, 20 kin of raw silk, 40 kin of floss, and 40 tan of cloth.

On this day Kudara no Nihiki, a man of the province of Settsu, presented to the Emperor a white agate.

9th day. An invitation was given to the three higher ecclesiastics, the Rishhi,[5] and also to the director and clerks of the Great Temple of the Great Palace, nine priests in all, and they were entertained at a lay[6] banquet. Moreover

1. Shuchō means red bird.—A.
2. Temmu Tennō.
3. Literally things with no end, i. e. without head or tail—non-sensica questions. Here is a specimen. " Why does a horse, after a rapid run, listen to the earth ? Why does a dog, when he goes slowly, raise his leg ? " —A.
4. A dye.—A.
5. A rank in the Buddhist priesthood.—A.
6. Not confined to vegetarian dishes.—A.

NEW YEAR FESTIVITIES

alms were given them of coarse silk, floss silk, and cloth, varying in value in the case of each.

10th day. The Princes and High Officials received a present of upper garments and trousers, one suit each.

13th day. Men of talent, scholars, professors of Philosophy,[1] and physicians, more than twenty persons in all, were summoned to the Palace. Food was given them and presents made to them.

14th day. At the hour of the cock[2] the Treasury Department at Naniha took fire and all the Palace was burnt. Some said that the fire broke out in the house of Kusuri, Ato no Muraji, and that it spread from there to the Palace. But the Arsenal offices were not burnt.

16th day. The Emperor invited the Princes and High Officials to a banquet in the Great Audience Hall, and made them presents of coarse silk, floss silk, and cloth, varying according to the rank of each.

On this day conundrums were put to the Ministers, and more presents of fine and coarse silk given to those who made the right answers on the spot.

17th day. A banquet was given in the hinder Palace.[3]

18th day. There was a great revel at Court.

On this day the Emperor took his place in front of the Imperial muro[4] building and made presents to performers, of various values. He also gave presents of clothing to singers.

---

1. Of the Yin and Yang system of Chinese philosophy.—A.
2. 6 p.m.—A.
3. The Empress-consort's rooms.—A.
4. For a long time there has been no mention of this kind of dwelling in the "Nihongi." Or perhaps Mimuro is simply the name of a particular building.—A.

ILLNESS AND DEATH OF AN EMPEROR

[A. D. 686]

Shuchō,[1] 6th month, 10th day. It was ascertained by divination that the Emperor's disease was owing to a curse from the Kusa-nagi sword.[2] The same day it was sent to the shrine of Atsuta, in Wohari, and deposited there.

12th day. Prayer was made for rain.

16th day. Prince Ise and a number of Officials were sent to the Temple of Asuka, to communicate to the priests the Emperor's commands, as follows :—" Of late our body is ill at ease, and We request that the dread power of the Three Precious Things may be invoked, in order to obtain repose for Our person. Let the Sōjō, and the general body of priests therefore put up prayers." Offerings of rare and valuable things were accordingly made to the Three Precious Things. On this day the three higher ecclesiastics, with the Risshi and the abbots[3] of the four temples, the directors, and the priests of professorial rank then in residence, received each alms of one suit of Imperial garments and one Imperial coverlet.

19th day. Public functionaries were sent to the Temple of Kahara to exhibit lanterns and make offerings of food.

---

1. Red-bird.
2. A sword found by Susanōwo no Mikoto in the tail of a dragon slain by him ; one of the three Imperial regalia.—Ed.
3. The Sinico-Japanese is Oshō, the equivalent of the Sanskrit Upashâya. Oshō is the polite word for a priest in Japan at the present day. The four temples were doubtless the great temples which remained under official administration after the disendowment measure (described Nihongi Vol.II. p. 346).—A.

ILLNESS AND DEATH OF AN EMPEROR

So there was a great vegetarian feast, and repentance was made for sin.

20th day. The priest Hōjin and Gishō were granted fiefs of thirty houses each, to support them in their old age.

22nd day.[1] The kitchen office[2] at Nabri was burnt.

Autumn, 7th month, 2nd day. The Emperor commanded that men should again wear leggings, and that women should let down their hair on their backs, as was formerly the practice.

On this day the Sōjō and Sōdzu came into the Palace, and performed a penitential service.

3rd day. The Emperor commanded the provinces to perform the ceremony of Oho-barahi.[3]

4th day. Half the commuted taxes were remitted throughout the Empire, and all forced labour was dispensed with.

5th day. Offerings were made to Kuni-gakari no Kami,[4] who dwells in the province of Kii, to the four shrines of Asuka, and to the Great God of Sumiyoshi.

8th day. One hundred priests were invited into the Palace, and made to read the Kon-kwō-myō Sutra.

10th day. There was lightning in the south, with a great clap of thunder. The buildings used by the Department of the Interior, for the storage of tax-cloth, met with destruction from Heaven. Some said that the fire broke out in the Palace of the Imperial Prince Osakabe, and that it spread to the Department of the Interior.

---

1. Something is wrong with the dates here.—A.
2. An agency for the supply of victuals for the Imperial table. These offices seem to have taken the place of some of the Be of more ancient times. The " Yengishiki " mentions such offices in Idzumi, Kii, Ahaji, Afumi, and Wakasa.—A.
3. Great Purification, a Shintō ceremony.
4. Said by the " Shiki " to be a Corean deity.—A.

ILLNESS AND DEATH OF AN EMPEROR

15th day. The Emperor gave orders that all matters of the Empire, without distinction of great and small, should be referred to the Empress-consort and the Prince Imperial.

On this day a general amnesty was granted.

16th day. Worship was paid to the Deities of Hirose and Tatsuta.

19th day. An Imperial edict was issued, as follows :—
" Let all common people throughout the Empire who, owing to poverty, have contracted debts in rice or in valuables, whether to the State or to private persons, on or before the 30th day of the 12th month of the year Kinoto Tori (685) be absolved from payment."

22nd day. The style of the year was changed to Shuchō, 1st year . . . The Palce was accordingly entitled the Palace of Asuka[1] no Kiyomibara.

28th day. Seventy persons of pure conduct[2] were selected to retire from the world. A feast of vegetable food was provided in the Palace in front of the Emperor's muro[3] residence.

In this month the Princes and Ministers made images of Kwannon,[4] for the Emperor's sake. Accordingly the Kwan-ze-on Sutra[5] was expounded in the Great Temple of the Great Palace.

8th month, 1st day. For the sake of the Emperor, eighty priests were received into religion.

2nd day. Priests and nuns, to the number of 100 in all,

---

1. Asuka is written with two Chinese characters which mean " flying-bird."—A.
2. Who practised the precepts of Buddhism.—A.
3. See Nihongi, Vol.II. p. 375.
4. In Sanskrit, Avalôkitês' vara.—A.
5. Part of the " Hokkekyō," or " Saddharma Pundarika Sūtra," called Fumonbon. Kwan-ze-on is another form of the word Kwannon.

ILLNESS AND DEATH OF AN EMPEROR

entered religion. Accordingly, 100 Bosatsu[1] were set up within the Palace, and 200 volumes of the Kwannon Sutra read.

9th day. On account of the illness of the Emperor, prayer was made to the (Shintō) Gods of Heaven and Earth.

13th day. Ihakatsu, Hada no Imiki, was sent to make offerings to the Great God of Tosa.

On this day the Prince Imperial, the Imperial Prince Ohotsu, and the Imperial Prince Takechi had each 400 houses added to their fiefs. The Imperial Princes Kahashima and Osakabe had each additions of 100 houses.

15th day. The Imperial Princes Shiki and Shigi received additions of 200 houses each.

The Temples of Hinokuma, Karu, and Ohokubo were each granted fiefs of 100 houses, limited to a term of thirty years.

23rd day. A fief of 200 houses was granted to the Temple of Kose.

9th month, 4th day. All, from the Princes of the Blood down to the Ministers, assembled in the Temple of Kahara, and put up vows for the Emperor's illness, etc., etc.

9th day. The Emperor's disease having shown no sign of abatement, he died in the principal Palace.

11th day. Lament was begun for him, and a temporary burial Palace erected in the South Court.

24th day. The Emperor was temporarily interred in the South Court and mourning began.

At this time the Imperial Prince Ohotsu conspired against the Prince Imperial.

27th day. At dawn, all the priest and nuns having made

---

1. Bodhisattva. The images of Kwannon made by the Princes and Ministers are probably meant.—A.

ILLNESS AND DEATH OF AN EMPEROR

lament in the Court of Temporary Interment, retired.

On this day, for the first time, offerings were made at the tomb and eulogies pronounced.

First of all, Aragama, Ohomi no Sukune, pronounced a eulogy regarding the Imperial Princes; next, Prince Ise, of Jō-dai-shi rank, pronounced a eulogy regarding the other Princes; next, Ohotomo, Agata no Mukahi no Sukune, of Jiki-dai-san rank, pronounced a eulogy regarding the officials of the Household generally; next, Prince Kahachi, of Jō-kwō-shi rank, pronounced a eulogy regarding the Ohotoneri of the right and left; next, Kunimi, Tahema no Mabito, of Jiki-dai-san rank, pronounced a eulogy regarding the Guards of the right and left; next, Tsukura, Unemo no Ason, of Jiki-dai-shi rank, pronounced a eulogy regarding the lady officials of the Palace; and next, Mabito, Ki no Ason, of Jiki-kwō-shi rank, pronounced a eulogy regarding the Stewards of the Palace.

28th day. All the priests and nuns again made lament in the Court of Temporary Interment.

On this day, Miaruji, Fuse no Ason, of Jiki-dai-shi rank, pronounced a eulogy regarding the Council of State; next, Maro, Isonokami no Ason, of Jiki-kwō-san rank, pronounced a eulogy regarding the judicial officers; next, Takechi-maro, Oho-miwa no Ason, of Jiki-dai-shi rank, pronounced a eulogy regarding the administrative officials; next, Yasumaro, Ohotomo no Sukune, of Jiki-kwō-san rank, pronounced a eulogy regarding the Treasury; and next, Ohoshima, Fujihara no Ason, of Jiki-dai-shi rank, pronounced a eulogy regarding the war officials.

29th day. The priests and nuns again raised lament.

On this day, Maro, Abe no Kunu no Ason, of Jiki-kwō-shi rank, pronounced a eulogy regarding the Board of

Punishments; next, Yumibari, Ki no Ason, of Jiki-kwō-shi rank, pronounced a eulogy regarding the Department of the Interior; next, Mushi-maro, Hodzumi no Ason, of Jiki-kwō-shi rank, pronounced a eulogy regarding the Governors of Provinces; next, the Ohosumi no Ata no Hayato, and the two Muma-kahi-be no Miyakko of Yamato and Kahachi each pronounced eulogies.

30th day. The priest and nuns made lament.

On this day, the Pèkché prince Nyang-u pronounced a eulogium on behalf of his father, Prince Chön-kwang. Next, the Miyakko of the various provinces, as they came, each pronounced his eulogy. There were also performances of all manner of singing and dancing.

From: Nihongi, Chronicles of Japan from the Earliest Times to A. D. 697, translated from the Original Chinese and Japanese by W. G. Aston. Transactions and Proceedings of the Japan Society London, Supplement I, 2 Vol. London, 1896. Kegan Paul, Trench, Trübner & Co., Ltd.

THE END OF A CONSPIRACY

[A. D. 686]

In the first year of Shuchō, on the ninth day of the ninth month, the Emperor Ame no Nunahara oki no Mabito[1] died. The Empress-consort presided over the Court and exercised control.

Winter, 10th month, 2nd day. The Imperial Prince Ohotsu's treason was discovered and he was placed under arrest. There were arrested at the same time Wotokashi, Yakuchi no Ason, of Jiki-kwō-shi rank, Hakatoko, Yuki no Muraji, of Lower Shōsen rank,[2] and also the Ohoto-neri Omi-maro, Nakatomi no Ason, Tayasu, Kose no Ason, a Silla priest named Hèng-sin, with Tobari, Toki no Michi-dzukuri, and others, more than thirty persons in all, who had been led astray by the Imperial Prince Ohotsu.

3rd day. Death was bestowed on the Imperial Prince Ohotsu in his house at Wosada. He was twenty-four years of age. His consort the Imperial Princess Yamanobe, hastened thither with her hair dishevelled and her feet bare, and joined him in death. All who witnessed sighed and sobbed.

The Imperial Prince Ohotsu was the third child of the Emperor Ame no Nunahara oki no Mabito. His demeanour was noble and his language refined. He was beloved by the Emperor Ame mikoto hirakasu wake.[3] When he grew to manhood he showed an eminent talent for learn-

1. Temmu Tennō.
2. This rank had been abolished some years before.—A.
3. Tenchi Tennō (661-671 A.D.)

THE END OF A CONSPIRACY

ing, and was very fond of writing. The practice of composing Chinese verses had its origin with Ohotsu.

29th day. An Imperial decree was issued as follows:—
" The Imperial Prince Ohotsu has been guilty of treason and has led astray officials and people, so that We, within the curtain, had no alternative.[1] The Imperial Prince Ohotsu has now perished. His followers deserve the same sentence as the Prince, but We pardon them all. Toki no Michi-dzukuri is however, banished to Idzu." It was further decreed, saying:—" We cannot bring ourselves to inflict punishment on the Silla priest Hèg-sin, who was an accomplice in the Imperial Prince Ohotsu's treason. He is therefore exiled to the temple of the province of Hida."

From: Nihongi, Chronicles of Japan from the Earliest Times to A. D. 697, translated from the Original Chinese and Japanese by W. G. Aston. Transactions and Proceedings of the Japan Society London, Supplement I, 2 Vol. London, 1896. Kegan Paul, Trench, Trübner & Co., Ltd.

---

1. The Empress (Jitō Tennō) is the speaker. Hence the phrase, " Within the curtain."—A.

SLAVES

[A. D. 689]

Jitō Kōgō, 3rd year. Autumn, 9th month, 22nd day. Komaro, Shimotsukenu no Ason, of Jiki-kwo-shi rank, represented to the Empress his desire to set free 600 slaves. His petition was granted.

[A. D. 691]

5th year 3rd month, 22nd day. An edict was issued, as follows :—" If a younger brother of the common people is sold by his elder brother, he should be classed with freemen ; if a child is sold by his parents, he should be classed with slaves ; persons confiscated into slavery by way of payment of interest on debts are to be classed with freemen, and their children, though born of a union with a slave, are also to be all classed with freemen."

Summer, 4th month, 1st day. An edict was issued, as follows :—" Slaves who have been manumitted in the time of the ancestor of a House, and already struck off the register of slaves, may not be claimed again as slaves by members of that House."

FLOOD AND RELIEF

[A. D. 692]

5th year. Intercalary 5th month, 3rd day. Great floods. Commissioners were sent to visit the districts and provinces one after another, making loans to those who, having met with disaster, were unable to support themselves, and allowing them to fish and cut wood in the hills and forests, the ponds and marshes.

An Imperial order was given that the Kin-kwō-miō Sutra should be expounded in the capital and in the four Home provinces.

4th day. The Buddhist priest Kwan-sei was given a present of fifteen hiki of coarse silk, thirty bundles of floss silk, and fifty tan of cloth, and he was commended for having made white lead.[1]

13th day. The Great Gods of Ise addressed the Empress, saying:—" Let the commuted taxes and forced labour for the provinces of Ise be remitted for this year. That being so, the thirty-five kind of red silk yarn forwarded by the two districts of the Gods should be reduced in value from next year."[2]

From: Nihongi, Chronicles of Japan from the Earliest Times to A. D. 697, translated from the Original Chinese and Japanese by W. G. Aston. Transactions and Proceedings of the Japan Society London, Supplement I, 2 Vol. London, 1896. Kegan Paul, Trench, Trübner & Co., Ltd.

1. Used as a cosmetic.—A.
2. The highly respectful character 奏 is used for the address of the Gods to the Empress. The interlinear Kana puts the respectful term tamaye in the mouths of the Gods. The districts referred to are Take and Watarahi.—A

IMPERIAL EDICTS OF LATE NARA PERIOD[1]

Discovery of Copper in Eastern Japan

This Edict is preceded in the Shoku Nihongi by the following statement:

In the 1st year of Wadō, 1st month of Spring (708) the District of Chichibu in the Province of Musashi sent an offering of copper to the Emperor, who pronounced this Edict.

The Edict, after the usual preamble, runs: It has been reported to Us that in the East of Our dominions in the province of Musashi soft copper,[1] naturally produced, has been found. It is Our opinion that this is a Treasure made manifest because the Gods that dwell in Heaven and the Gods that dwell on the Earth have deigned to enrich and bless us. Therefore We decree that, because of this precious Sign which has been manifested by the Gods of Heaven and Earth, the name of this Era shall be

---

1. "These edicts, recorded in the Shoku Nihongi (completed 797) are, as nearly as possible in pure Japanese, while the Edicts in the earlier Chronicles (Nihongi and Kojiki) are in Chinese." (Sansom).

2. Soft Copper. Naturally produced. The reading is doubtful, but the characters show that what is intended is copper, perhaps native copper or else a high-grade ore, in such a form as to be easily worked. It is by no means certain that this is the first discovery of copper in Japan. It was certainly scarce, since it was before this imported from Corea, but the reason for the present Edict was, more probably, that the copper was in an easily workable form. The Shoku Nihongi states that mint officials were appointed at this time. Vide Aston's Translation of the Nihongi II, p. 415, where there is a reference to copper from Inaba in 698, ten years previously.

In any case, copper was discovered late in Japan, which is surprising in view of the fact that it is now one of the chief copper-producing countries. I believe it is established that in Europe copper was known in the late Neolithic period.—Sansom.

changed and the fifth year of Kei-Un shall be called the first year of Wado.[1] The Edict continues (but in Chinese) to declare an Amnesty for certain sorts of offenders, bestows rewards upon aged people and persons who have displayed the virtues of filial piety or connubial faithfulness, promotes certain officials; and exempts the province of Musashi from certain levies, and the district of Chichibu from all contributions, for one year.

Ceremony and Music

The Sovereign According-to-the-Word deigns respectfully to speak. He says: The Sovereign Sage, whose name is to be spoken with awe, that ruled the Great Land of Many Islands in the Kiyomibara Palace of Asuka, in governing and ordering the Realm, even as a God deemed that to control and soften both high and low, keeping them tranquil and peaceful, it was necessary to have everywhere and always these two things: Ceremony and Music.

Therefore He invented and composed this Dance, and We knowing this and desiring that it shall be received and handed on for ever, as lastingly as Heaven and Earth, have caused this August Child the Princess Imperial to learn it and humbly received it as a charge and now present it before Our August Sovereign.[2]

---

1. Wadō if of course, soft copper; and small coins, struck in the first year of Wadō, are preserved in the Shōsōin.—(Sa).

2. This Edict is in Book XV. where it is stated that in Tempyo XV, 5th month (743), the Princess Imperial danced at a banquet given to the high officials in the Palace. The edict was read by Tachibana no Sukune to the Dowager Empress (Genshō), and the Princess Imperial is she who later became Empress Kōken.—Sa.

The "Sovereign Sage" is Temmu Tennō.—"Everywhere and always" is a possible rendering of tairakeku nagaku, but it is a phrase which constantly occurs with the meaning of "peacefully and lastingly."

Discovery of Gold in Eastern Japan

He says :—

This is the Word of the Sovereign who is the Servant of the Three Treasures, that he humbly speaks before the Image of Rōshana.

In this land of Yamato since the beginning of Heaven and Earth, Gold, though it has been brought as an offering from other countries, was thought not to exist. But in the East of the land which We rule, the Lord Michinoku Kudara no Kyōfuku of the Junior Fifth Rank, has reported that in his territory, in the district of Ōda, Gold has been found.

Hearing this we were astonished and rejoiced, and feeling that this is a Gift bestowed upon us by the love and blessing of Rōshana-butsu, We have received it with reverence and humbly accepted it, and have brought with Us all Our officials to worship and give thanks.

This We say reverently, reverently, in the Great Presence of the Three Treasures, whose name is to be spoken with awe.[1]

Ceremony and Music. Rei to Gaku to. This theory of government is of course purely Chinese, and is that which was developed by Confucius. Gaku includes both music and dancing. "This Dance." It was called the Dance of the Five Seasons (go setsu no mai).—Sa.

1. This Edict appears in Book XVII, where it is stated that in Tempyo Shobo I, 4th month of summer (749), the Emperor Shomu proceeded in state to the Tōdaiji and entered the front part of the Hall of the Image of Rushana-Butsu, and took up his position facing North towards the Image. The Empress, the Princess Imperial, the Ministers, Nobles, and civil and military functionaries were all present, the latter being drawn up on ranks at the end of the Hall. The Sadaijin Tachibana no Sukune Moroye was sent forward to address the Buddha in the Sovereign's name.

This is in some ways the most remarkable document of the collection. It will be noticed that the language used by the Sovereign is very humble. He does not refer to his divine ancestry, but describes himself as the servant

IMPERIAL EDICTS OF LATE NARA PERIOD

ON THE DEATH OF A MINISTER

On the death of the Sadaijin Fujiwara no Nagate. Expresses grief at the loss of a loyal servant. " Lamenting and bewailing and grieving and mourning, We weep August tears." It continues as follows :

From to-day shall We not hear the Words of Our Minister on the Business of the State ? From tomorrow shall We not see his labours on Our behalf. As the days and months pile up, more and more shall We grieve. As the years pass on, ever lonelier shall We feel. With whom now shall We go in company to relish the lovely hues of Spring and Autumn ? Who will go with Us to the pure places of the hills and streams ?

From: The Imperial Edicts in the Shoku-Nihongi, translated with Introduction and Notes by G. B. Sansom. Transactions of the Asiatic Society of Japan, Second Series, Vol. 1, 1923-4.

of the Three Treasuries, that is Buddha, the Law and the Priesthood. The word used for his address to the image is mōsu, used of a subject reporting to the throne. ' Facing North ' is the position of a subject when granted audience.

" Image of Rushana." Roshana or Rushana is the phonetic transcript of Locana, i. e., according to Professor Anezaki, Shaka as revealed in the Kegon Sutra. It is not, as sometimes stated, an abbreviation of Birushana, which stands for Vairocana. The identification of Dainichi (i. e. Birushana, Moha-Vairocana) with the Sun Goddess belongs to a later stage, during the development of Shingon doctrine in Japan.—Gold previous to this is always mentioned in the Chronicles as coming from Korea, either as a gift or as tribute. With regard to the name of the official concerned, note that Kudara is the Japanese for Pek-che, one of the Korean kingdoms.—Sa.

HEIAN PERIOD
(A.D. 794—1185)

A GOVERNOR TRAVELS
Ki no Tsurayuki
1. The Departure

[A. D. 935.]

28 JAN. One year on the twenty-first day of the twelfth month 'a certain personage'[1] left home at the Hour of the Dog (8:00 p. m.), which was the beginning of this modest record. He had just completed the usual period of four or five years as Governor of a Province; everything had been wound up, documents etc. had been handed over, and now he was about to go down to the place of embarkation; for he was to travel on shipboard. All sorts of people, both friends and strangers, came to see him off, including many who had served him faithfully during the past years, and who sorrowed at the thought of losing him that day. There was endless bustle and confusion; and so with one thing and another the night drew on.

29 JAN. 22nd day. He prayed for a calm voyage to the Land of Izumi. Fujiwara no Tokisane came to 'turn his horses head,'[2] although he was to travel by sea. Upper, middle, and lower classes all drank too heavily, and, wonderfully to relate, there they were on the edge of the salt sea itself all useless and incompetent!

30 JAN. 23rd day. A certain man, called Yagi no Yasu-

---

1. The author. As he writes in Japanese, in an epoch in which a well educated man was expected to do his literary work in Chinese, he assumes the language, the sentiments and the style of a woman-diarist. It was Ki no Tsurayuki who compiled (and wrote the famous preface of) the great collection of Heian-Poetry, the Kokinshū. He died in 946—Ed.

2. "An old expression corresponding to our 'stirrup cup'; it gradually came to mean any kind of farewell present..."—P.

nori, although he was of too high rank to have been one of his regular attendants in the Province, openly made him a farewell present. Perhaps he had not made a very good Governor; but still, the country-folk usually on an occasion like this just said good-bye and then disappeared; and here was a kind heart which was not ashamed to come back again. This word of praise for him is not due to the present he brought!

31 JAN. 24th day. The Chief Priest made him a farewell present; and accordingly everybody, high and low, even the very boys, got so intoxicated, that those who did not know how to write one word found that their feet had playfully trodden the word ' ten '[1] in the sand.

1 FEB. 26th day. Still at Government House, where the entertainment grew boisterous; the host and even the servants became uproarious. With loud voices Chinese poems were declaimed; and the host, ' the visitor ' and the other guests recited Japanese verses. The Chinese poems are not recorded here; but the following is the Japanese verse composed by the Governor, as host:

> *From the Capital*
> *Far across the sea I came,*
> *Came to see my Lord;*
> *But alas! 'twas all in vain,*
> *For we now must part again.*

Whereupon ' the former Governor ' composed this in reply:

> *I, too, travelled far*
> *O'er the stormy road of waves*
> *White with crested foam;*

---

1. which is similar to our sign for plus.—P.

Scarce, I think, another man
Would have faced the risks we ran!

There were also verses composed by many others, but they were quite worthless. Having recited these, the late and the present Governors descended together; the present and the late hosts went forth hand and hand, in good fellowship and the best of spirits.

2. DELAY

6 FEB. New Year's Day. Still they remained at the same place. The byakusan[1] had been placed for safe-keeping during the night in the ship's cabin; but the wind which is usual at this time of the year got up and blew it all into the sea. They had nothing left to drink, no potatoes, no seaweed and no rice-cakes; the neighborhood could supply nothing of this kind, and so their wants could not be satisfied. They could do nothing more than suck the head of a trout. What must the trout have thought of everybody sucking it in turn! That day he could think of nothing but the Capital, and talk of nothing but the straw rope stretched across the Gates of the Imperial Palace, the mullet heads and the holly.[2]

7 FEB. 2nd day. Still at Ōminato. The Chief Priest sent a gift of food and sake.

8 FEB. 3rd day. In the same place. I wonder if the wind and waves had a tender feeling for him, as they seemed to wish to delay him for some time? He certainly had no tender feeling for them!

---

1. Lit. 'white powder,' vegetabilic composition added to the sake.
2. These references are all to the customs and ceremonies of the New Year. For details see Mr. Porter's note 14, p. 137.

A GOVERNOR TRAVELS

9 FEB. 4th day. No start was made, as a high wind was still blowing. Masatsura presented a gift of sake and other good things. A man who came with presents like this ought not to have come in vain, but there was literally nothing to offer him; and, though it all looked lively enough, his spirits were very low.

10 FEB. 5th day. As the wind and waves had not gone down, they still remained at the same spot, and many people constantly came to call on him.

11 FEB. 6th day, is the same as yesterday.

*   *   *

14 FEB. 9th day. They set out from Ominato the first thing in the morning and rowed on, intending to stop at Nawa. All united in coming to bid him farewell (now that they were passing the boundaries of the Province); among many others, Fujiwara no Tokisane, Tachibana no Suehira, and Hasabe no Yukimasa, &c. From the day he left his Official Residence, people all the way along the route had come to see him off, and they all did it from kindness of heart; in fact, their kind hearts seemed to be as bottomless as the sea. At this spot, then, they parted and rowed on, for it was here that these people had come to see him off. After this, as they rowed gently forward, those who remained upon the sea-shore grew further and further away, and they in turn could no longer see those in the boat; from the shore they could not speak to the ship, and, if the ship called to them, it was all in vain. This being so, he could only recite the following verse to himself:

> *Far across the sea*
> *In my heart I fly to you*

DELAY

Bidding you farewell;
But no written word, alas!
From the ship to you may pass.

From: The Tosa Diary, translated from the Japanese by William N. Porter. London Henry Frowde, 1912.

SERVANT QUARTER'S TALES
Ochikubo Monogatari, ca. A.D. 975

1. Preparations for a Third Night

THE next night being the Third Night,[1] Akogi[2] wondered what she could arrange, and how she could serve them ricecakes. Again, having no one else to advise her, she wrote to her aunt, the wife of Izumi no Kami.[3] 'I received with great pleasure the things I asked you for,' she wrote. 'Thank you very much indeed. Again it may seem strange but I need some rice-cakes to-night for a certain reason. And also I should like a little fruit to serve with them as is usual. We thought that the guest would be staying only a little while, but the main building will be in an unlucky direction for him for forty-five days. May I therefore keep the furniture longer? And also may I have a washing-basin? I am sorry that I am giving you so much trouble by asking you so much, but I have no one else that I can ask.'

Meanwhile the Lord had sent this poem—

> *Absence the stronger*
> *Has made my love; let us be*

---

1. The Third Night of the consummation of the union was at this time most important, for it was customary for the bridegroom then to meet the bride's parents for the first time. If he did not come on the Third Night, therefore, it was understood that he wished the affair to end.—Wh.—On the Ochikubo Monogatari and ancient Japanese marriage customs see Appendix VII.
2. Servant-maid of the unhappy Lady who has been visited two times by the Lord of this story.
3. Provincial Governor.

PREPARATIONS FOR A THIRD NIGHT

As are a figure
And its shade in a mirror—

The same day the Lady answered for the first time—

Inseparable
Though now we may seem to be,
This thought saddens me—
Your love may be as fleeting
As a shade in a mirror.

The answer came from the house of Izumi no Kami for Akogi. 'Because I love you as I loved the one who is now dead,' her aunt wrote, ' and as we have no daughter, we had decided to adopt you and bring you up, giving you every attention possible. However to our great regret, you refused our offer. As for the furniture, keep it as long as you need it. I am sending you a washing-basin. It is very strange that you have not one already, for every maid in a noble's mansion ought to have such things. Why have you not told me before? As for the rice-cakes, it will be very easy for me to send you some; I will have them made at once. Do you need these things, because tonight is your Third Night[1] when you take a husband? I should very much like to see him. Oh, how I wish to see you also! Let me know everything in future. A governor in power is said to be very wealthy and my husband being a governor now, I can send you anything you wish.' The letter being in such a friendly strain, it made Akogi very happy.

'Why do you need rice-cakes?' the Lady asked, when Akogi showed her this letter.

---

1. That is when the union is regularised. The aunt deduces from the request for mochi and fruit that it is a question of a Third Night Feast. —Wh.

SERVANT QUARTER'S TALES

'Oh, I have a purpose,' Akogi said smilingly.

Two fine basins and a beautiful table had arrived with the letter, and with it, a bag containing white rice and fruit and dried food-stuffs, separated from each other by pieces of paper, and all packed very nicely. In order that she could serve the rice-cakes to them in grand style that night, Akogi set out the fruit and the chestnuts.

As night fell, the rain which had stopped for a while began to fall again in torrents. However just when Akogi was beginning to think that the rain had prevented her aunt from sending the rice-cakes, a man with an umbrella arrived, carrying a chest of magnolia wood. Her joy was beyond compare! Looking into the chest, she wondered how her aunt could have done so much in such a short time. There were two kinds of kusa-mochi, and two kinds of rice-cakes for the Third Night ceremonies and mochi of all kinds of shapes, some small and some cut into all kinds of curious shapes.

'Your request was unexpected,' her aunt's accompanying letter read, 'and I am sorry that, having to make them in a hurry, I was not able to make them as I like them.'

The messenger being in a hurry to return on account of the rain, she gave him only some saké and sent him back with this note to express her heartfelt gratitude, "Whatever words I may use to express my thanks, they cannot but sound too commonplace.'

Akogi was delighted that everything was now ready; she took some of the mochi in on a tray to the Lady.

*   *   *

The Lord, wearing only a single thickness of white clothing, went out unattended except by Tachihaki,[1] under

---

1. Attendant of the Lord.

PREPARATIONS FOR A THIRD NIGHT

the same umbrella, both feeling it very disagreeable to have to go out in such weather. They secretly opened the gate and stole out and made their way with great difficulty along the bad roads in the pitch darkness. Then at the crossing of two narrow lanes, they fell in with a procession of men with torches, evidently the retinue of some great noble.

The road was so narrow that it was impossible to avoid being seen, but they walked on the side of the road and held their umbrella to screen their faces.

'Stop a moment, you walking there,' one of the men in the procession said. 'This is very suspicious, walking about like this in the rain in the middle of the night. We shall arrest you.'

The two stood still, feeling very embarrassed, while the men brandished their torches.

'They have white legs. Perhaps they are not thieves,' one of them said.

'Upper class pilferers may have white legs though,' said another, and as he prepared to go on, he continued, " Why do you remain standing? Sit down.'

So the two had to sit down there, where there was much stinking filth.

'Why do you hide your faces under that umbrella?' another of a rougher character said, pulling aside the umbrella, and moving his torch about to see them as they sat among the filth. 'They are both wearing drawers; they are only poor men on their way to visit their sweet-hearts.'

'That is so,' they all agreed and went on their way.

'That must be one of the Emon no Kami[1] going the rounds,' the Lord said, as he rose to his feet. 'I thought I should have died, expecting every minute to be arrested

---

1. One of the Commanders, Right or Left, of the Bodyguard.—Wh.

as a suspicious person. It was funny calling us white-legged thieves,' and they laughed very heartily as they talked over the incident.

'Well, it is a pity, but we had better go home. We are all filthy. If we go to them in this stinking state, they will be very distant with us,' said the Lord to Tachihaki's great amusement.

'When you come to her in the rain like this, she will realise how very much you love her and she will think that the smell is the smell of musk. Our destination is near and your house a long way off. I hope you will decide to go on.'

The Lord agreed, thinking that it would be a shame to allow all his labour in coming so far to be in vain.

With great difficulty they opened the door, and entered. At Tachihaki's apartment, they both washed their feet.

"Get up before dawn. We must get away while it is still dark. We must not stay too long or we shall look very funny going home in this state,' said the Lord, who went then to tap on the lattice. . . .

Vengeance

'This year, the festival of the Kamo Shrine will be very splendid,' someone said to the Saemon no Kami, so he decided to take the whole household to see it, as there was little to amuse them in the mansion.

'Have a new carriage made. Let the servants have new robes, and let them look very nice,' the Saemon no Kami[1] said, and they all busied themselves in the preparations.

On the day of the festival a notice-board was erected in the main street at Ichijō[2] so that no one else could take that

---
1. Commander of the Gate-guards of the Left.
2. in Kyōto.

position. They therefore did not need to leave the house so early.

There were five carriages for the twenty older servants and two carriages for four young maids and four under-servants. The Saemon no Kami was with them, so there were many men of the Fourth and Fifth Rank as runners. In addition there were the Lord's younger brothers, the one formerly a Chamberlain but now a Shōshō, and the younger, mentioned before as a boy but who was now Hyōe no Suke.[1] 'We will go and see the procession with you,' they had said, and they had therefore come in their own carriages with their own attendants. Altogether there were more than twenty carriages.

When at last the party arrived at the place where the notice-board had been erected, they saw that on the opposite side of the road, there were standing two carriages, an old one of palm-leaf, and the other a basket-work carriage.

'Have my brothers' carriages placed just opposite ours, that is, on the opposite side of the street, for I want to have them near us,' the Saemon no Kami commanded.

'Have those carriages pulled on a little so that these carriages can be put there,' one of his men called out to the servants of the carriages on the opposite side of the street. However, they refused to move.

The Lord therefore asked his men to find out whose carriages they were, and discovered that they belonged to the old Chūnagon. 'I do not care whether they belong to a Chūnagon or a Dainagon,[2]' the Lord said. 'Why have they been placed here? They must have seen the

---

1. Colonel of the Military Guards.
2. Chūnagon : Counsellor of Middle Rank, Dainagon : Great Councellor. This Chūnagon here is the father of the Saemon no Kami's Lady who had been cruelly treated by the Chūnagon's second wife.—Ed.

SERVANT QUARTER'S TALES

notice-board. There is plenty of room further along the street. Tell them to pull along a little.'

The attendants went across and took hold of the carriages. The servants of the other carriages remonstrated. 'What are you doing? What very hot-tempered fellows you are! Your swaggering lord is of the same rank as ours, a Chūnagon. Does he want the whole street of Ichijō for himself? That is unreasonable,' they protested.

'Even the ex-Emperor, the Crown Prince and the Sai-in[1] in awe give way before our Lord,' a violent-tempered one of them retorted.

'Your lord may be of the same rank as ours,' another answered, ' but they cannot be mentioned in the same breath.'

As his brothers' carriages had not yet been brought into position, the Lord called for the Saemon no Jō.[2] 'See that those carriages are taken a little distance away,' he ordered.

The Saemon no Jō and his men therefore took hold of the carriages and dragged them away. The number of attendants on the other side was small, and they could make no resistance. There were a few runners but they said, 'It is useless. We cannot fight against them. We could kick the Dajōdaijin behind, but we cannot lay a finger on this Lord's ox-driver.'

They took the carriages and placed them inside someone's front gate and left them there. The people inside peeped out. 'What a mishap! What shall we do now?' they said.

(Though the Lord was the Commander of the Gate Guards and might seem fierce in the eyes of the world, he was very loving and gentle).

1. The Imperial Princess in charge of the Kamo Shrine.
2. Tachihaki, Korenari.

VENGEANCE

The silly old man Tenyaku no Suke[1] was inside. 'I will ask them to make room for us,' he said and alighted hurriedly from the carriage. 'Do not act so cruelly in this matter. If we had put our carriages where you had put your notice-board, you would have been justified in becoming angry with us. Why do you do this when the carriages were placed on the opposite side of the road? You should think of the consequences before you do such a thing. We shall have our revenge on you,' the foolish old man threatened.

The Saemon no Kurōdo[2] was very glad when he saw that it was the Tenyaku no Suke whom he had long been wishing to meet again.

The Saemon no Kami also recognised Tenyaku. 'Korenari,' he called out, 'Why do you allow that fellow to talk like that?'

Korenari understood. He winked to the servants who were ready for any violence and they rushed on the old man.

'You tell us to think of the consequences, old man. What are you going to do to the Lord?' one asked and knocked off the old man's hat with his long fan. And when everyone saw his thin queue and his bald and shining head, they shook with laughter. The old man covered his head with his sleeve and tried to retreat to his carriage, but the men closed on him and each gave him a kick, saying, 'What will be the consequences of that?' to their hearts' content.

'I am dying,' cried the old man, but he had hardly breath to say it from the cruel way in which they were treating him.

1. Chief tool of the Chūnagon's wife.—Ed.
2. Tachihaki, Korenari.

'Stop that. Stop that,' shouted the Lord, but he did not intend that they should. After knocking him down and trampling on him, they hung him partly in the carriage and dragged it still further away. The attendants belonging to it would not come near out of fear, for they had grown wiser by experience. They stood not far away, but behaved as if they were strangers. When the carriages had been left in the middle of the road up a lane, they slowly returned to the carriage and lifted up the shafts. It had all been a very shameful spectacle.

All the people in the carriage, even the old Kita no Kata,[1] decided that they must return home without waiting to see the procession. They hurriedly brought up the oxen and then one of the straps that held the carriage on the axle and which had been weakened in the contest broke with a 'futsu, futsu.' Then the carriage fell off the wheels into the middle of the road with a thud, 'hata.'

The low class people all around saw it and laughed until they shook. The servants who had been knocked over, their feet in the air, when the carriage fell, could not replace the carriage quickly. 'Today has been the most Unlucky Day for us. We have come to the depths of shame,' one of them said, snapping his fingers in his excitement and grief.

The feelings of the people in the carriage can only be left to the imagination. All were weeping; and the old Kita no Kata wept more than all, for she was sitting in the rear end of the carriage while her daughters were in front, and so she had had further to fall. With difficulty she crawled back into the carriage again for her elbow was dislocated and wept and sobbed, 'oi-oi.'

1. The wife of the Chūnagon.

VENGEANCE

'What is this tribulation a retribution for?' she said as she wept.

'Do not make such a noise,' her daughters urged her unfeelingly.

From: Ochikubo Monogatari, or the Tale of Lady Ochikubo, translated by Wilfried Whitehouse, M. A., J. L. Thompson & Co. (Retail), Ltd. Kobe; Kegan Paul, Trench, Trübner & Co., Ltd. London, 1934.

A LADY-IN-WAITING
Sei Shōnagon

1. Arrival at Court

WHEN I first entered her Majesty's services[1] I felt indescribably shy, and was indeed constantly on the verge of tears. When I came on duty the first evening, the Empress was sitting with only a three-foot screen in front of her, and so nervous was I that when she passed me some picture or book to look at, I was hardly capable of putting out my hand to take it. While she was talking about what she wanted me to see—telling me what it was or who had made it—I was all the time wondering whether my hair was in order. For the lamp was not in the middle of the room, but on a stand immediately beside where we sat, and we were more exposed than we should have been even by daylight. It was all I could do to fix my attention on what I was looking at. Only part of her Majesty's hand showed, for the weather was very cold and she had muffled herself in her sleeves; but I could see that it was pink and very lovely. I gazed and gazed. To an inexperienced home-bred girl like me it was a wonderful surprise to discover that such people as this existed on earth at all. At dawn I hurried away, but the Empress called after me, saying I seemed to be as frightened of the daylight as the ugly old God of Katsuragi.[2] I lay down again,

---

1. The authoress, daughter of Kiyohara no Motosuka who died as Governor of Bingo in 990, entered in 991 at the age of twenty-four the court of Empress Sadako, who then was fifteen years old. The pillow-book deals with the decade from 991 to 1000.—Ed.

2. Who is so unhappy about his appearance that he hides all day and only comes out at night.—W.

purposely choosing an attitude in which she could not get a full view of me. The shutters had not yet been opened. But soon one of the ladies came along and the Empress called out to her, "Please open those things!" She was beginning to do so, when the Empress suddenly said, "Not now." and, laughing, the lackey withdrew. Her Majesty then engaged me in conversation for some time, and said at last: "Well, I expect you are wanting to be off. Go as soon as you like." "And come back in good time to-night," she added. It was so late when I got back to my room that I found it all tidied and opened up for the day. The snow outside was lovely. Presently there came a message from the Empress saying it was a good opportunity for me to wait upon her in the morning. "The snow-clouds made it so dark," she said, "that you will be almost invisible." I could not bring myself to go, and the message was repeated several times. At last the head-girl of our room said: "You mustn't shut yourself up here all the time. You ought to be thankful to get a chance like this. Her Majesty would not ask for you unless she really wanted you, and she will think it very bad manners if you do not go." So I was hustled off, and arrived once more in the Imperial Presence, in a state of miserable embarrassment and confusion.

2. Holiday-Problems

A Court lady, when she is on a holiday, needs to have both her parents alive.[1] She will get on best in a house where people are always going in and out, where there is a great deal of conversation always going on in the back rooms, and where at the gate there is a continual clatter

---

1. Shōnagon's father died before she went to Court.—W.

A LADY-IN-WAITING

of horsemen. Indeed, she would far rather have too much noise than too little.

It is very annoying if one is living in some one else's house and a friend comes from Court, either openly or in secret, just to ask how long one will be away or to apologize for not having written ("I did not even know you were on holiday...")—it is, as I say, extremely annoying, particularly if he is a lover, to have the owner of the house coming and making a scene ("very dangerous...at this time of night too," and more in the same style) merely because one has opened the front door for a moment, to let the visitor in. Then later on : "Is the big gate locked?" To which the porter grunts in an injured tone: "There's someone here still. Am I to lock him in?" "Well, lock up directly he goes," says the landlord. "There have been a lot of burglaries round here lately." All of which is not very pleasant to over-hear.

After this the master of the house is continually poking out his head to see whether the visitor is still there, to the great amusement of the footmen whom the guest has brought with him. Most alarming of all is to hear these footmen doing an imitation of the landlord's voice. What a row there will be if he hears them!

It may happen that someone, who neither appears to be nor indeed is in any way a lover, finds it more convenient to come at night. In that case he will not feel inclined to put up with the churlishness of the family, and saying : "Well, it is rather late; and as it seems to be such a business for you to open the gate..." he will take his departure.

But if it is someone of whom the lady is really fond, and after she has told him again that she dare not receive him, he nevertheless goes on waiting outside her room till dawn ; at which point the porter, who has during his nightly rounds continually lingered regretfully by the gate, exclaims in a tone intended to be heard : " The morning's come " (as though such a thing had never happened before !) " and that front gate has been[1]—open all night," whereupon in broad daylight, when there is no longer any point in doing so, he locks the gate—all that sort of thing is very trying.

As I have said, with real parents of one's own, it would be all right. But step-parents can be a nuisance. One is always wondering how they will take things ; and even a brother's house can be very tiresome in this way.

Of course, what I really like is a house where there is no fuss about the front gate, and no one particularly minds whether it is midnight or morning. Then one can go out[2] and talk to whoever it may be—perhaps one of the princes, or of the lords attached to his Majesty's service—sit all through a winter's night with the shutters open, and after the guest has gone, watch him make his way into the distance. If he leaves just at daybreak, this is very agreeable, particularly if he plays upon his flute as he goes. Then, when he is out of sight, one does not hurry to go to bed, but discusses the visitor with someone, reviews the poems he made, and so gradually falls to sleep.

" I saw someone, who had no business here , in the corridor early this morning. There was a servant holding an umbrella over him. He was just going away. . ." So I heard one of the girls say, and suddenly realized that it was to a visitor of mine that she was referring !

However, I really didn't know why she should de-

---

1. The adverb he uses (raisō to), evidently a very emphatic one, was a a slang expression of the time, the exact meaning of which is uncertain.—W.
2. Out to the front of the house.—W.

A LADY-IN-WAITING

scribe him as "having no business here." As a matter of fact, he is only a chige,[1] a person of quite comfortable eminence, whom I have every right go know, if I choose.

Presently a letter came from the Empress, with a message that I was to reply instantly. Opening it in great agitation, I saw a drawing of a huge umbrella; the person holding it was entirely hidden, save for the fingers of one hand. Underneath was written the quotation: "Since the morning when dawn broke behind the fringe of the Mikasa[2] Hills..."

The whole affair was a trival one, but her Majesty might easily have been cross about it, and when the letter came I was actually hoping that no one would mention the matter to her. And now, instead of a scolding, came only this joke, which, though it humiliated me, was really very amusing. I took another piece of paper and drawing upon it the picture of a heavy rainstorm, I wrote underneath: "It is a case of much cry and no rain."

3. Table Manners

The things that workmen eat are most extraordinary. When the roof of the eastern wing was being mended, there were a whole lot of workmen sitting in a row and having dinner. I went across to that side of the house and watched. The moment the things were handed to them, they gulped down the gravy, and then, putting their bowls aside, ate up all the vegetables. I began to think that they were going to leave their rice, when suddenly they fell upon it and in a twinkling it had all disappeared.[3]

[1]. A courtier not admitted on to the Imperial dais.—W.
[2]. Mikasa means "Three Umbrellas."—W.
[3]. The Japanese code of good manners demands that after each morsel of vegetables or fish some rice should be taken and that dishes should not be eaten one after the other, but that one should help oneself alternately to each of several dishes served on a tray.—Ed.

There were several of them sitting there together and they all ate in the same way ; so I suppose it is a habit of builders. I can't say I think that it is a very attractive one.

4. Annoying Things

It is particularly annoying if a letter goes astray and gets delivered to someone to whom one would never have dreamt of showing it. If the messenger would simply say straight out that he has made a mistake, one could put up with it. But he always begins arguing and trying to prove that he only did as he was told. It is this that is so trying, and if there was not always someone looking on, I am sure I should rush at him and strike him.

To plant a nice hagi[1] or susuki,[2] and then find someone with a long-box and gardening tools who has dug them up and is carrying them away—is a painful and annoying experience. The provoking part of it is that if a male even of the humblest description were on the spot, the wretch would never dare to do so. When one stops him and and expostulates, he pretends he has only thinned them out a bit, and hurries off. I really cannot tell you how annoying it is.

One is staying with a provincial Governor or some small official of that kind, and a servant comes from some grand house. He speaks and behaves with the utmost rudeness and an air as much as to say " I know I am rude ; but people like you can't punish me for it, so what do I care ? " I find that very annoying.

A man picks up a letter that one does not want him to see and takes it with him into the courtyard, where he stands reading it. At the first moment one rushes after

---

1. Lespedeza bicolor.—W.
2. Eularia japonica.—W.

him in rage and desperation; but at the curtains one is obliged to stop, and while one watches him reading one can hardly prevent oneself from swooping down upon him and snatching it away.

A lady is out of humour about some trifle, and leaving her lover's side goes and establishes herself on another couch. He creeps over to her and tries to bring her back, but she is still cross, and he, feeling that this time she has really gone too far, says: "As you please," and returns to the big bed, where he ensconces himself comfortably and goes to sleep. It is a very cold night and the lady, having only an unlined wrap to cover herself with, soon begins to suffer. She thinks of getting up; but everyone else in the house is asleep and she does not know what to do or where to go. If she must needs have this quarrel, it would have been better, she thinks, to start it a little earlier in the evening. Then she begins to hear strange noises both in the women's quarters and outside. She becomes frightened and softly creeps towards her lover, plucks at the bedclothes, and raises them. But he vexingly pretends to be fast asleep; or merely says: "I advise you to go on sulking a little longer."

Small children and babies ought to be fat. So ought provincial governors, or one suspects them of being bad-tempered. As regards appearance, it is most essential of all that the boys who feed the carriage-oxen should be presentable. If one's other servants are not fit to be seen, they can be stowed away behind the carriage. But outriders, or the like, who are bound to catch the eye, make a painful impression if they are not perfectly trim. However, if it is too obvious that one's men servants have been lumped together behind the carriage in order to escape notice, this in itself looks very bad.

It is a mistake to choose slim, elegant youths on purpose that they may look well as footmen, and then let them wear trousers that are grimy at the ends and hunting-cloaks or the like that have seen too much wear. The best that can be hoped is that people will think they are walking beside your carriage by chance and have nothing to do with you.

But it is a great convenience that all one's servants should be handsome. Then if they should happen to tear their clothes or make themselves in any way shabby or untidy, it is more likely to be overlooked.

Officers of State, who have official attendants allotted to them, sometimes spoil the effect by allowing their page-boys to go about dirty and ill-kept.

Whether a gentlemen is at home or on an official mission or staying with friends he ought always to have round him quantities of handsome page-boys.

For secret meetings summer is best. It is true that the nights are terribly short and it begins to grow light before one has a wink of sleep. But it is delightful to have all the shutters open, so that the cool air comes in and one can see into the garden. At last comes the time of parting, and just as the lovers are trying to finish off all the small things that remain to be said, they are suddenly startled by a loud noise just outside the window. For a moment they make certain they are betrayed; but it turns out only to be a crow that cried as it flew past.

But it is pleasant, too, on very cold nights to lie with one's lover, buried under a great pile of bed-clothes. Noises such as the tolling of a bell sound so strange. It seems as though they came up from the bottom of a deep pit. Strange, too, is the first cry of the birds, sounding so muffled and distant that one feels sure their beaks are still tucked under their wings. Then each fresh note gets shriller and nearer.

From: The Pillow Book of Sei Shōnagon, translated by Arthur Waley, London, George Allen and Unwin, 1928.

THE HOUSE BEAUTIFUL
Murasaki Shikibu

1. On Ladies

It was the season of the long rains. For many days there had not been a fine moment and the Court was keeping a strict fast. The people at the Great Hall were becoming very impatient of Genji's long residence at the Palace, but the young lords, who were Court pages, liked waiting upon Genji better than upon anyone else, always managing to put out his clothes and decorations in some marvellous new way. Among these brothers his greatest friend was the Equerry, Tō no Chūjō, with whom above all other companions of his playtime he found himself familiar and at ease. This lord too found the house which his father-in-law, the Minister of the Right, had been at pains to build for him, somewhat oppressive, while at his father's house he, like Genji, found the splendours somewhat dazzling, so that he ended by becoming Genji's constant companion at Court. They shared both studies and play and were inseparable companions on every sort of occasion, so that soon all formalities were dispensed with between them and the inmost secrets of their hearts freely exchanged.

It was on a night when the rain never ceased its dismal downpour. There were not many people about in the palace and Genji's rooms seemed even quieter than usual. He was sitting by the lamp, looking at various books and papers. Suddenly he began pulling some letters out of the drawers of a desk which stood near by. This aroused

Tō no Chūjō's curiosity. " Some of them I can show to you " said Genji, " but there are others which I had rather. . . ." " It is just those which I want to see. Ordinary, commonplace letters are very much alike and I do not suppose that yours differ much from mine. What I want to see are passionate letters written in moments of resentment, letters hinting consent, letters written at dusk. . . . "

He begged so eagerly that Genji let him examine the drawers. It was not indeed likely that he had put any very important or secret documents in the ordinary desk ; he would have hidden them away much further from sight. So he felt sure that the letters in these drawers would be nothing to worry about. After turning over a few of them, " What an astonishing variety ! " Tō no Chūjō exclaimed and began guessing at the writers' names, and made one or two good hits. More often he was wrong and Genji, amused by his puzzled air, said very little but generally managed to lead him astray. At last he took the letters back, saying " But you too must have a large collection. Show me some of yours, and my desk will open to you with better will." " I have none that you would care to see," said Tō no Chūjō, and he continued : " I have at last discovered that there exists no woman of whom one can say " Here is perfection. This is indeed she." There are many who have the superficial art of writing a good running hand, or if occasion requires of making a quick repartee. But there are few who will stand the ordeal of any further test. Usually their minds are entirely occupied by admiration for their own accomplishments, and their abuse of all rivals creates a most unpleasant impression. Some again are adored by over-fond parents. These have been since childhood guarded behind lattice windows[1] and no knowledge of them is allowed to reach the outer-world, save that of their excellence in some accomplishment or art; and this may indeed sometimes arouse our interest. She is pretty and graceful and has not yet mixed at all with the world. Such a girl by closely copying some model and applying herself with great industry will often succeed in really mastering one of the minor and ephemeral arts. Her friends are careful to say nothing of her defects and to exaggerate her accomplishments, and while we cannot altogether trust their praise we cannot believe that their judgment is entirely astray. But when we take steps to test their statements we are invariably disappointed."

He paused, seeming to be slightly ashamed of the cynical tone which he had adopted, and added "I know my experience is not large, but that is the conclusion I have come to so far." Then Genji, smiling: "And are there any who lack even one accomplishment?" "No doubt, but in such a case it is unlikely that anyone would be successfully decoyed. The number of those in whom nothing but good can be found is probably equal. I divide women into three classes. Those of high rank and birth are made such a fuss of and their weak points are so completely concealed that we are certain to be told that they are paragons. About those of the middle class everyone is allowed to express his own opinions, and we shall have much conflicting evidence to sift. As for the lower classes, they do not concern us."

---

1. Japanese houses were arranged somewhat differently from ours and for many of the terms which constantly recur in this book (kichō, sudare, sunoko, etc.) no exact English equivalents can be found. In such cases I have tried to use expressions which without being too awkward or unfamiliar will give an adequate general idea of what is meant.—W.

THE HOUSE BEAUTIFUL

The completeness with which Tō no Chūjō disposed of the question amused Genji, who said " It will not always be so easy to know into which of the three classes a woman ought to be put. For sometimes people of high rank sink to the most abject positions; while others of common birth rise to be high officers, wear self-important faces, redecorate the inside of their houses and think themselves as good as anyone. How are we to deal with such cases ? "

At this moment they were joined by Hidari no Uma no Kami and Tō Shikibu no Jō, who said they had also come to the Palace to keep the fast. As both of them were great lovers and good talkers, Tō no Chūjō handed over to them the decision of Genji's question, and in the discussion which followed many unflattering things were said. Uma no Kami spoke first. " However high a lady may rise, if she does not come of an adequate stock, the world will think very differently of her from what it would of one born to such honours; but if through adverse fortune a lady of highest rank finds herself in friendless misery, the noble breeding of her mind is soon forgotten and she becomes an object of contempt. I think then that taking all things into account, we must put such ladies too into the " middle class." But when we come to classify the daughters of Zuryō,[1] who are sent to labour at the affairs of distant provinces,—they have such ups and downs that we may reasonably put them too into the middle class.

" Then there are Ministers of the third and fourth classes without Cabinet rank. These are generally thought less of even than the humdrum, ordinary officials. They are usually of quite good birth, but have much less responsibility than Ministers of State and consequently much greater

---

1. Provincial officials. Murasaki herself came of this class.—W.

peace of mind. Girls born into such households are brought up in complete security from want or deprivation of any kind, and indeed often amid surroundings of the utmost luxury and splendour. Many of them grow up into women whom it would be folly to despise; some have been admitted at Court, where they have enjoyed a quite unexpected success. And of this I could cite many, many instances."

" Their success has generally been due to their having a lot of money," said Genji smiling. " You should have known better than to say that," said Tō no Chūjō, reproving him, and Uma no Kami went on: " There are some whose lineage and reputation are so high that it never occurs to one that their education could possibly be at fault; yet when we meet them we find ourselves exclaiming in despair " How can they have contrived to grow up like this?""

" No doubt the perfect woman in whom none of these essentials is lacking must somewhere exist and it would not startle me to find her. But she would certainly be beyond the reach of a humble person like myself, and for that reason I should like to put her in a category of her own and not to count her in our present classification.

" But suppose that behind some gateway overgrown with vine-weed, in a place where no one knows there is a house at all, there should be locked away some creature of unimagined beauty—with what excitement should we discover her! The complete surprise of it, the upsetting of all our wise theories and classifications, would be likely, I think, to lay a strange and sudden enchantment upon us. I imagine her father rather large and gruff; her brother, a surly, ill-looking fellow. Locked away in an utterly blank and uninteresting bed-room she will be subject to odd flights of fancy, so that in her hands the arts that others learn as trivial accomplishments will seem strangely full of meaning and importance; or perhaps in some particular art she will thrill us by her delightful and unexpected mastery. Such a one may perhaps be beneath the attention of those of you who are of flawless lineage. But for my part I find it hard to banish her. . ." and here he looked at Shikibu no Jō, who wondered whether the description had been meant to apply to his own sisters, but said nothing. " If it is difficult to choose even out of the top class. . ." thought Genji, and began to doze.

He was dressed in a suit of soft white silk, with a rough cloak carelessly hung over his shoulders, with belt and fastenings untied. In the light of the lamp against which he was leaning he looked so lovely that one might have wished he were a girl; and they thought that even Uma no Kami's "perfect woman," whom he had placed in a category of her own, would not be worthy of such a prince as Genji.

The conversation went on. Many persons and things were discussed. Uma no Kami contended that perfection is equally difficult to find in other spheres. The sovereign is hard put to it to choose his ministers. But he at least has an easier task than the husband, for he does not entrust the affairs of his kingdom to one, two or three persons alone, but sets up a whole system of superiors and subordinates.

But when the mistress of a house is to be selected, a single individual must be found who will combine in her person many diverse qualities. It will not do to be too exacting. Let us be sure that the lady of our choice possesses certain tangible qualities which we admire; and if in other ways she falls short of our ideal, we must be patient

ON LADIES

and call to mind those qualities which first induced us to begin our courting.

But even here we must beware; for there are some who in the selfishness of youth and flawless beauty are determined that not a dusk-flick shall fall upon them. In their letters they choose the most harmless topics, but yet contrive to colour the very texture of the written signs with a tenderness that vaguely disquiets us. But such a one, when we have at last secured a meeting, will speak so low that she can scarcely be heard, and the few faint sentences that she murmurs beneath her breath serve only to make her more mysterious than before. All this may seem to be the pretty shrinking of girlish modesty; but we may later find what held her back was the very violence of her passions.

Or again, where all seems plain sailing, the perfect companion will turn out to be too impressionable and will upon the most inappropriate occasions display her affections in so ludicrous a way that we begin to wish ourselves rid of her.

Then there is the zealous house-wife, who regardless of her appearance twists her hair behind her ears and devotes herself entirely to the details of our domestic welfare. The husband, in his comings and goings about the world, is certain to see and hear many things which he cannot discuss with strangers, but would gladly talk over with an intimate who could listen with sympathy and understanding, someone who could laugh with him or weep if need be. It often happens too that some political event will greatly perturb or amuse him, and he sits apart longing to tell someone about it. He suddenly laughs at some secret recollection or sighs audibly. But the wife only says lightly " What is the matter ? " and shows no interest.

This is apt to be very trying...[1]

1. The discussion continues.—Ed.

THE HOUSE BEAUTIFUL

2. The Festival of Red Leaves

The imperial visit to the Red Sparrow Court was to take place on the tenth day of the Godless Month. It was to be a more magnificent sight this year than it had ever been before and the ladies of the Palace were disappointed that they could not be present.[1] The Emperor too could not bear that Fujitsubo[2] should miss the spectacle, and he decided to hold a grand rehearsal in the Palace. Prince Genji danced the 'Waves of the Blue Sea.' Tō no Chūjō was his partner; but though both in skill and beauty he far surpassed the common run of performers, yet beside Genji he seemed like a mountain fir growing beside a cherry-tree in bloom. There was a wonderful moment when the rays of the setting sun fell upon him and the music grew suddenly louder. Never had the onlookers seen feet tread so delicately nor head so exquisitely poised; and in the song which followed the first movement of the dance his voice was sweet as that of Kalavinka[3] whose music is Buddha's Law. So moving and beautiful was this dance that at the end of it the Emperor's eyes were wet, and all the princes and great gentlemen wept aloud. When the song was over and, straightening his long dancer's sleeves, he stood waiting for the music to begin again and at last the more lively tune of the second movement struck up,—then indeed, with his flushed and eager face, he merited more than ever his name of Genji the Shining One. The Princess Kōkiden did not at all like to see her step-son's beauty arousing so much enthusiasm and she said sarcastically " He is altogether too beautiful. Presently we shall have a god coming down

---
1. They were not allowed to leave the palace.—W.
2. Empress at that time involved in a love-affair with Prince Genji.—Ed.
3. The bird that sings in Paradise.—W.

from the sky to fetch him away."[1] Her young waiting-ladies noticed the spiteful tone in which the remark was made and felt somewhat embarrassed. As for Fujitsubo, she kept on telling herself that were it not for the guilty secret which was shared between them the dance she was now witnessing would be filling her with wonder and delight. As it was, she sat as though in a dream, hardly knowing what went on around her.

Now she was back in her own room. The Emperor was with her. "At to-day's rehearsal" he said, 'The Waves of the Blue Sea' went perfectly." Then, noticing that she made no response, "What did you think of it?" "Yes, it was very good," she managed to say at last. "The partner did not seem to me bad either," he went on; "there is always something about the way a gentlemen moves and uses his hands which distinguishes his dancing from that of professionals. Some of our crack dancing-masters have certainly made very clever performers of their own children; but they never have the same freshness, the same charm as the young people of our class. They expended so much effort on the rehearsal that I am afraid the festival itself may seem a very poor affair. No doubt they took all this trouble because they knew that you were here at the rehearsal and would not see the real performance."

* * *

On the day of the festival the royal princes and all the great gentlemen of the Court were in attendance. Even the Heir Apparent went with the procession. After the music-boats had rowed round the lake dance upon dance

---

1. In allusion to a boy-prince of seven years old whom the jealous gods carried off to the sky. W. (The tale of Ganymed, according to Le Coq, had come to be known in the Far East in Hellenistic or Roman times. Ed.)

THE HOUSE BEAUTIFUL

was performed, both Korean and of the land beyond the sea.[1] The whole valley resounded with the noise of music and drums. The Emperor insisted upon treating Genji's performance at the rehearsal as a kind of miracle or religious portent, and ordered special services to be read in very temple. Most people thought this step quite reasonable; but Princess Kōkiden said crossly that that she saw no necessity for it. The Ring[2] was by Emperor's order composed indifferently of commoners and noblemen chosen out of the whole realm for their skill and grace. The two Masters of Ceremony, Sayemon no Kami and Uyemon no Kami, were in charge of the left and right wings of the orchestra. Dancing-masters and others were entrusted with the task of seeking out performers of unusual merit and training them for the festival in their own houses. When at last under the red leafage of tall autumn trees forty men stood circle-wise with their flutes and to the music that they made a strong wind from the hills sweeping the pine-woods added its fierce harmonies, while from amid a wreckage of whirling and scattered leaves the Dance of the Blue Waves suddenly broke out in all its glittering splendour,—a rapture seized onlookers that was akin to fear.

The maple-wreath that Genji wore had suffered in the wind and thinking that the few red leaves which clung to it had a desolate air, the Minister of the Left[3] plucked a bunch of chrysanthemums from among those that grew before the Emperor's seat and twined them in the dancer's wreath.

1. China.—Ed.
2. Those who stand in a circle round the dancers while the latter change their clothes.—W.
3. Reading "Sadaijin," not "Sadaisho."—W.

"CHINESE BANQUET"

At sunset the sky clouded over and it looked like rain. But even the weather seemed conscious that such sights as this would not for a long while be seen again, and till all was over not a drop fell. His Exit Dance, crowned as he was with this unspeakably beautiful wreath of many coloured flowers, was even more astonishing that that wonderful moment on the day of the rehearsal and seemed to the thrilled onlookers like the vision of another world. Humble and ignorant folk sitting afar on tree-roots or beneath some rock, or half-buried in deep banks of fallen leaves—few were so hardened that they did not shed a tear. Next came the "Autumn Wind" danced by Lady Jōkyōden's son[1] who was still a mere child. The remaining performances attracted little attention, for the audience had had its full of wonders and felt that whatever followed could not spoil the recollection of what had gone before.

That night Genji was promoted to the First Class of the Third Rank and Tō no Chūjō was promoted to intermediate standing between the First and Second Classes of the Fourth Rank. The gentlemen of the court were all promoted one rank. But although they celebrated their good fortune with the usual rejoicings they were well aware that they had only been dragged in Genji's wake and wondered how it was that their destinies had come to be linked in this curious way with those of the prince who had brought them this unexpected piece of good fortune.

3. "Chinese Banquet"

About the twentieth day of the second month the Emperor gave a Chinese banquet under the great cherry-tree of the Southern Court. Both Fujitsubo and the Heir

---

1. Another illegitimate son of the Emperor, Genji's step-brother.—W.

Apparent were to be there. Kōkiden, although she knew that the mere presence of the Emperss was sufficient to spoil her pleasure, could not bring herself to forego so delightful an entertainment. After some promise of rain the day turned out magnificent; and in full sunshine, with the birds singing in every tree, the guests (royal princes, noblemen and professional poets alike) were handed the rhyme words which the Emperor had drawn by lot, and set to work to compose their poems. It was with a clear and ringing voice that Genji read out the word "Spring" which he had received as the rhyme-sound of his poem. Next came Tō no Chūjō who, feeling that all eyes were upon him and determined to impress himself favourably on his audience, moved with the greatest possible elegance and grace; and when on receiving his rhyme he announced his name, rank, and titles, he took great pains to speak pleasantly as well as audibly. Many of the other gentlemen were rather nervous and looked quite pale as they came forward, yet they acquitted themselves well enough. But the professional poets, particularly owing to the high standard of accomplishment which the Emperor's and Heir Apparent's lively interest in Chinese poetry had at that time diffused through the Court, were very ill at ease; as they crossed the long space of the garden on their way to receive their rhymes they felt utterly helpless. A simple Chinese verse is surely not much to ask of a professional poet; but they all wore an expression of the deepest gloom. One expects elderly scholars to be somewhat odd in their movements and behaviour, and it was amusing to see the lively concern with which the Emperor watched their various but always uncouth and erratic methods of approaching the Throne. Needless to say a great deal of music had been arranged for. Towards dusk the delightful dance known as the Warbling of Spring Nightingales was performed, and when it was over the Heir Apparent, remembering the Festival of Red Leaves, placed a wreath on Genji's head and pressed him so urgently that it was impossible for him to refuse. Rising to his feet he danced very quietly a fragment of the sleeve-turning passage in the Wave Dance. In a few moments he was seated again, but even into this brief extract from a long dance he managed to import an unrivalled charm and grace. Even his father-in-law who was not in the best of humour with him was deeply moved and found himself wiping away a tear.

"And why have we not seen Tō no Chūjō?" said the Heir Apparent. Whereupon Chūjō danced the Park of Willow Flowers, giving a far more complete performance than Genji, for no doubt he knew that he would be called upon and had taken trouble to prepare his dance. It was a great success and the Emperor presented him with a cloak, which everyone said was a most unusual honour. After this the other young noblemen who were present danced in no particular order, but it was now so dark that it was impossible to discriminate between their performances.

4. An Imperial Companion

It will be remembered that after Rokujō's death Genji decided that her daughter Princess Akikonomu had best come and live with him till the time came for her Presentation at Court. At the last minute, however, he altered his mind, for such a step seemed too direct a provocation to Princess Akikonomu's admirer, the young ex-Emperor Suzaku. But though he did not remove her from her palace in the Sixth Ward he felt his responsibilities towards this unfortunate orphan very keenly and paid her many lengthy visits. He had now definitely arranged with Fujitsubo that Akikonomu was soon to enter the Emperor's Palace, but he was careful not to betray in public any knowledge of this plan, and to the world at large he seemed merely to be giving the girl such general guidance and support as might be expected from a guardian and family friend.

Suzaku was indeed bitterly disappointed at the intelligence that the Princess had been handed over to a mere infant such as the present Emperor. He often thought of writing to her but at the same time dreaded the scandal which would ensue if his attachment became known. When however the day of Presentation at last arrived, his caution suddenly deserted him, and he sent to Akikonomu's palace an assortment of the most costly and magnificent gifts which his treasury could supply—comb-boxes, scrap-boxes, cases for incense-jars; all of the most exquisite workmanship and material; with these was a supply of the most precious perfumes both for burning and for the scenting of clothes, so that the bales in which these gifts arrived scented the air for full league on every side. This extravagant magnificence, besides relieving Suzaku's feelings, had another very definite object. It was particularly intended to annoy the lady's guardian, to whom, as Suzaku very well knew, the contents of these packages would immediately be shown. It so happened that Genji was actually at Akikonomu's palace when the scented bales arrived; her servants at once showed them to him and told him whence they came. He picked up at random one of a pair of comb-boxes; it was a work of fascinating elegance and delicacy. Near it was a box for combs such as are worn in the hair, decorated with a pattern of flowers.

In the very centre of one petal was an inscription. Looking closer he read the poem:

> *' Come not again!'*[1]
> *Because it fell to me,*
> *Who least would have it so,*
> *At Heaven's command your exile to ordain;*
> *To others, not to me who bade you go,*
> *You come again!*

*   *   *

She wrote no letter, but only the poem:

> *" Come not again!" I wept to hear those words,*
> *Thinking you willed it so,*
> *When Heaven's command my exile did ordain;*
> *Now hearing that it grieved you I should go,*
> *I weep again.*

The messengers who had brought the presents were richly rewarded and sent upon their way. Genji would very much have liked to see her reply, but she refused to show it to him.

She was small and frail. How well Suzaku, with his almost girlish beauty, would have suited her; while as for the Emperor, he was years her junior, scarcely out of the nursery. Did she too (though she certainly breathed no word of complaint) secretly resent the steps which he had taken for her worldly advancement? This idea troubled him sorely; but it was by now far too late to undo the arrangement, and the best he could do was to stay with her for a little while and advise her as kindly and discreetly as possible how to conduct herself in the new life that was before her. He then interviewed the Court

---

1. The formula with which the Emperor despatches the Vestal of Ise.—W.

THE HOUSE BEAUTIFUL

chamberlains who were to arrange her Presentation, and having settled everything satisfactorily with them he made his way to the Inner Palace. He did not wish it to appear that he was himself standing sponsor for the new arrival nor that he was in the Palace as her relative or guardian. He therefore gave his coming the appearance of an ordinary ceremonial visit.

Princess Akikonomu's palace was famous for the unusual number of good-looking gentlewomen who were in service there. Many of these had recently been living at their homes, but they now assembled in full force, and arriving with their mistress at Court created a most dazzling impression. Were Rokujō alive, with what solicitude would she be watching over that day's momentous proceedings, thought Genji, as he saw the procession arrive; and remembering her singular gifts and lively intelligence, he felt how great a loss she was not to himself only, but to the whole life of the Court. So rare indeed (as it now seemed to him) was her perfection both of mind and person that he seldom encountered among his acquaintances talent or accomplishment of any kind without immediately recalling how slender these attainments would seem if set beside those of Lady Rokujō.

On the day of the Presentation Fujitsubo was at the Palace. When she told the Emperor that some one new coming to see him, he listened very earnestly and attentively. He was an intelligent and lively child, very forward for his age. After telling him all about the princess, " So you see she is rather an important lady," Fujitsubo continued, " and when she comes this evening you must be very polite to her and not play any of your tricks. . ." The Emperor said nothing, but he thought to himself that if the lady were indeed so grown up and so important, far from wanting to tease her he would be very frightened of her indeed.

Great was his delight then when very late that evening there arrived at the Palace a very shy, shrinking girl, very small and fragile, not indeed looking like a grown-up person at all. He thought her very pretty; but he was much more at his ease with Chūjō's little daughter, who had lived at the Palace for some while and was very sociable and affectionate, while the new princess was terribly silent and shy. Still, though he found her rather difficult to get on with, he felt, partly owing to the deference with which, as Prince Genji's ward, she was treated by every one else at Court, and partly owing to the magnificence with which she was served and apparelled—he felt that she was in some way which he did not understand a person of very great importance. In the evenings indeed he allowed the one to wait upon him as often as the other; but when he wanted a partner in some game or some one to amuse him the early part of the day, it was seldom Akikonomu for whom he sent.

5. BROTHERS AND SISTERS, AND A CHERRY-TREE

It was the third month, which is the real season of cherry-blossom, for not only are the boughs laden with it but the very air quavers with a storm of failing flowers. At Tamakatsura's palace a profound stillness reigned. No visitor had set foot there all day, and it seemed so unlikely that anyone would come that Himegimi and her sister were sitting at the window, both of them handsome, lively girls of about seventeen to eighteen.

Himegimi herself was certainly the more striking of the two, and her beauty was so thoroughly in the style fashionable at the moment that it seemed inconceivable she would not do better for herself than marry into an ordinary clan.

She wore a white dress lined with dark purple, and a skirt of a tint that recalled the globe-flower, as fold on fold it spilled its yellow shimmer on the floor. There was about her a singular air of competence and self-possession.

Her sister was dressed in a light reddish-brown, a colour which suited[1] the long, rippling tresses of her hair, She was very tall, but graceful and adroit in her movements. Her expression was more serious than that of her sister, and she looked as though she were capable of far deeper feelings.

Himegimi, the elder girl, was generally considered the more attractive of the two. On this particular occasion they were sitting opposite one another playing draughts, an occupation that can show a woman's charms to great advantage, with its dangling tresses and raising and sinking of the head. Their younger brother Jiju was with them, ' to see that they did not cheat,' he said. Presently the two elder brothers, Sakon no Chujo and Uchuben, looked into the room. ' Jiju has stolen a march upon us,' they said. ' Look, their ladyships have taken him on as referee in a game of draughts.' And with a rather patronizing air, complete men of the world, they advanced towards the draughts-board, leaving it to the ladies-in-waiting to make room for them.

' It is too bad,' said Sakon no Chujo, ' that while I am slaving at the Palace Jiju should step in and supplant me here.' ' And what about me ? " said Uchuben. ' My work in the Council of State takes up far more time, and I might easily be forgiven for neglecting my courtly duties in this house, were I so faithless as to do so.'

The girls had stopped their game and were sitting looking in front of them with an air of slight bewilderment that

---

1. A brownish tinge is not unknown in Japanese women's hair.—W

was very engaging. Sakon no Chujo knew how much, both at the Palace and wherever he went, he missed the late Minister's support. And as he looked at his sisters tears filled his eyes at the thought that their case was worse than his own. But he was now twenty-seven. He was beginning to have some influence, and he must use the whole of it to do for these girls some part at least of what his father would have done.

Out in the garden there was, among the many flowering trees, one particular cherry-tree with a scent that far exceeded that of all the rest. Sakon sent someone to pluck a branch and set it in his sister's hands.

'What blossom!' Himegimi said. 'There is no flower like it!' 'That is the tree,' said Sakon no Chujo, 'about which we had a quarrel when we were small. Each of you said that it was yours, and I said it belonged to me. Father said it was Himegimi's, and mother said it was Wakagimi's[1] tree. But no one said it was mine, and I remember that though I did not cry or make a fuss, I was very unhappy about it. It is growing old itself—this cherry-tree,' he went on, 'and makes one feel old along with it. So many people that once shared it with us are gone now.' He spoke sadly, yet half smiling. The sisters had seldom seen him in so serious a mood. He was married now, and lived with his wife's people, so that he could seldom spend a quiet hour like this at his mother's house. But to-day he had been determined to come, simply for the sake of this tree.

It was strange to think that this full-grown man was Tamakatsura's son, for she looked far younger than her age, and had indeed retained much of her beauty; and if the ex-Emperor Ryozen continually asked about her inten-

1. The younger sister.

tions with regard to Himegimi, it was not so much the daughter as the mother who was in his thoughts. For turning the matter over in his mind he saw no other prospect of his ever meeting Tamakatsura again.

About his sister's future Sakon no Chujo had decided views. 'Everything has its time,' he said, 'and Ryozen's is long past. He is, I grant, still a fine-looking man; but even if he were the handsomest and most attractive person in the world, his present situation would make his life a depressing one to share. It is the same with everything. The zithern and the flute with their tunes, the trees with their blossom, the birds with their song—each keeps to its own season and then only can please the eye or ear. But the Crown Prince, now. . . .'

'Oh come,' broke in Tamakatsura, 'she is not wanted there. His attention is already fully occupied. If Higekuro were alive, we could take the risk; but now we must arrange something that will make her future, if not brilliant, at any rate secure.'

When Sakon no Chujo went away his sisters resumed their game of draughts. It was to be the best out of three, and the winner, they laughingly decided, should have the cherry-tree for her own. As it was getting dark they moved the board as close as possible to the window, and their respective waiting-women, raising the blinds, gathered round, each bent on the victory of her own side.

Presently, as usual, Kurodo no Shosho arrived and went straight to Jiju's room; but Jiju had gone out with his brothers. There seemed indeed to be no one about, and as the door of the corridor leading to the women's apartments was ajar, Kurodo stepped lightly towards it and looked in. He was dumbfounded at his own good fortune. His heart stood still as it might have done if Buddha himself had suddenly risen up in front of him. It was misty as well as late, but soon among the mass of dark figures he distinguished the sharp contrasts of a 'cherry'[1] dress. Yes, that surely was she. He gazed and gazed, that he might at least have something to remember 'when the flowers were fallen.'[2] He saw her clearly now; but her beauty filled him only with a greater sadness. Better now than ever before he knew how much it was that he was doomed to lose.

The young girls in attendance, who were for the most part very lightly and negligently clad, presented a charming spectacle in the evening light. The elder sister lost the match. 'Where is the Korean[3] fanfare?' someone wittily asked. 'The trouble has always been,' said one of Wakagimi's ladies, 'that although you have a tree of your own, for it is nearest to your lady's room, you people would insist year after year that this other one was your tree. Well, that's over any way!' The 'junior side,' elated by its victory, was becoming quite truculent.

Kurodo had not the least idea what all this was about. But the conversation amused him, and he longed to join in it. This however was for the moment out of the question, for to break in upon a party of ladies whose costumes and attitudes showed so clearly that they were counting on not being disturbed, would be the height of ill-breeding. He slipped away and, hoping that before long a better opportunity would occur, hung about somewhere in the dark.

1. The robe that Himegimi wore was called a 'cherry dress.'—A.
2. In allusion to the old poem: 'I will dye my dress to the deepest cherry hue, that when the flowers are fallen I may have something to remember them by.'—A.
3. After the horse races when the 'junior side' won a Korean fanfare was played.—A.

THE HOUSE BEAUTIFUL

It was a windy evening, and now the cherry-blossom, for the possession of which the two sisters had contended, was tumbling in great showers to the ground.

'Though you would not be mine, uneasy, faithless blossoms, grows my heart, to see the night-wind rise.' Such was Himegimi's poem, and her maid Saisho: 'A brittle victory, that at the wind's first breath casts all its guerdon shivering to the ground.' And Wakagimi: 'Though flower from branch be this world's windy law, because the tree is mine, my heart can have no rest.'[1] And her maid, Taiu: 'Wise flowers that fall towards the margin[2] of the lake, and lapping surf-like drift to your own side.'

At this, one of Wakagimi's page-boys went to the foot of the tree and collected an armful of petals which he brought back, reciting: 'Though the great winds of heaven scatter them, mine are they, mine to gather as I will—these blossoms of the cherry-tree.' To which Nareki, a little girl in Himegimi's service answered: 'Were your sleeve wide enough, even the perfume, O selfish folk, you would enfold, I think, and keep it for your own.'[3]

From: The Tale of Genji, by Lady Murasaki, translated from the Japanese by Arthur Waley. Vol. I, II, V. George Allen & Unwin, London 1932.

---

1. Play of words on utsurou (1) change ownership, (2) wilt.—A.
2. Play of words on migi (1) the 'junior side,' the right. (2) The margin of a pool or lake.—A.
3. The little girl has in mind the old poem: 'Oh that my sleeve were wide as the great heavens above. Then would the storms of spring no longer at their will destroy the budding flowers.'—A.

PAGES FROM MURASAKI SHIKIBU'S DIARY

(A. D. 1007—1010)

1. At the Mansion of the Prime Minister

As the autumn season approaches the Tsuchimikado[1] becomes inexpressibly smile-giving. The tree-tops near the pond, the bushes near the stream, are dyed in varying tints whose colours grow deeper in the mellow light of evening. The murmuring sound of waters mingles all the night through with the neverceasing recitation[2] of sutras which appeal more to one's heart as the breezes grow cooler.

The ladies waiting upon her honoured presence are talking idly. The Queen hears them; she must find them annoying, but she conceals it calmly. Her beauty needs no words of mine to praise it, but I cannot help feeling that to be near so beautiful a queen will be the only relief from my sorrow. So in spite of my better desires (for a religious life) I am here. Nothing else dispels my grief[3] —it is wonderful!

It is still the dead of night, the moon is dim and darkness lies under the trees. We hear an officer call, "The outer doors of the Queen's apartment must be opened. The maids-of-honour are not yet come—let the Queen's secretaries come forward!" While this order is being given the three-o'clock bell resounds, startling the air. Immedi-

---

1. Tsuchimikado: the residence of Prime Minister Fujiwara, the father of the Queen.—D.—O.
2. Priests are praying for the easy delivery of the Queen, who has gone to her parents' house before the birth, in accordance with old Japanese custom.—D.—O.
3. The writer of this diary lost her husband in 1001.—D.—O.

ately the prayers at the five altars[1] begin. The voices of the priests in loud recitation, vying with each other far and near, are solemn indeed. The Abbot of the Kanon-in Temple, accompanied by twenty priests, comes from the eastern side building to pray. Even their footsteps along the gallery which sound to'-do-ro to'-do-ro are sacred. The head priest of the Hoju Temple goes to the mansion near the racetrack, the prior of the Henji Temple goes to the library. I follow with my eyes when the holy figures in pure white robes cross the stately Chinese bridge and walk along the broad path. Even Azaliah Saisa bends the body in reverence before the deity Daiitoku. The maids-of-honour arrive at dawn.

I can see the garden from my room beside the entrance to the gallery. The air is misty, the dew is still on the leaves. The Lord Prime Minister is walking there; he orders his men to cleanse the brook. He breaks off a stalk of ominaeshi (flower maiden) which is in full bloom by the south end of the bridge. He peeps in over my screen! His noble appearance embarrasses us, and I am ashamed of my morning (not yet painted and powdered) face. He says, " Your poem on this! If you delay so much the fun is gone! " and I seized the chance to run away to the writing-box, hiding my face—

> *Flower-maiden in bloom—*
> *Even more beautiful for the bright dew,*
> *Which is partial, and never favours me.*

" So prompt! " said he, smiling, and ordered a writing-box to be brought (for himself).

His answer:

1. Altars before Fudō, Gosansé, Gunsari, Daiitoku, Kongōyasha.—D.-O.

A STATE BANQUET AND ITS END

The silver dew is never partial.
From her heart
The flower-maiden's beauty.

One wet and calm evening I was talking with Lady Saishō. The young Lord[1] of the Third Rank sat with the misu[2] partly rolled up. He seemed maturer than his age and was very graceful. Even in light conversation such expresssions as "Fair soul is rarer than fair face" come gently to his lips, covering us with confusion. It is a mistake to treat him like a young boy. He keeps his dignity among ladies, and I saw in him a much-sought-after romantic hero when once he walked off reciting to himself:

Linger in the field where flower-maidens are blooming
And your name will be tarnished with tales of gallantry.

Some such trifle as that sometimes lingers in my mind when really interesting things are soon forgotten—why?

2. A STATE BANQUET AND ITS END

The first day of the Frost month was the fiftieth day after the birth. The persons who were to present themselves came in full dress. The sight before her presence was like a picture of a poet's assembly. Many kichō[3] were arranged along the east side of the Queen's dais from the inner room to the veranda. The Royal dining-table was placed towards the south front of the house. At the west side was prepared the Queen Dowager's dinner. It was

---

1. Yorimichi, the Prime Minister Fujiwara Michinaga's son, who was then sixteen years old.—D.-O.
2. Misu: a thin finely woven bamboo curtain, behind which one may see but not be seen, hung before great personages and women's apartments.—D.-O.
3. Kichō: a kind of screens used in upper-class houses.—O.-D.

placed on a tray of aloe wood. I don't know what kind of a stand it was on because I did not see it. She wore a grape-coloured kimono trimmed with five folds and red uchigi. Those serving the dinner were Lady Saishō and Lady Sanuki. The maids-of-honour dressed their hair with saishi and bands. Lady Dainagon served the August Prince's dinner at the east side—a little dining-table, plate, stand for chopsticks, with a central decoration representing a bit of seashore—all as small as playthings for dolls. At the east end where the sudaré was a little rolled up, there were in waiting such ladies as Ben-no-Naishi, Lady Nakatsukasa, Lady Koshōshō; as I was inside I could not see in great detail. That night Lady Shō, the nurse, was permitted to wear a dress of honourable colour. She seemed still girlish, as she took the August Prince in her arms and gave him to the Lord Prime Minister who was within the dais. He came out quietly and they were plainly seen in the flickering light of the torches. It was very lovely. The August Prince was dressed in red brocade with shaded skirt—exquisitely pretty. The mochi[1] was given to him by the Lord Prime Minister. The seats of the courtiers had been prepared at the west side of the east building; there were two ministers present. They came out to the bridge and were very drunk and boisterous.

As the torches burnt low, the Major-General of the Fourth Rank was called to light lanterns. Boxes and baskets of food,[2] the Prime Minister's gifts, were borne in by the attendants and piled up on the balcony near the railing. Some of the boxes were to be taken to the King's

---

1. Mochi: a cake made of beaten rice flour paste.—D.-O.
2. These dainty white wooden boxes of food arranged in a way pleasing to the eye are still a feature of Japanese life. They are distributed, with varying contents, at weddings and funerals, sold at railway stations, and carried on picnics.—D.-O.

kitchen, and as the next day was to be a day of abstinence for religious devotion they were carried away at once.

*   *   *

The Queen's First Officer came to the misu and asked if the court nobles should be invited there. As the answer was "yes," every one came led by the Prime Minister, and approached the east door. Ladies stood in two or three rows; the misu was rolled up by those who were nearest it, Lady Dainagon, Lady Koshōshō, and others. The Minister of the Right came dancing wildly and made a hole in the kichō behind which ladies were sitting. They laughed, saying, "He has long passed the age for that." He did not notice, but made a great many unbecoming jokes, taking away ladies' fans. The August Prince's First Officer took a saké cup[1] and stepped out; he sung a song; although it was unaccompanied by dancing it was very delightful. Farther towards the east, leaning against a door-post, the General of the Right was standing, studying the ladies' sleeves and the skirts of their garments showing below the misu. He is different from other men. The ladies, thinking that after all the intoxicated men were only trying to seem young and irresistible, made light of their behavior and said, "It is nothing, nobody else will behave so." Compared with such men the General is far superior. He was afraid of the saké cup, and when it came to him passed it by, singing the song which begins "One Thousand and Ten Thousand Ages," The First Officer of the Light Bodyguard said, "I think Lady Murasaki[2] must be some-

---

1. At banquets a great cup was used which could contain one or two quarts of liquor. When this was circulated among the guests each was expected to empty the cup, and it was the pride of the drinker to toss it off in one draught.—D.–O.

2. The young heroine of Genji Monogatari.—O.–D.

where here!" I listened, thinking, "How can she be here in a place where there is no such graceful person as Prince Genji?"[1] The Minister of the Right said, "Sanmi-no-Suké [officer of the third rank], accept this cup!" When the officer came out from below the Lord Keeper of the seal [an inferior position] the drunken man wept. The King's Adviser, leaning in a corner, was flirting with Lady Hyobu. The Prime Minister did not forbid even unmentionable jokes. It was an awful night of carousal, so after the ceremony I signalled to Lady Saishō and we hid ourselves, but there came noisily the Prime Minister's sons and Lieutenant-General Saishō, so, although we two had remained hidden behind the screen, even this was taken away and we were captives. "Compose a poem each, and you shall be excused," said the Lord Prime Minister. I was frightened and helpless, and made haste to comply:

How can I number the years of the Prince!
One thousand, nay, eight thousand, may he live and more.

"Well done!" said he, reciting it twice, and he answered immediately:

O would I might live the life of a crane—
Then might I reckon the years of the Prince
Up to one thousand!

He was much intoxicated, but the poem had feeling, for it came from his innermost desire. The child cherished in this way will have a very bright future. Even such as I can imagine the thousand prosperous years of His August Highness! He felt satisfied with his own poem and said, "Has Your Majesty heard the poem? I have made a poem!" and then—"I am worthy to be your father and

---

1. The hero of Genji Monogatari.—O.-D.

you are worthy to be my daughter—Mother is smiling, she must think she is happy. She may be thinking she has got a good husband!" said he in extreme intoxication. As is usual with drunken persons all were listening. His wife seemed to be embarrassed by this conversation and retired. "Mother will be angry if I do not follow her," said he, and went through the dais hurriedly muttering, "Excuse me, Your Majesty, but a child is adored because of its father!" and everybody laughed.

3. THE QUEEN AND HER LADIES-IN-WAITING

Our Queen of perfect mind, enviably lovely, is reserved and never obtrusive, for she believes that few who are forward can avoid blunders. In fact, imperfect wit is worse than reserve. Our Queen when she was very young was much annoyed to hear persons of shallow culture saying vulgar, narrow things with conceit, so she favoured ladies who made no mistakes, and childlike persons pleased her very well. This is why our ladies have become so retiring. As Her Majesty grows older, she begins to see the world as it is, the bad and good qualities of the human heart. Reserve or boldness—she knows neither is good. The court nobles rather look down on us—"Nothing interesting here!" they seem to say. The Queen knows this, but she knows we cannot please everybody. If we stumble, hideous things may happen. Yet we must not be faint-hearted and bashful either, so Her Majesty says, but our old habits are not so easily shaken off, and all the young nobles of the present day are, on their side, only indulgent pleasure-seekers.

The ladies around the Abbess, who indulge in aesthetic pursuits, gazing at the moon and admiring flowers, may talk only of these things to the nobles, boastfully and intentionally,and the nobles might say that it is difficult to find ladies with whom they can chatter light-heartedly morning or evening, or discuss interesting topics occasionally; although, as I haven't heard them say it, I don't know really what they think. In general conversation it is awkward to say profound things. It is far better to speak with simplicity, and the nobles seem to think so. The difficulty is to understand the occasion and adapt one's self to it.

When the First Official of Her Majesty comes to report to her, the delicate, shy ladies-in-waiting cannot meet him on common ground, or converse fluently, not because they are deficient in words or thoughts, but because of their extreme timidity. They fear their faults may be noticed so they cannot decide what to say. Others [Abbess ladies] may not be so. Even women of high birth must follow the general custom when they become ladies-in-waiting at the Court, but many behave as if they were still daughters at home.

From: Diaries of Court Ladies of Old Japan, translated by Annie Shepley Omori and Ptofessor Kochi Doi, Kenkyusha Co., Tokio 1935.

A VOYAGE AND A DREAM
Sarashina Diary

1. A Small Girl Starts for the Capital

I was brought up in a distant province[1] which lies farther than the farthest end of the Eastern Road. I am ashamed to think that inhabitants of the Royal City will think me an uncultured girl.

Somehow I came to know that there are such things as romances in the world and wished to read them. When there was nothing to do by day or at night, one tale or another was told me by my elder sister or stepmother, and I heard several chapters about the shining Prince Genji.[2] My longing for such stories increased, but how could they recite them all from memory? I became very restless and got an image of Yakushi Buddha[3] made as large as myself. When I was alone I washed my hands and went secretly before the altar and prayed to him with all my life, bowing my head down to the floor. " Please let me go to the Royal City. There I can find many tales. Let me read all of them."

When thirteen years old, I was taken to the Royal City. On the third of the Long-moon month,[4] I removed (from my house) to Imataté, the old house where I had played as a child being broken up. At sunset in the foggy twi-

---

1. Her father (Fujiwara) Takasue was appointed Governor of Kazusa in 1017, and the authoress who was then nine years old, was brought from Kyōto to the Province. O.-D.
2. Prince Genji: the hero of Genji-monogatari.
3. Yakushi Buddha: " The Buddha of Healing," or Sanscrit, Bhaisajya-guru-Vaiduryaprabhah. O.-D
4. Original, Nagatsuki, September.—O.-D.

light, just as I was getting into the palanquin, I thought of the Buddha before which I had gone secretly to pray—I was sorry and secretly shed tears to leave him behind.

Outside of my new house (a rude temporary, thatched one) there is no fence nor even shutters, but we have hung curtains and sudaré.[1] From that house, standing on a low bluff, a wide plain extends towards the South. On the East and West the sea creeps close, so it is an interesting place. When fogs are falling it is so charming that I rise early every morning to see them. Sorry to leave this place.

On the fifteenth, in heavy dark rain, we crossed the boundary of the Province and lodged at Ikada in the Province of Shimofusa. Our lodging is almost submerged. I am so afraid I cannot sleep. I see only three lone trees standing on a little hill in the waste.

The next day was passed in drying our dripping clothes and waiting for the others to come up.[2]

On the seventeenth, started early in the morning, and crossed a deep river. I heard that in this Province there lived in olden times a chieftain of Mano. He had thousand and ten thousand webs of cloth woven and dipped them (for bleaching) in the river which now flows over the place where his great house stood. Four of the large gate-posts remained standing in the river.

---

1. Ancient ladies avoided men's eyes and always sat behind sudare (finely split bamboo curtains) through which they could look out without being seen.—O.-D.
2. High personages, Governors of Provinces or other nobles, travelling with a great retinue, consisting of armed horsemen, foot-soldiers, and attendants of all sorts both high and low, together with the luggage necessary for prolonged existence in the wilderness. From Tokyo to Kyōto nowadays the journey is about twelve hours. It took about three months in the year 1017. O.-D.

A SMALL GIRL STARTS FOR THE CAPITAL

Hearing the people composing poems about this place, I in my mind:

> *Had I not seen erect in the river*
> *These solid timbers of the olden time*
> *How could I know, how could I feel*
> *The story of that house?*

That evening we lodged at the beach of Kurodo. The white sand stretched far and wide. The pine-wood was dark—the moon was bright, and the soft blowing of the wind made me lonely. People were pleased and composed poems. My Poem:

> *For this night only*
> *The autumn moon at Kurodo beach shall shine*
>   *for me,*
> *For this night only!—I cannot sleep.*

Early in the morning we left this place and came to the Futoi River[1] on the boundary between Shimofusa and Musashi. We lodged at the ferry of Matsusato[2] near Kagami's rapids,[3] and all night long our luggage was being carried over.

My nurse had lost her husband and gave birth to her child at the boundary of the Province, so we had to go to the Royal City separately. I was longing for my nurse and wanted to go to see her, and was brought there by my elder brother in his arms. We, though in a temporary lodging, covered ourselves with warm cotton matting, but my nurse, as there was no man to take care of her, was lying in a wild place (and) covered only with coarse matting. She was in her red dress.[4]

1. Futoi River is called the River Edo at present. O.-D.
2. Matsusato, now called Matsudo. O.-D.
3. Kagami's rapids, now perhaps Karameki-no-se. O.-D.
4. Under-dress.—Ed.

A VOYAGE AND A DREAM

The moon came in, lighting up everything, and in the moonlight she looked transparent. I thought her very white and pure. She wept and caressed me, and I was loath to leave her. Even when I went with lingering heart, her image remained with me, and there was no interest in the changing scenes.

The next morning we crossed the river in a ferry-boat in our palanquins. The persons who had come with us thus far in their own conveyances went back from this place. We, who were going up to the Royal City, stayed here for a while to follow them with our eyes; and as it was a parting for life all wept. Even my childish heart felt sorrow.

Now it is the Province of Musashi.[1] There is no charm in this place. The sand of the beaches is not white, but like mud. People say that purple grass[2] grows in the fields of Musashi, but it is only a waste of various kinds of reeds, which grow so high that we cannot see the bows of our horsemen who are forcing their way through the tall grass.

*   *   *

We crossed it (the Sumida-river) in a boat, and it is the Province of Sagami. The mountain range called Nishitomi is like folding screens with good pictures. On the left hand we saw a very beautiful beach with long-drawn curves of white waves. There was a place there called Moro-koshi-ga-Hara[3] (Chinese Field) where sands

---

1. The country side of modern Tokio.—Ed.
2. Common Gromwell, Lithospermum.—O.-D.
3. According to "Sagami-Fudoki," or "The Natural Features of Sagami Province," this district was in ancient times inhabited by Koreans. The natives could not distinguish a Korean from a Chinese, hence the name of Chinese Field. A temple near Oiso still keeps the name of Koraiji, or the Korean temple.—O.-D.

are wonderfully white. Two or three days we journeyed along that shore. A man said: " In Summer pale and deep Japanese pinks bloom there and make the field like brocade. As it is Autumn now we cannot see them." But I saw some pinks scattered about blooming pitiably. They said : " It is funny that Japanese pinks are blooming in the Chinese field."

There is a mountain called Ashigara (Hakone) which extends for ten and more miles and is covered with thick woods even to its base. We could have only an occasional glimpse of the sky. We lodged in a hut at the foot of the mountain. It was a dark moonless night. I felt myself swallowed up and lost in the darkness, when three singers came from somewhere. One was about fifty years old, the second twenty, and the third about fourteen or fifteen. We set them down in front of our lodging and a karakasa (large paper umbrella) was spread for them. My servant lighted a fire so that we saw them. They said that they were the descendants of a famous singer called Kobata. They had very long hair which hung over their foreheads ; their faces were white and clean, and they seemed rather like maids serving in noblemen's families. They had clear, sweet voices, and their beautiful singing seemed to reach the heavens. All were charmed, and taking great interest made them come nearer. Some one said, " The singers of the Western Provinces are inferior to them," and at this the singers closed their song with the words, " if we are compared with those of Naniwa " (Ōsaka).[1] They were pretty and neatly dressed, with voices of rare

---

[1]. This seems to be the last line of a kind of song called Imayō, perhaps improvised by the singers ; its meaning may be as follows : " You compare us with singers of the Western Provinces ; we are inferior to those in the Royal City, we may justly be compared with those of Osaka."—O.-D.

A VOYAGE AND A DREAM

beauty, and they were wandering away into this fearful mountain. Even tears came to those eyes which followed them as far as they could be seen; and my childish heart was unwilling to leave this rude shelter frequented by these singers.

Next morning we crossed over the mountain.[1] Words cannot express my fear[2] in the midst of it. Clouds rolled beneath our feet. Halfway over there was an open space with a few trees. Here we saw a few leaves of aoi[3] (Asarum caulescens). People praised it and thought strange that in this mountain, so far from the human world, was growing such a sacred plant. We met with three rivers in the mountain and crossed them with difficulty. That day we stopped at Sekiyama. Now we are in Suruga Province. We passed a place called Iwatsubo (rock-urn) by the barrier of Yokobashiri. There was an indescribably large square rock through a hole in which very cold water came rushing out.

Mount Fuji is in this Province. In the Province where I was brought up (from which she begins this journey) I saw that mountain far towards the West. It towers up painted with deep blue, and is covered with eternal snow. It seems that it wears a dress of deep violet and a white veil over its shoulders. From the little level place of the top smoke was going up. In the evening we even saw burning fires there.[4] The Fuji River comes tumbling down from

---

1. Hakone Mountain has now become a resort of tourists and a place of summer residence.—O.-D.
2. Fear of evil spirits which probably lived in the wild, and of robbers who certainly did.—O.-D.
3. Aoi, or Futaba-aoi. At the great festival of the Kamo shrine in Kyōto the processionists crowned their heads with the leaves of this plant, so it must have been well known.—O.-D.
4. Mount Fuji was then an active volcano.—O.-D.

that mountain. A man of the Province came up to us and told us a story.

"Once I went on an errand. It was a very hot day, and I was resting on the bank of the stream when I saw something yellow come floating down. It came to the bank of the river and stuck there. I picked it up and found it to be a scrap of yellow paper with words elegantly written on it in cinnabar. Wondering much I read it. On the paper was a prophecy of the Governors (of provinces) to be appointed next year. As to this Province there were written the names of two Governors. I wondered more and more, and drying the paper, kept it. When the day of the announcement came, this paper held no mistake, and the man who became the Governor of this Province died after three months and the other succeeded him."

There are such things. I think that the gods assemble there on that mountain to settle the affairs of each new year.

2. THE WIDOW

1058. On the fifth day of the Tenth month all became like a dream.[1] My sorrows could be compared to nothing in this world.

Now I knew that my present state had been reflected in the mirror offered to the Hasé Temple (about twenty-five years before by her mother) where some one was seen weeping in agony. The reflection of the happier one had not been realized. That could never be in the future.

On the twenty-third we burnt his remains with despairing hearts, my boy, who went down with him last Au-

1. Her husband died. O.-D.

A VOYAGE AND A DREAM

tumn, being dressed exquisitely and much attended, followed the bier weeping in black clothes with hateful things (mourning insignia) on them. My feeling when I saw him going out can never be expressed. I seemed to wander in dreams and thought that human life must soon cease here. If I had not given myself to idle fictions (she herself had written several) and poetry, but had practised religious austerities night and day, I would not have seen such a dream world.

At Hasé Temple a cedar branch was cast down to me by the Inari god and this thing (the loss of her husband) would not have happened if I had visited the Inari shrine on my way home. The dreams which I had seen in these past years which did me pray to the Heaven Illuminating Honoured Goddess meant that I should have been in the Imperial Court as a nurse, sheltered behind the favour of the King and Queen—so the dream interpreter interpreted my dream, but I could not realize this. Only the sorrowful reflection in the mirror was realized unaltered. O pitiful and sorrowful I! Thus nothing could happen as I willed, and I wandered in this world doing no virtuous deed for the future life.

Life seemed to survive sorrows, but I was uneasy at the thought that things would happen against my will, even in the future life. There was only one thing I could rely on.

Ceaseless tears—clouded mind:
Bright scene—moon-shadow.[1]

On the thirteenth of the Tenth month (1055) I dreamed one night this dream:

There in the garden of my house at the farthest ledge

1. Chinese poem.—Ed.

THE WIDOW

stood Amitabha Buddha! He was not seen distinctly, but as if through a cloud. I could snatch a glimpse now and then when the cloud lifted. The lotus-flower pedestal was three or four feet above the ground; the Buddha was about six feet high.

Golden light shone forth; one hand was extended, the fingers of the other were bent in form of benediction. None but I could see him, yet I felt such reverence that I dared not approach the blind to see him better. None but I might hear him saying, "Then this time I will go back, and afterwards come again to receive you." I was startled and awoke into the fourteenth day. This dream only was my hope for the life to come.[1]

I had lived with my husband's nephews, but after the sad event we parted not to meet again. One very dark night I was visited by the nephew who was living at Rokuhara; I could not but welcome so rare a guest.

No moon, and darkness deepens
Around Obasutè. Why have you come?
It cannot be to see the moon![2]

After that time (the death of her husband) an intimate friend stopped all communication.

She may be thinking that I
Am no more in this world, yet my days
Are wasted in weeping.

In the Tenth month I turned, my eyes full of tears towards the intensely bright moon.

---

1. At the death Lord Buddha coming on a cloud appears to the faithful one and accompanies the soul to Heaven. O.-D.
2. The point of this is in the name of the place, Obasuté, which may be translated, "Aunt Casting Away," It is a place famous for the beauty of its scenery in moonlight.—O.-D.

A VOYAGE AND A DREAM

*Even into the mind always clouded with grief,
There is cast the reflection of the bright moon.*

Years and months passed away. Whenever I recollected the dream-like incident (of his death) my mind was troubled and my eyes filled so that I cannot think distinctly of those days.

My people went to live elsewhere and I remained alone in my solitary home. I was tired of meditation and sent a poem to one who had not called on me for a long time.

*Weeds grow before my gate
And my sleeves are wet with dew,
No one calls on me,
My tears are solitary—alas !*

She was a nun and she sent an answer :

*The weeds before a dwelling house
May remind you of me !
Bushes bury the hut
Where lives the world-deserted one.*

From : Diaries of Court Ladies of Old Japan, translated by Annie Shepley Omori and Kochi Doi, Tokyo, Kenkyusha Co., 1935.

KAMAKURA PERIOD
(A.D. 1185—1392)

ROMANCE AND CHIVALRY

Heike-Monogatari

1. Early Dancing Girls

Now not only did this priestly statesman[1] hold the whole country in the hollow of his hand, but, neither ashamed at the censure of the world, nor regarding the derision of the people, he indulged in the most surprising conduct. For example, in the Capital there were two famous Shirabyōshi[2] who were sisters, named Giō and Ginyo, both young girls and very skilled in their art. The elder, Giō, was beloved by Kiyomori, and her younger sister also was in high favour with everyone. So they were enabled to build a good house for their mother, who was granted a monthly income of a hundred koku of rice, and a hundred kwan in money by Kiyomori. Their family was consequently rich and honoured, fortunate beyond the lot of most people. Now the origin of Shirabyōshi in our country was in the reign of Tobain when Shima-no-chisai and Waka-no-mae appeared as dancers. In the beginning the Shirabyōshi wore the " Suikan " or silk court robe and " tate-eboshi " or black court headdress, with a white dirk in their belt, when they danced, and it was like the dancing of a man; but from the middle age the headdress and sword were disused, and they danced only in the white " Suikan," hence they were called Shirabyōshi.

But among the Shirabyōshi of the Capital, when they

---

1. Kiyomori (1118–1181), the Leader of the Heike or Taira House.
2. " White Rhythm Makers," dancers, the prototype of the classical Geisha.—Ed.

heard of the good fortune of Giō, there were some who hated her and some who were envious. Those who envied her said: " Ah! how fortunate is Giō Gozen, if we do even as she does we too may become prosperous in like manner; " so they added the syllable " Gi " to their names to see if they too might not obtain good luck. Some called themsleves Giichi, Giji, Gifuku, or Gitoku. Those who hated her said, " Surely it is not a matter of the name or character with which it is written, fortune is the result of disposition inherited from a previous existence; " and so few of them took such a name.

Now it came to pass that, three years afterwards, another skilful Shirabyōshi appeared; and she was a maiden of sixteen years of age, born in the province of Kaga, and her name was Hotoke. And when the people of the Capital, both high and low, saw her, they said that although from of old times many Shirabyōshi had been seen there, one so dexterous as she had not been beheld; and she too was in exceeding great favour with all. And in the course of time Hotoke Gozen said: " Though I have made sport for the whole Empire, yet this great Taira minister who now is the source of all fortune and prosperity has not yet deigned to summon me; after the manner of entertainers I will e'en go uninvited." So she forthwith proceeded to the Palace in Nishihachijo. On her arrival, a servant entered the presence of the minister and announced: " Hotoke Gozen, now so famous in this city is without." Then the Lay-priest grew very angry and replied " How then! do not these players attend only when they are called? Why it is that she has come unbidden? Whether she be called God or Buddha (Hotoke), it is not suitable that she come here while Giō is present. Bid her depart at once."

Hotoke Gozen was already retiring at those unkind

words, when Giō said to the Minister " It is surely the usual custom that players should attend unbidden, and moreover it is because she is still young and innocent that she has thus intruded on you—so it will be most unkind to speak harshly and send her away—how greatly will she be shamed and distressed by it; as I myself have trodden the same path, I cannot but remember these things. If you will not deign to allow her to dance or to sing, yield, I pray you, so far as to call her back and receive her in audience; if you then dismiss her, it will be a favour indeed worthy of her deep gratitude." To this the Priest-Minister answered: " Since you wish it to be so, I will see her and then dismiss her : " and he sent a servant to call her.

Hotoke Gozen, having been thus harshly treated, was even then entering her carriage to return when she was summoned and turned back again. The Minister met her and granted her an audience. Thus Hotoke, though it seemed unlikely that she would gain an audience, yet through the kindness of Giō, who thus imported for her, was not only able to enter the Minister's presence, but further it happened that he, wishing to hear her voice, directed that she should sing a song of the kind called " Imayo : " and thus she sang :

" When I first enjoyed the sight of your bountiful presence,

'Twas like the evergreen pine, flourishing age after age.

Like to the pond on whose rocks is basking the turtle thrice blessed,

Numberless storks beside it happily preening their wings."

And those who heard it were greatly wondering at her

skill and her beauty, and pressed her to repeat it even to three times. The Lay-priest also was greatly diverted and said: " Since you are so skilful at Imayo you must also be able to dance well; we wish to see one of your dances." Then the drums were ordered to be beaten and she danced forthwith. Now Hotoke Gozen was renowned for the beauty of her hair and features, and her voice was no less exquisite; how then should she fail in the dance? So when she put forth all her skill and charm in dancing, Kiyomori was enraptured and his heart turned wholly toward her. But when Hotoke Gozen said to him: " Did I not present myself uninvited, and when almost rejected was I not only brought back by the entreaty of Giō Gozen? I pray thee grant me leave that I may return quickly;" the Lay-monk by no means agreed to the proposal, and thinking that she was only embarrassed because of the presence of the other, proposed to send Giō away.

But Hotoke Gozen answered " How can this be? If we were to remain here both together, I should be most embarrassed, and if your Excellency send away Giō Gozen and keep me alone, how ashamed will she not feel in her heart? Indeed it will be most painful to her. If you deign to think of me again in the future, I am always able to come at your call. I beg that to-day I may be allowed to retire."

Kiyomori, seeing how the matter lay, straightway ordered Giō to leave the Palace, and to that end sent a messenger three times. Although Giō had expected this thing from long before, she did not think that it would come to pass to-day or to-morrow. But as the Nyūdō continually repeated this unreasonable demand, there was nothing for her but to sweep her room clean and to go. Even those who meet under the shade of the same tree, or who greet each other by the riverside, since it is owing to relations in a previous existence, ever feel pain at parting with each other; how much more grievous a thing it is, when two have been together in affection for the space of three years. So in regret and grief she shed unavailing tears. Thus as it was a thing that must be, Gio went forth, but ere she went she wrote on the Shōji this verse, thinking to bring perchance to remembrance the forgotten image of one who was gone.

> *Whether fresh and green*
> *Or in sere and yellow leaf,*
> *Grasses of the field,*
> *When the autumn comes at length,*
> *Meet with the same hopeless fate.*

2. Autumn Leaves: a Boy-Emperor and his Servants

While Takakura Tennō[1] was on the Throne everybody declared that his consideration for others surpassed even that of the Mikados of the periods Enki and Tenryaku, and though generally speaking it was after he had attained to years of discrimination that he obtained his reputation for wisdom and benevolence, yet his disposition was kind and gentle from his earliest childhood.

During the period Shoan, when His Majesty was only about ten years old, being extremely fond of the tinted leaves of autumn, he had a little hill-garden made, in the north enclosure of the Palace, and planted it with maple and " haze " trees that redden beautifully in that season, calling it " The Hill of Autumn Tints " and from morning

---

1. Son of Emperor Shirakawa II. He came to throne as a boy of 8 years in 1169 and ruled until 1180, one year before his death.—Ed.

till evening he never seemed to tire of looking at it. But one night a late autumn gale blew violently and scattered the leaves everywhere in confusion, so the next morning, when the Palace servants went round early as usual to clean the grounds, they swept up all the fallen leaves and the broken branches as well, and as it was a bleak and cheerless morning they made a fire with them in the court of the Nuidono, and heated some sake to warm themselves.

Soon afterwards the Kurando[1] in waiting, hastening to inspect the garden before the Emperor should see it, and finding nothing there, enquired the reason and the servants told him. " What ? " he exclaimed, " how could you dare to treat the garden that the Emperor is so fond of in such a way ? You deserve to be imprisoned or banished at least, and I too may very likely incur the Imperial displeasure." Just then the Emperor, coming out to see his favourite trees as soon as he had left his bed-chamber, was surprised to find they had all disappeared, and the Kurando told him what had happened. To his surprise His Majesty was not at all angry, but only laughed and quoted the Chinese poem by Haku-raku-ten (Po-chu-i) about warming wine in the woods by burning maple-leaves. " I wonder " he said, " who can have taught it them. Really they are quite esthetes."

3. The Death of a Poet-Warrior

Satsuma-no-kami Tadanori, the Commander of the western army, clad in a dark-blue hitatare and a suit of armour with black silk lacing, and mounted on a great black horse with a saddle enriched with lacquer of powdered gold, was calmly withdrawing with his following of a hund-

---

1. High Court official, originally an Archivist.—Ed.

THE DEATH OF A POET-WARRIOR

red horsemen, when Okabe-no-Rokuyata Tadazumi of Musashi espied him and pursued at full gallop, eager to bring down so noble a prize.

"This must be some great leader!" he cried. "Shameful! to turn your back to the foe!" Tadanori turned in the saddle, "We are friends! We are friends!" he replied, as he continued on his way. As he turned, however, Tadazumi had caught a glimpse of his face and noticed that his teeth were blackened. "There are none of our side who have blackened teeth," he said, "This must be one of the Heike Courtiers." And overtaking him, he ranged up to him to grapple. When his hundred followers saw this, since they were hired retainers drawn from various provinces, they scattered and fled in all directions, leaving their leader to his fate.

But Satsuma-no-kami, who had been brought up at Kumano, was famous for his strength, and was extremely active and agile besides, so clutching Tadazumi he pulled him from his horse, dealing him two stabs with his dirk while he was yet in the saddle, and following them with another as he was falling. The first two blows fell on his armour and failed to pierce it, while the third wounded him in the face but was not mortal, and as Tadanori sprang down upon him to cut off his head, Tadazumi's page, who had been riding behind him, slipped from his horse and with a blow of his sword cut off Tadanori's arm above the elbow.

Satsuma-no-kami, seeing that all was over and wishing to have a short space to say the death-prayer, flung Tadazumi from him so that he fell about a bow's length away. Then truning toward the west he repeated: "Kōmyō Henjō Jippō Sekai, Nembutsu Shujō Sesshu Fusha; O Amida Nyorai, who sheddest the light of Thy Presence through the ten quarters of the world, gather into Thy Radiant Heaven all who call upon Thy Name!" And just as his prayer was finished, Tadazumi from behind swept off his head.

Not doubting that he had taken the head of a noble foe, but quite unaware who he might be, he was searching his armour when he came across a piece of paper fastened to his quiver, on which was written a verse with this title: "The Traveller's Host, a Flower."

> *Seeking where I may lodge on my weary way, in the evening*
> *Under a tree I lie; now is my host but a flower.*

Wherefore he knew that it could be none but Satsuma-no-kami.

Then he lifted up the head on his sword's point and shouted with a loud voice: "Satsuma-no-kami Dono, the demon-warrior of Nippon, slain by Okabe-Rokuyata Tadazumi of Musashi!" And when they heard it, all, friends and foes alike, moistened the sleeves of their armour with their tears exclaiming: "Alas! what a great captain has passed away! Warrior and artist and poet; in all things he was pre-eminent."

4. An Amazon

Now Kiso[1] had brought with him from Shinano two beautiful girls named Tomoe and Yamabuki, but Yamabuki had fallen sick and stayed behind in the Capital. Tomoe had long black hair and a fair complexion, and her face was very lovely; moreover she was a fearless rider whom

---

1. Kiso Yoshinaka, cousin of the Minamoto-Leader Yoritomo, later his adversary.—Ed.

neither the fiercest horse nor the roughest ground could dismay, and so dexterously did she handle sword and bow that she was a match for a thousand warriors, and fit to meet either god or devil. Many times had she taken the field, armed at all points, and won matchless renown in encounters with the bravest captains, and so in this last fight, when all the others were slain or had fled, among the last seven there rode Tomoe.

At first it was reported that Kiso had escaped to the north either through Nagasaka by the road of Tamba, or by the Ryūge pass, but actually he had turned back again and ridden off toward Seta, to see if he could hear aught of the fate of Imai Kanehira. Imai had long valiantly held his position at Seta till the continued assaults of the enemy reduced his eight hundred men to but fifty, when he rolled up his banner and rode back to Miyako to ascertain the fate of his lord; and thus it happened that the two fell in with each other by the shore at Ōtsu. Recognizing each other when they were yet more than a hundred yards away, they spurred their horses and came together joyfully.

Seizing Imai by the hand, Kiso burst forth: "I was so anxious about you that I did not stop to fight to the death in the Rokujō-kawara, but turned my back on a host of foes and hastened off here to find you." "How can I express my gratitude for my lord's consideration?" replied Imai; "I too would have died in the defence of Seta, but I feared for my lord's uncertain fate, and thus it was that I fled hither." "Then our ancient pledge will not be broken and we shall die together," said Kiso, "and now unfurl your banner, for a sign to our men who have scattered among these hills."

So Imai unfurled the banner, and many of their men who

had fled from the Capital and from Seta saw it and rallied again, so that they soon had a following of three hundred horse. "With this band our last fight will be a great one," shouted Kiso joyfully, "who leads yon great array?" "Kai-no-Ichijō Jirō, my lord." "And how many has he, do you think?" "About six thousand, it seems." "Well matched!" replied Yoshinaka, "if we must die, what death could be better than to fall outnumbered by valiant enemies? Forward then!"

That day Kiso was arrayed in a hitatare of red brocade and a suit of armour laced with Chinese silk; by his side hung a magnificent sword mounted in silver and gold, and his helmet was surmounted by long golden horns. Of his twenty-four eagle-feathered arrows, most had been shot away in the previous fighting, and only a few were left, drawn out high from the quiver, and he grasped his rattan-bound bow by the middle as he sat his famous grey charger, fierce as a devil, on a saddle mounted in gold. Rising high in his stirrups he cried with a loud voice; "Kiso-no-Kwanja you have often heard of; now you see him before your eyes! Sama-no-kami and Iyo-no-kami, Asahi Shōgun, Minamoto Yoshinaka am I! Come! Kai-no-Ichijō Jirō! Take my head and show it to Hyōye-no-suke Yoritomo! "Hear, men!" shouted Ichijō-no-Jirō in response "On to the attack! This is their great Capaitn! See that he does not escape you now! And the whole force charged against Kiso to take him. Then Kiso and his three hundred fell upon their six thousand opponents in the death fury, cutting and slashing and swinging their blades in every direction until at last they broke through on the farther side, but with their little band depleted to only fifty horsemen, when Doi-no-Jirō Sanehira came up to support their foes with another force of two thousand.

Flinging themselves on these they burst through them also, after which they successively penetrated several other smaller bands of a hundred or two who were following in reserve.

But now they were reduced to but five survivors, and among these Tomoe still held her place. Calling her to him Kiso said: "As you are a woman, it were better that you now make your escape. I have made up my mind to die, either by the hand of the enemy or by mine own, and how would Yoshinaka be shamed if in his last fight he died with a woman?" Even at these strong words, however, Tomoe would not forsake him, but still feeling full of fight, she replied: "Ah, for some bold warrior to match with, that Kiso might see how fine a death I can die." And she drew aside her horse and waited. Presently Onda-no-Hachirō Moroshige of Musashi, a strong and valiant samurai, came riding up with thirty followers, and Tomoe, immediately dashing into them, flung herself upon Onda and grappling with him dragged him from his horse, pressed him calmly against the pommel of her saddle and cut off his head. Then stripping off her armour she fled away to the Eastern Provinces.

5. The Beginning of the Final Fight

Now the two hosts of the Genji and Heike faced each other scarcely thirty chō distant on the water; and as the tide was running strongly through Moji, Akama and Dan-no-ura,[1] the Heike ships were carried down by the current against their will, while the Genji were naturally able to

---

[1] From the description of the battle of Dannoura (1185), finally won by the Genji (Minamoto). "From this time, until the restoration of 1868, Japan was governed by successive dynasties of military dictators, nearly all of them sprung from Minamoto stock." (Sir George Sansom).—Ed.

advance on them with the tide. Kajiwara with his sons and retainers to the number of fourteen or fifteen, stuck close to the shore, and catching on with rakes to some ships of the Heike that went astray, they boarded them and sprang from one ship to the other, cutting their men down both at bow and stern and doing great deeds. And their merit that day has been specially recorded.

Thus both armies joined battle all along the line, and the roar of their war-cries was such as to be heard even to the highest heavens of Brahma, and to cause the deity deep under the earth to start in amazement. Then Tomomori, coming forth on to the deck-house of his ship, shouted to his men in a mighty voice: "Even in India and China and also in our country, with the most renowned leader and the bravest warriors an army cannot prevail if fate be against it. Yet must our honour be dear to us, and we must show a bold front to these Eastern soldiers. Let us then pay no heed to our lives, but think of nothing but fighting as bravely as we may." Hidano-Saburō Saemon Kagetsune again repeated this proclamation to the samurai. "Ho! these Eastern fellows may have a great name for their horsemanship," shouted Aku-shichi-byōye Kagekiyo, "but they know nothing about sea fights, and they will be like fish up a tree, so that we will pick them up one by one and pitch them into the sea!" "And let their Commander Kurō Yoshitsune be the special object of your attack," added Etchū-no Jirōhyōye Moritsugu, "he is a little fellow with a fair complexion and his front teeth stick out a bit, so you will know him by that. He often changes his clothes and armour, so take care he doesn't escape you!" "Who cares for that wretched little fellow?" replied Aku-shichi, "Cheer up, my brave

THE BEGINNING OF THE FINAL FIGHT

comrades; we'll soon pick him up under our arms and fling him into the sea!"

After Shin-Chūnagon Tomomori had thus addressed his men he took a small boat and rowed across to the ship of the Daijin Munemori. "Our own men look well enough," said he, "only Awa-no-Mimbu Shigeyoshi seems doubtful in his allegiance. I pray you let me take off his head." "But he has served us well so far," replied Munemori, "so how can we do this only on suspicion? Anyhow, let him be summoned." So Shigeyoshi came into the presence of Munemori. He was attired in a hitatare of yellowish red colour with a little black in it, and armour laced with light red leather. "How now, Shigeyoshi? Do you intend treachery?" said Munemori, "for your conduct to-day has a suspicious look. Do you tell your men of Shikoku to bear themselves well in the fight, and don't play the dastard." "Why should I play the dastard?" said Shigeyoshi as he retired from before the Daijin. Meanwhile Tomomori had been standing by with his hand gripping his sword-hilt hard enough to break it, casting meaning looks at Munemori to intimate his wish to cut Shigeyoshi down, but as the latter gave no sign he could do nothing.

So the Heike divided their thousand vessels into three fleets. In the van rowed Yamaga-no-Hyōtōji Hidetō with five hundred ships, and after him came the Matsuura with three hundred more; last of all came the Heike nobles with two hundred. Now Yamaga-no Hyōtōji who led the van was the strongest archer in all Kyūshu, and he chose five hundred men who drew the bow better than most, though not equal to himself, and placed them in the bows of his ships, shoulder to shoulder, so that they let fly a volley of five hundred arrows at once.

The fleet of the Genji was the more numerous with its three hundred ships, but as their men shot from various places here and there, their force did not show to advantage. Yoshitsune himself, who was fighting in the forefront of the battle, was greatly embarrassed by the arrows of the foe which fell like rain on his shield and armour. So, elated by their victory in the first attack, the Heike pressed onward, and the roar of their shouting mingled with the booming of their war-drums that continuously sounded the onset.

Now on the side of the Genji, Wada-no-Kotaro Yoshimori did not go on shipboard, but mounted his horse and sat himself firmly in the saddle with his feet deep in the stirrups, riding into the midst of the Heike host and letting fly his arrows right and left. A famous archer he had always been, and no enemy within the space of three cho escaped his arrows, but one shaft he shot an extroardinary distance on which was a request to return it to the marksman. When it was withdrawn by order of Tomomori it was seen to be feathered with white-wing-feathers of the crane mixed with black ones of the wild-goose, a plain bamboo shaft thirteen handbreaths and three fingers long, inscribed at the space of a handbreath from the lashing on the butt with the name Wada-no-Kōtarō Yoshimori painted in lacquer.

Among the Heike too there were some fine archers, but none who could do a feat like this. After a while however, Nii-no-Kishirō Chikakiyo of Iyo stepped forward and shot it back again. It flew to a distance of more than three cho and struck deep into the left arm of Miura-no-Ishi Sakon-no-Taro, who was standing about a tan behind Wada. " Ha-ha ! " laughed Miura's men as they came crowding around, " Wada-no-Kōtarō boasts no one can

THE BEGINNING OF THE FINAL FIGHT

equal him at shooting, and he has been put to shame openly." Then Yoshimori, angered at this, sprang into a small boat and pressed on into the midst of the foe, drawing his bow lustily so that very many of his adversaries were killed and wounded. . . .

After this both sides set their faces against each other and fought grimly without a thought for their lives, neither giving way an inch. But as the Heike had on their side an Emperor endowed with the Ten Virtues and the Three Sacred Treasures of the Realm, things went hard with the Genji and their hearts were beginning to fail them, when suddenly something that they at first took for a white cloud, but which soon appeared to be a white banner floating in the breeze, came drifting over the two fleets from the upper air and finally settled on the stern of one of the Genji ships, hanging on by the rope.

From: Heike Monogatari, translated by Professor A. L. Sadler. Transactions of the Asiatic Society of Japan, Vol. XLVI, Part II, 1918 and Vol. XLIX, Part I, 1921.

THIS WORLD OF CALAMITIES
Kamo no Chōmei, 1212 A. D.

Fire, Famine, Plague, and Earthquake

Now since first I had conscious knowledge of the world about me, have some forty Springs and Summers gone by, and of many strange events have I had experience.

On the 28th day of the 4th month of 3 Angen (May 28th, 1177) while a violent storm was raging about the hour of the dog (7-8 p. m.), a fire broke out in the dragon (south-east) quarter of the city and extended to the Dog and Hog (north-west) Quarter as far as the Shuzaku Gate,[1] the Daigoku Hall,[2] the Daigaku Ryō,[3] and the Mimbushō[4]—in the course of the one night the whole was reduced to ashes. Folks say the fire began in a cottage used as a temporary hospital situated in the lane known as Higuchitomi.

Favoured by the wind the conflagration spread fanwise. Distant houses were smothered in the smoke, the nearer spaces were enveloped in coils of flame. The air was filled with clouds of dust, which reflected the blaze, so that the whole neighbourhood was steeped in a glow of fire amid which tongues of flame darted over the adjoining streets. Amid such horrors who could retain a steady mind?

Some choked by the smoke, fell to the ground; others in their bewilderment ran straight into the flames trying

---

1. Gate of the Red Sparrow—in the middle of the south face of the Palace at Kyōto.—D.
2. Or Hachishō-In, Hall of the Eight Boards of Government.—D.
3. The University of Chinese Learning, etc.—D.
4. One of the Eight Boards—answering nearly to the Home Office.—D.

FIRE, FAMINE, PLAGUE, AND EARTHQUAKE

to save their property, and were burnt to death; great stores of wealth were utterly destroyed—in very truth the loss was incalculable.

Sixteen mansions of Kugyō (high court-officers) were consumed, and innumerable smaller houses. A full third of the city was destroyed. Thousands of persons perished, horses and cattle beyond count.

How foolish are all the purposes of men—they build their houses, spending their treasure and wasting their energies, in a city exposed to such perils!

Again on the 29th of the hare (4th) month of 4 Jijō (May 25th, 1180) a hurricane devastated the city from the Nakamikado Kyōgoku[1] quarter as far as Rokujō.[2] Not a single house was left standing within the circuit of several wards. Some were levelled with the ground, some were left with beams and uprights alone standing, the cross-pieces of the gateways were blown off in some cases and carried three or four chō (one chō = 360 yards) away, fences were blown down, and neighbouring compounds thus thrown into one. Needless to say, the contents of houses were scattered in all directions, while the shingles filled the air like leaves in winter, and clouds of dust like smoke obscured the sky and blinded one's eyes. The roar of the wind was fearful, one could not hear a word spoken, the storm seemed a true hell-blast.

Not only were houses destroyed, but the number of those who were injured or maimed in their attempts to save their dwellings was incalculable. The wind finally veered towards the Goat and Ape quarter (south-west) and did much harm in that region. It was a whirlwind, but what

1. In the northern part of the capital.—D.
2. In the southern part of the capital.—D.

a one! An extraordinary hurricane! people doubted not it portended some evil of like dimensions.

Again, in the same year in the waterless (6th) month a change of capital was suddenly made, against all expectation. Kyōto had already been the capital for some centuries since its choice by the Mikado Saga[1] (A. D. 810–823).

As there was no sufficient reason for this removal the people were discontented beyond words. Their complaints, however, were of no avail, and the Mikado and his Court betook themselves to Naniwa in Settsu.

Who, then, if he regard the ways of the world, would care to remain in the deserted city? Therefore those who hankered after place and rank and courted great men's favour strove their utmost to forestall their fellows in removing, if only by a single day. Others whose home was lost, whose hopes were frustrated, and whom the world neglected, remained sorrowfully behind.

The mansion of those who have vied with each other in the height of their roods (i.e. in wealth and show) fell into ruin, houses were demolished, and the parts floated down the Yodo to the new city; gardens were turned visibly into mere fields. Even men's dispositions changed, only horses and harness were thought of, and were there none to use ox-drawn carriages. Lands in the south and west rose in demand, and property in the north and eastern provinces fell in value.

At this juncture he had occasion to visit the new capital and found it too confined for the due laying out of streets

---

1. Kyōto was really founded by Emperor Kwanmu in 784, but the next Mikado, Heizei, resided for three years at the former capital, Nara (hence he is often known as the Nara Mikado), so that the founding of Kyōto is ascribed to his successor, Saga. The removal was decreed at the instance of the famous Taira-no-Kiyomori.—D.

FIRE, FAMINE, PLAGUE, AND EARTHQUAKE

and avenues. To the north lay the slopes of a chain of hills, on the south it was washed by the sea. The roar of the waves sounded everlastingly in one's ears, the briny gales blew everlastingly in one's face, the Palace right among the hills reminded one of the Round Timber palace,[1] though it was not without design and elegance.

Daily were dwellings taken to pieces and sent down the river to be rebuilt in the new City-Royal, yet many were the open spaces and few the completed mansions, and while the old capital was desolated the new town was unfinished, and men seemed to themselves to be drifting with the clouds.

The old inhabitants were unhappy because their property was lost, and the newcomers had to live amid the unpleasant bustle of construction. As one scanned the ways one saw carriage-folk on horseback and vestments of state and elegance replaced by common tunics. The grace of manners of the former capital all at once vanished, and country fashions reigned.

Such were clear signs of public disturbance; every day grew the agitation, and the minds of folk became unsettled.

---

1. The Empress Saimei died in A.D. 661 at Asakura in Tosa, where she was at the head of an army assembled to assist the Koreans against China. Her son Tenji lived in the same place, mourning for her, and ordered his palace to be constructed of Kuroki (timber with the bark on), which later Mikados imitated on ascending the throne as a symbol of frugality and humility (a Chinese, not a purely Japanese idea). He made (or caused some court poet to make) the following verse on the occasion :—

>Asakura ya
>Ki no marudono ni
>Ware woreba
>Nanori wo shitsutsu
>Yuku wa taga ko zo!
>(Manyoshū)

" In a rude palace, at Asakura, of round unbarked timber, dwell I, and as men pass shouting their names, I ask whose sons they be."—D.

Nor was this confusion without cause, and when the Winter came the people could not be restrained from returning to Kyōto. But what became of the houses that had been pulled down and removed? We know not, but this we know, that the old state of the city was not restored.

According to dim tradition, in the wise days of old the sovrans[1] ruled compassionately, their palaces had but thatched roofs, nor were the eaves adjusted to them (no verandahs—a luxury?—D). When no smoke was seen ascending from the hearths the taxes were remitted. One knows only too well how ill these modern days compare with the days of yore.

Once more—it would be in Yōwa (A. D. 1181), but so long ago is it one cannot be sure—for two whole years a famine raged in the land, a very miserable time. Either there were droughts in Spring and Summer, or floods and storms in Autumn and Winter. So the evil went on, and of the five grains[2] no crops were reaped. To till the land in Spring was vain, in Summer to plant was foolishness, in Autumn there was no reaping, in Winter nothing to store.

So that many people in the different provinces deserted the land and crossed the frontiers (of their proper districts? —D.), or fled from their homes to pick up a living among the wild hills. Many prayers of various kinds were offered up, and unusual rites were practised, but without avail.

The town, of course, depends upon the country, but nothing came from the country, and so it was that the

---

1. The Mikado Nintoku (A.D. 313–399 official chronology) is more particularly referred to.—D.

2. Rice, Wheat, Awa (Setaria, Italian Millet), Kibi (Sorghum panicum miliaceum), and Hiye (p. frumentaceum).—D.

FIRE, FAMINE, PLAGUE, AND EARTHQUAKE

city lost, so to speak, its countenance. While folk begged for aid they offered their goods recklessly for sale, but caught never a purchaser. Gold was held cheap and grain dear. Beggars whined in misery by the roadsides, dinning one's ears with their cries, and so in misery came to an end the first of those two years.

The following year it was hoped matters would mend, but instead a plague was added to the famine, and more and more vain the prayers offered up appeared to be. It seemed as if the whole population would starve to death like the fish in the proverbial pool (none of which survive on its drying up—D.).

At last even men who wore hats and whose feet were covered and who were well dressed began to go around begging from house to house. Such poor wretches would often fall to the ground from weakness as one looked at them wondering how they could stand on their feet. The number of those who perished of hunger is incalculable, they lay dead under walls and by roadsides, and as there were none to carry away the bodies the air was filled with the stink of their corruption, and sorry indeed were the sights that met one's eyes. Of course, the banks of the river[1] were impassable for horses and vehicles (because they were crowded with corpses).

Even the poor woodcutters lost their vigour, and faggots became scarce, so that men in their helplessness destroyed their own dwellings and took the wood to market, but the value of a man's load was not enough to buy a single day's food. A strange thing was that among these faggots were to be seen pieces of wood painted with red

---

1. The dry parts of the bed of the river are meant—foreshores, a sort of no man's land. The river, of course, is the Kamogawa.—D.

lead or showing patches of gold and silver foil. On inquiry it was discovered that destitute wretches had plundered the temples of images of Buddha and broken sacred vessels and ornaments for mere firewood. That one should be born into such a world of dross and evil as to witness so sinful a deed, which I, alas, did!

Pitiful scenes there were. There was a sort of rivalry in death among those men or women who could not bear to be separated. What food one of such a pair procured by begging would be reserved to keep the other alive, while the first one was content to die. Both sexes displayed this tender self-sacrifice. With parents and children it was almost the rule for the parent to die first. And there were cases in which infants were found lying by the corpses of their dead parents and trying to suck the mother's breast.

In the great temple of Ninwa (Benevolence and Peace) was a chief priest of the Jison (Compassion and Respect) temple named Okurakyo Ryūgyō, who, moved by commiseration for the countless numbers who died, made arrangements, with the help of other saintly men, to write on the foreheads of the dead the holy character A as a seal to Buddha.

He kept count of the bodies marked during the fourth and fifth months, and found in the portion of the capital bound by Ichijō on the north and Kujō on the south, Kyōgoku on the east and Sujaku on the west, altogether about 42,300 corpses.

To these must be added many others in different quarters of the city and in the suburbs to give a correct idea of the vast numbers of deaths that took place at this time. Lastly, must be counted in the numbers of those who perished in the provinces.

Not very long before, under the Mikado Sutoku, in the

period Chōshō (A. D. 1132-4), a like catastrophe occurred, but the details are unknown to me—what I saw with my own eyes was strange and terrible enough.

Again, in 2 Genryaku[1] (A. D. 1185), a great earthquake occurred. It was not an ordinary one. Hills were shattered and dammed up the rivers, the sea toppled over and flooded the shore-lands, the earth gaped and water roared up through the rents, cliffs were cleft and the fragments rolled down into the valleys, boats sculled along the beach were tossed inland upon the shore, horses on the roads lost the ground beneath their roofs ; all round the capital it is hardly necessary to add, in various places not a single building was left entire ; house or temple, tower or chapel,[2] some were rent and cracked, others were thrown down ; the dust rose into the air like volumes of smoke.

The roar of the quaking earth mingled with the crash of falling buildings was like thunder. To remain within doors was to run the risk of being crushed : to rush out of doors was to be swallowed up in some gaping fissure, unless you had wings to fly up into the air, or could ride on the clouds like a dragon. In the midst of all these horrors one felt that of all dreadful things an earthquake is the most dreadful.

Amid all this ruin I will mention a piteous case. The son of a samurai, six or seven years of age only, had built himself a little play-hut under a shed against a wall, in which he was amusing himself, when suddenly the wall collapsed and buried him flat and shapeless under its ruins, his eyes protruding an inch from their orbits. It was sad

---

1. Bramsen gives Genryaku one year only : 1. Bunji is probably intended, the nengō were sometimes changed in the course of the year.—D.

2. Tomb-chapel or mortuary shrines.—D.

beyond words to see his parents embracing his dead body and hear their unrestrained cries of distress. Piteous indeed it was to see even a samurai, stricken down with grief for his son thus miserably perished, foregetting his dignity in the extremity of his grief.

Such violent shocks did not last long, but the aftershocks continued and twenty or thirty times a day were repeated with a force that under ordinary circumstances would have been felt as most alarming. This went on for some weeks, the shocks diminishing in frequency from four or five to two or three in a day, or even one only, with intervals of quiet days, but for three months the disturbance continued. The other three of the four great calamities, flood, fire, and storm, leave the great earth almost unchanged —not so earthquakes.

Long ago in the period Saiko (A. D. 854-6) it is said there was a great earthquake which did vast damage, and amongst other calamities threw down the august head of the great Buddha of the temple of Todai. But that earthquake was far from being as disastrous as the one described, and people accordingly for some time talked of nothing but the misery of this world and the foulness and frivolity of the human heart. Days and months, however, summed up to years, and years passed, and after a time no one so much as spoke a word about the great earthquake of Genryaku.

From: Hōjōki, translated by Victor Dickins, London, 1927.

AN AESTHETE-RECLUSE
Yoshida Kenkō, 1283—1350

1. The Right Life

WANTON and heedless must one hold those who, forgetting the benevolent rule of the great ones of old, reckless of the people's sorrow and the country's harm, delight to exhaust all forms of luxury, and live withal cramped by their own magnificence. In Kujō Dono's admonitions to his descendants it is written, "From your headdress and your garments to your horse and your carriage, be content with what you have, and do not seek for elegance and splendour." So, in his august writings on palace affairs, the Mikado Juntoku[1] says, "In all things for the Emperor's use plainness is desirable."

2. On Taste

There is a charm about a neat and proper dwelling house, although this world, 'tis true, is but a temporary abode. Even the moonshine seems to gain in friendly brilliancy, striking into the house where a good man lives in peaceful ease.

The man is to be envied who lives in a house, not of the modern, garish kind, but set among venerable trees, with a garden where plants grow wild and yet seem to have been disposed with care, verandas and fences tastefully arranged, and all its furnishings simple but antique.

A house which multitudes of workmen have devoted

---

1. Son of Emperor Toba II; he abdicated in 1221.—Ed.

all their ingenuity to decorate, where rare and strange things from home and abroad are set out in array, and where even the trees and shrubs are trained unnaturally such is an unpleasant sight, depressing to look at, to say nothing of spending one's days therein. No, gazing on it, can one but reflect how easily it might vanish in a moment of time.

The appearance of a house is in some sort an index to the character of its occupant.

There is a story that Saigyō,[1] when he saw that the Minister Go-Tokudaiji had stretched ropes across the roof of his residence in order to keep the kites from settling there, exclaimed, " And if the kites do settle there, what harm can they do ? This then is the sort of man his Lordship is ! ", and ever after refused to visit him.

So, when I once saw ropes stretched on the palace roof of His Highness Prince Aya-No-Koji, I remembered this story, but then I heard people say that the truth was, His Highness could not bear to see the frogs in his pond caught by crows that settled there in flocks, and I thought this is a very praise-worthy action, and after all, we cannot tell but what Go-Tokudaiji had some good reason for what he did.

3. Going to the Country Side

It wakes one up to go away from home for a time, no matter wither. Rambling and exploring about the countryside you come upon a host of unwonted sights in rustic spots and mountain hamlets. You get a messenger to take letter to the capital, and you write and say " Do not forget to send me so and so by the next opportunity." All

---

1. Famous monk-poet (1118–1190). Some of his finest poems may be found in Waley's " Uta," pp. 100–102.—Ed.

this is in its way amusing. Of course you have a thousand things to think of in such a place.

Pleasant also to slip away and go into retreat in some mountain temple.

4. Sensibility

It is a great relief and very pleasant, when you have neglected to write for a long time, and, thinking "How angry she must be with me!", you feel conscious of your guilt and do not know how to approach her, to get a message from a woman, saying "I want a manservant. Can you spare me one?" Such a disposition (i.e. free from malice—Sa.) is very admirable, so people say,—and with reason.

5. Scene at a Country Temple

Once I saw emerging from within a coarse, bamboo-plaited gate a very young man, of important mien, wearing a rich silken hunting-robe, whose hue the moon obscured, but which was embroidered in deep colours. Attended by one small boy, he took the path stretching far away among the rice fields, brushing through the young plants wet with dew, and playing to himself the while with unspeakable sweetness on a flute. As he went on, little thinking that there was one who listened with admiration, curious to see where he was going I followed him with my eyes until he ceased to play, and went in at a temple gate by the foot of the hill.

A carriage propped up on its shafts attracts more attention here in the country than in the Capital. I enquire of my servants and they reply, "Such and such a prince is now here. It is no doubt some Buddhist rite they are performing." Priests and others are assembled in the Hall, and on the cool evening breeze comes a pervading odour of incense. The way in which the maids of honour take care that their garments shall not flutter in the breeze they make as they pass along the gallery to the royal apartments, shews that they are careful to preserve decorum even here in this hillside village where none can see them.

Here the Autumn moor, in wanton luxuriant growth, is flooded with the heavy fall of dew; insects sing noisily; and the water in the pipes flows with a soothing sound. The clouds seem to gather and disperse more rapidly than in the sky of the Capital, the moon to wear a more variable complexion.

6. A Glimpse

One day towards the close of Spring in calm and lovely weather, I came upon a seemly house, in a garden stretching far back, grown with venerable trees and strewn with faded blossoms. I could not pass without a look, and, peeping in, I saw that all the shutters on the Southern side were down, giving the place a deserted air; but facing East the doors were thrown open, and through a rent in the blind I saw a handsome young man of about twenty, who, though quite at his ease, was sitting there dignified and calm, reading a volume spread out before him on the desk.

I felt a great desire to find out who and what manner of man he was.

7. On Accomplishments

Of a man's abilities first comes a knowledge of the teachings of the Sages, by a clear understanding of Literature.

Next is handwriting, which should be studied, even though not as an object in itself, as an aid to learning.

Next should be learned the art of Medicine. Without Medicine, a man cannot care for his own body, nor help others, nor perform his duties to parents and his lord.

Next come Archery and the Riding of a Horse, from among the Six Accomplishments, and they certainly must be given attention.

A knowledge of Letters, Arms and Medicine cannot in truth be done without; and a man who will learn these cannot be said to be an idle person.

"Food is man's Heaven," and it must be accounted a great virtue in a man to know how to prepare well-tasting food.

Next is Handicraft, which has a thousand uses.

Beyond these, too many accomplishments are a source of shame to high and low. Skill in poetry, talent for music are fine and admirable qualities; but though Sovereign and subject may prize them, nowadays a condition of things has been reached where it would seem foolish to (expect to) govern a state by their means. Though gold is superior, it cannot equal iron in the multitude of its uses.

8. On Marriage

A wife is a thing a man ought not to have. I like to hear a man say "I am still living alone," and so on. To hear it said, "So-and-so is getting married," or "He has taken such-and-such a wife, and they are now living together" lowers him extremely in my estimation. For one thinks poorly of a man who marries a quite ordinary person because, forsooth, he has made up his mind she is a fine woman; while, if she is a handsome woman, and he cares for and cherishes her as if she were his own Image of Buddha, then one wonders how he can go so far. More regrettable still is it in the case of a woman who manages the work of the household; and grievous when children come, and she nurses and loves them. When she becomes a nun after her husband's death, and grows old, her condition is mean though he is no longer alive.

Living day in, day out with a woman, of whatever sort she may be, she must lose her attraction and become disliked. The woman, too, must grow indifferent. It is by keeping apart, and going to stay with her from time to time, that an intimacy is reached that even the passing of months and years will not destroy.

It is a pleasant change then to go and stay from time to time.

From: The Tsuredzure-gusa by Yoshida Kenko, translated by G. B. Sansom. Transactions of the Asiatic Society of Japan, 1st Series, Vol. 39.

A WORLD OUT OF JOINT

Nijō Gawara no Rakushu

An anonymous placard exposed at the market-place in the early part of the fourteenth century gave the following picture of the metropolis :—

The things that abound in the capital now are night-attacks ; robberies ; forged Imperial decrees ; calls to arms ; galloping messengers ; empty tumults ; decapitations ; recusant priests and tonsured laymen ; degraded nobles and upstart peers ; gifts of estates and confiscations of property ; men rewarded and men slaughtered ; eager claimants and sad petitioners ; baggage consisting of manuscripts only ; sycophants and slanderers ; friars of the Zen and priests of the Ritsu ;[1] leaps to fortune and neglected talents ; shabby hats and disordered garments ; holders of unwonted batons and strangers asking the path to the Palace ; Imperial secretaries who affect widsom, but whose falsehoods are more foolish than the folly of fools ; soldiers saturated with finery, who wear hats like cooking-boards and strut about fashionably at the fall of evening in search of beautiful women to love ; wives who simulate piety but live lives abominable to the citizens ; official hunters holding each an emaciated hawk that never strikes quarry ; leaden dirks fashioned like big swords and worn with the hilts disposed for ready drawing ; fans with only five ribs ; gaunt steeds ; garments of thinnest silk ; second-hand armour hired by the day ; warriors riding to their offices in palanquins ; plebeians in brocade robes ; civilians in war panoply and surcoats ; archers so

---

[1]. Buddhist Sects.—Ed.

A WORLD OUT OF JOINT

ignorant of archery that their falls from their horses outnumber their arrows; new exercises of arms without any teacher to show their methods; Kyōto and Kamakura seated side by side making verselets. All over the country poetasters abound and literary critics are still more numerous. Hereditary vassals and new retainers practise equal license; a lawless society of Samurai. Dogmimes which forestalled the ruin of Kamakura are all the fashion here. Men meet everywhere to drink tea and light incense, while the fires of the watch-house in each street burn in rude sheds built with three boards and festooned with official curtains. Many samurai are stil without residences, and many half-built houses disfigure the city. Vacant spaces swept last year by conflagrations are counted lucky sites to-day. Deserted dwellings stand desolate. Discharged samurai troop through the streets, preserving their official strut, but without any business except to make obeisances to one another. The oldtime hills of blossom and groves of peach are unvisited. Men and horses crowd the Imperial city. Samurai with high- sounding titles, relics of past glory, would fain lay aside these encumbrances, but men who in the morning were foddering beasts of burden, find themselves in the evening with full purses and in high favour on account of some petty service rendered to the Emperor. Merit is neglected on the one hand, lawlessness is exalted on the other. The recipients of fortune doubt its reality, and can only trust blindly to their Sovereign who bestowed it. A strange thing, truly, the unification of the nation! A lucky fellow I, who have seen these singular events come to pass, and now jot down a fraction of them!

From: Japan, its History, Art and Literature, by Captain F. Brinkley, Boston and Tokyo 1901, Vol. II.

ASHIKAGA AND MOMOYAMA PERIODS
(1392—1568)

THE ACTOR AND HIS PUBLIC
Kwanze Seami Motokiyo, about A.D. 1363-1444

1. On Patrons

WHEN a Sarugaku[1] is performed it is necessary that exactly the right moment should be chosen for the sashi[2] and issei.[3] It is bad to begin them too soon and bad to begin them too late. When the actor leaves the gaku-ya[4] and advances on to the hashigakari[5] he should pause for a moment to scan his audience. He must not begin to chant till he hears a simultaneous murmur of " Now he is going to begin ! " arise in every part of the theatre. If he waits thus till he has secured everyone's attention, his opening will produce the proper effect.

But if he is an instant late, attention will have slackened and he will fail to move the hearts of the multitude (lit. " 10,000 people "). He ought to begin his first chant standing two-thirds of the way up the hashigakari; the second phrase should be changed at the end of the hashigakari, on the edge of the stage itself.—

The actor should not stare straight into the faces of the audience, but look between them. When he looks in the direction of the " honourable " (the Daimyōs) he must

---

1. One of the earlier forms of the Nō play, originally connected with the sacred Shintō-Dance (Kagura)—Ed.
2. I think Sashi must here mean the waki's opening words.—W.— For detailed explanation of the technical terms see Noël Péri, Cinq Nō, Paris 1927. The shite may be compared to the protagonist, the Waki to the deuteragonist of the Greek scene.
3. Issei, the shite's first chant.—W.
4. Green-room.
5. A bridge-like passage connecting the green-room with the stage.

not let his eyes meet theirs, but must slightly avert his gaze.

At palace-performances or when acting at a banquet, he must not let his eyes meet those of the Shogun or stare straight into the Honourable Face. When playing in a large enclosure he must take care to keep as close as possible to the side where the Nobles are sitting; if in a small enclosure as far off as possible. But particularly in palace-performances and the like he must take the greatest pains to keep as far away as he possibly can from the August presence.

Again, when the recitations are given at the palace it is equally essential to begin at the right moment. It is bad to begin too soon and fatal to delay too long.

It sometimes happens that the "noble gentlemen" do not arrive at the theatre until the play has already reached its Development and Climax. In such cases the play is at its climax, but the noble gentlemen's hearts are ripe only for Introduction.

If they, ready only for Introduction, are forced to witness a Climax, they are not likely to get pleasure from it. Finally even the spectators who were there before, awed by the entry of the "exalted ones." become so quiet that you would not know they were there, so that the whole audience ends by returning to the Introductory mood. At such a moment the Nō cannot possibly be a success. In such circumstances it is best to take Development-Nō and give it a slightly "introductory" turn. Then, if it is played gently, it may win the August Attention.

It also happens that one is suddenly sent for to perform at a Shogunal feast or the like. The audience is already in a "climax-mood"; but "introductory" Nō must be played. This is a great difficulty. In such circumstances

ON PATRONS

the best plan is to tinge the introduction with a nuance of development. But this must be done without " stickiness," with the lightest possible touch, and the transition to the real Development and Climax must be made as quickly as possible.

In old times there were masters who perfected themselves in Nō without study. But nowadays the nobles and gentlemen have become so critical that they will only look with approbation on what is good and will not give attention to anything bad.

Their honourable eyes have become so keen that they notice the least defect, so that even a masterpiece that is as pearls many times polished or flowers choicely culled will not win the applause of our gentlemen to-day.[1]

At the same time, good actors are becoming few and the Art is gradually sinking towards its decline. For this reason, if very strenuous study is not made, it is bound to disappear altogether.

When summoned to play before the noble gentlemen, we are expected to give the regular " words of good-wish " and to divide our performance into the three parts, Introduction, Development and Climax, so that the pre-arranged order cannot be varied. But on less formal occasions, when, for example, one is playing not at a Shogunal banquet but on a common, everyday (yō no tsune) stage, it is obviously unnecessary to limit oneself to the set forms of " happy wish."

*   *   *

---

1. Seami wrote his notes on the Nō in 1423, according to Waley (l. c., p. 35).

The history of the Nō in its present form begins with Seami's father Kwanami Kiyotsugu.—Ed.

THE ACTOR AND HIS PUBLIC

Further Advice to Actors

One's style should be easy and full of graceful yūgen,[1] and the piece[2] selected should be suitable to the audience. A ballad (ko-utai) or dance-song (kuse-mai) of the day will be best. One should have in one's repertory a stock of such pieces and be ready to vary them according to the character of one's audience.

In the words and gestures (of a farce, kyōgen) there should be nothing low. The jokes and repartee should be such as suit the august ears of the nobles and gentry. On no account must vulgar words or gestures be introduced, however funny they may be. This advice must be carefully observed.

Introduction, Development and Climax must also be strictly adhered to when dancing at the palace. If the chanting proceeds from an " introductory-mood," the dancing must belong to the same mood—when one is suddenly summoned to perform at a riotous banquet, one must take into consideration the state of the noble gentlemen's spirits.

*   *   *

Peoples' tastes differ; to suit the dispositions of " ten thousand " men is a task of unrivalled difficulty. Yet one's model should be the actor who is successful wher-

---

1. Yūgen, one of the most untranslatable words, means according to Waley, " What lies beneath the surface," the subtle, as opposed to the obvious, the dint as opposed to the statement. It is applied to the natural grace of a boy's movements, to the gentle restraint of a nobleman's speech and bearing, " a white bird with a flower in its beak."—Ed.
2. The piece to be used as an introduction. Modern performances are not confined to full Nō. Sometimes actors in plain dress recite without the aid of instrumental music, sitting in a row, or one actor may recite the piece, with music (this is called Hayashi) or the piece may be mimed without music (this is called Shimai).—W.

ever he appears throughout the whole Empire. There are three ways to success, by the eyes, by the ears and by the heart.

A play which appeals successfully to the eye is one to which from the beginning the whole audience succumbs. The style of the dancing and chanting is agreeable to them; the spectators, high and low, burst into applause; the whole theatre wears an air of gaiety. Not only connoisseurs, but even people without knowledge of Nō, are saying to themselves with one accord, "How enjoyable!"

But the actor must beware. If the play is too great a success, everything he does will begin to delight the audience equally. They will be in such a state of exultation and continuous appreciation that the play will begin to fatigue them.

The actor too will exhaust himself in his excitement. In such cases he must hold himself in and restrain his movements in order to give a little repose to the audience. He must, I say, give people time to rest and breathe, and play the exciting passages quietly. Then he will regain his power over the hearts of the audience and the latter part of the play will gain in strength; nor will he progressively lose his power to move as he proceeds from play to play.

From: Nō-Plays, translated by Arthur Waley, London 1921, George Allen and Unwin, Ltd.

THE CULT OF TEA
Sen Rikyū, A.D. 1521-1591

1. Whoever wishes to enter this Way must be his own teacher.
2. Learn by observation. And he is a fool who criticizes others while yet he has not learnt.
3. Be sympathetic to those who are anxious to learn and teach them all you know.
4. Don't be ashamed to ask anyone for information. This is the foundation of all proficiency.
5. Three things are needed to attain skill: Love of the subject, ability and perseverance.
6. In the technique of Tea there must be strength and no weakness, but bad habits must be got rid of.
7. But don't think strength alone will do. Strength is weakness and lightness is firmness.
8. Whenever you use any utensil take it lightly and put it down firmly.
9. Don't listen to those who say that anything will do for Usu-cha.[1] It should be as carefully served as any other kind.
10. Don't trouble too much about the technique of Koi-cha.[2] It is the quality of the Tea that is, after all, most important.
11. And the quality of the Tea, is this. That the water should be hot, that there should be no froth nor any hard lumps in it.

---

1. " Thin tea," not do strong as Koi-cha, and made more informally.
2. " Thick tea," the best kind, made with the most of ceremony.

THE CULT OF TEA

12. And the only way to understand this quality is by the experience of making Koi-cha.
27. Sticking to rules in arranging Charcoal is no good if the kettle doesn't boil.
35. Kettles have a lot of fancy names, but all the same they are all kettles.
36. A picture should be hung in the Tokonoma according to the way the Tokonoma faces.
41. When you put down a utensil after moving it do so lingeringly as though parting from someone beloved.
43. When you give flowers to other people take care that they are only slightly opened.
50. When hot water is ladled there are three things to remember. Not to take up too much, to ladle hot water from the bottom, and cold from the middle of the vessel, and not to raise the ladle too high in air.
51. When hot water is ladled into the Tea-bowl the arm should move from the elbow.
52. When either hot or cold water is ladled out, one should think rather of carrying than of drawing it.
53. When Tea is whisked this too should be done from the elbow and not from the wrist.
54. When a scroll of poetry is hung in the Tokonoma there must not be any other verses in the room.
55. When you show a scroll with an inscription on the outside, this is to be shown in silence and then the scroll unrolled for inspection.
61. In ancient times at an Evening Tea there was neither picture nor flower in the Tokonoma.
77. If a Cha-no-yu party is given after a flower-viewing

THE CULT OF TEA

excursion no painting of flowers and birds may be displayed.

78. When a guest drops in unexpectedly and Tea is served it should be done in the Informal style.
83. By observing one performance of Cha-no-yu you can see whether a man is good or bad or self-conscious or the reverse.
84. If the performer is too quick or too slow or is defective in some point one describes him as one " whose Tea accent is bad."
85. Taste consists in handling heavy things lightly and light things firmly.
86. If you put a Bonseki (Tray landscape) into the Tokonoma a landscape picture should be avoided, for they will clash.
87. Though it is not usual to display a Tea-jar or Tea-caddy in a Tokonoma with a wooden floor, yet there is a way of doing it successfully.
88. When you inspect a hanging scroll or a flower arrangement you should sit respectfully three feet from the Tokonoma.
89. Practice means doing these things from the beginning to the end, and then going over it again back to the beginning.
90. When you make Tea, fix your attention on the Tea-whisk, and take care that it does not strike the bottom of the Tea-bowl.
91. Use your eye and then your ear, sniff the incense and ask questions, and then you will understand.
92. Consider all you have learnt as useless rubbish, and all that is written about it as so much waste paper.
93. Water both cold and hot, Tea-napkins and Tea-

THE CULT OF TEA

whisks, chop-sticks, tooth-picks and ladles cannot be too fresh and clean.

94. Cha-no-yu must be simple and full of hospitable feeling, but the utensils may be the first that come to hand.

95. If you have one kettle it is quite enough for Cha-no-yu. Only stupidity needs a lot of utensils.

96. But to hide away utensils that you happen to have and to pretend you haven't got them is equally stupid.

97. Cha-no-yu consists merely in boiling water and making tea. Then in drinking it.

98. In former days there were no special rules about these things, but now I lay them down for the future.

99. Cha-no-yu is the plum-blossom and the winter chrysanthemum, the autumn leaves, the green bamboo and the withered branch and the frosty dawn.

100. Though you may cleave to these rules and sometimes break them, and though you don't take them seriously, don't quite forget them.

From: The Hundred Articles of Sen Rikyū in the translation of Professor Sadler, Appendix to Okakura Kakuzō: The Book of Tea, Angus and Robertson Limited, Sydney (Australia), 1932.

AN EPILOGUE

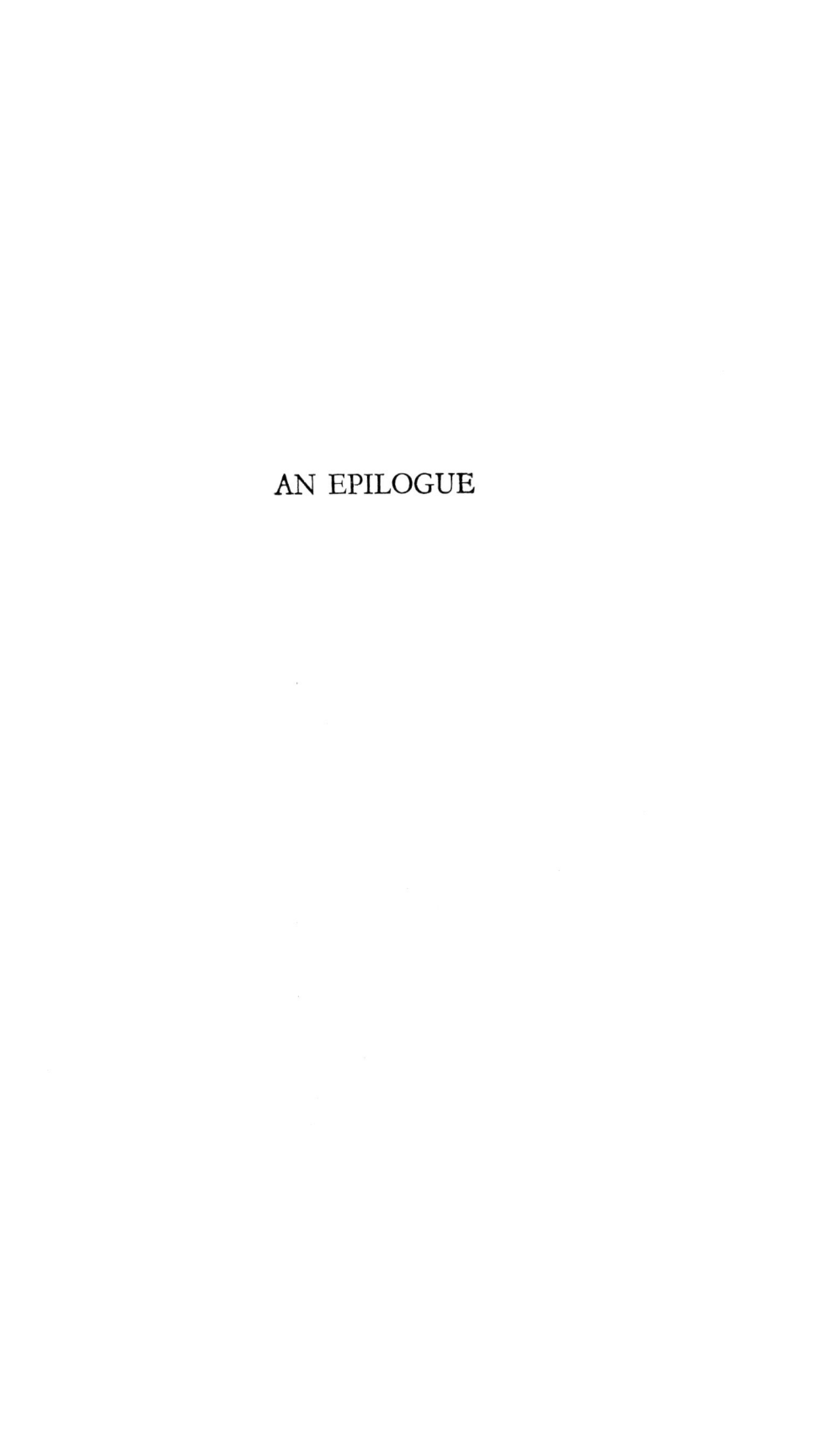

DELIVERY

Motokiyo Kwanze Seami

The following monody, from the Nō-play Shunkwan, is taken, according Mr. Waley, from an ancient Kōwaka dance " Jō ga Shima " (Sulphur Island), contrasting the piety of two worshippers of the Deity of Kumano and the "amoral mysticism" of Shunkwan, abbot of the Zen temple Hosshōji. The three had been banished by the Taira to that island, also called Devil's Island, on the shore of Satsuma in South Kyūshū. But the two Kumano-worshippers had been permitted to return by an act of amnesty. Shunkwan, left behind on the desert island, remains unrepentant. " But as for the God of Kumano, I have no faith in him." The Deity of Kumano, in Kii, a peninsula south of Yamato, was the object of a very important buddho-shintoist cult during the middle-ages.

The Kōwaka is described by Mr. Waley, p. 17, as a " recitation accompanied by rhythmical tapping with the fan." A performance, under this name, by villagers of Fukuoka prefecture, in the Nihon Seinen Kwan, Tokio, autumn 1935, revealed a soldier-like march rhythm of a surprisingly clear trochaic structure, rarely if ever found in later Japanese music.

Editor's Note.

Shunkwan Sings:

Then lonely, lonely these two to worship went ;
On the wide sea they gazed,
Roamed on the rugged shore ;
Searching ever for a semblance
Of the three Holy Hills.
Now, where between high rocks
A long, clear river flowed :
Now, where tree tops soar

DELIVERY

Summit on summit upward to the sky.
And there they planned to set
The Mother-Temple, Hall of proven **Truth** *;*
And here the Daughter-Shrine,
The Treasury of Kan.
There far to northward aiming
To a white cliff they came, where from the clouds
Swift waters tumbled down.
Then straightway they remembered
The Hill of Nachi, where the Dragon God,
Winged water-spirit, pants with stormy breath
And fills the woods with awe.
Here reverently they their Nachi set.
The Bonze Shunkwan mounted to a high place ;
His eye wandered north, south, east and west.
A thousand, thousand concepts filled his heart.
Suddenly a black cloud rose before him,
A heavy cloak of cloud ;
And a great rock crashed and fell into the sea.
Then the great Bonze in his meditation remembered
An ancient song :
" The wind scattered a flower at Buddha's feet ;
" A boulder fell and crushed the fish of the pool.
" Neither has the wind merit, nor the boulder blame ;
" They know not what they do."
" The Five Limbs are a loan," he cried, " that must be repaid ;
A mess of earth, water, air, fire.
And the heart—void, as the sky ; shapeless, substanceless !
Being and non-being
Are but twin aspects of all component things.
And that which seems to be, soon is not.

DELIVERY

But only contemplation is eternal."
So the priest : proudly pillowed
On unrepentance and commandments broke.

From: Nō-Plays, translated by Arthur Waley, London 1921, George Allen and Unwin Ltd.

SEVEN APPENDICES:

LAWS, RULES AND CUSTOMS

I.

The Laws of Prince Shōtoku

[A. D. 604]

Summer, 4th month, 3rd day. The Prince Imperial in person prepared for the first time laws. There were seventeen clauses, as follows :—

1. Harmony is to be valued,[1] and an avoidance of wanton opposition to be honoured. All persons are influenced by class-feelings, and there are few who are intelligent. Hence there are some who disobey their lords and fathers, or who maintain feuds with the neighbouring villages. But when those above are harmonious and those below are friendly, and there is concord in the discussion of business, right views of things spontaneously gain acceptance. Then what is there which cannot be accomplished!

2. Sincerely reverence the three treasures. The three treasures, viz. Buddha, the Law and the Priesthood, are the final refuge of the four generated beings,[2] and are the supreme objects of faith in all countries. What man in what age can fail to reverence this law? Few men are utterly bad. They may be taught to follow it. But if they do not betake them to the three treasures, wherewithal shall their crookedness be made straight?

3. When you receive the Imperial commands, fail not scrupulously to obey them. The lord is Heaven, the vassal is Earth. Heaven overspreads, and Earth upbears.

---

1. From the " Lunyu," or " Analects " of Confucius.—A.
2. That is, the beings produced in transmigration by the four processes of being born from eggs, from a womb, moisture-bred, or formed by metamorphosis (as butterflies from caterpillars). Some editions omit the phrase Buddha, the Law and Priesthood.—A.

APPENDIX I

When this is so, the four seasons follow their due course, and the powers of Nature obtain their efficacy. If the Earth attempted to overspread, Heaven would simply fall in ruin. Therefore is it that when the lord speaks, the vassal listens : when the superior acts, the inferior yields compliance. Consequently when you receive the Imperial commands, fail not to carry them out scrupulously. Let there be a want of care in this matter, and ruin is the natural consequence.

4. The Ministers and functionaries should make decorous behaviour their leading principle, for the leading principle of the government of the people consists in decorous behaviour.[1] If the superiors do not behave with decorum, the inferiors are disorderly : If inferiors are wanting in proper behaviour, there must necessarily be offences. Therefore it is that when lord and vassal behave with propriety, the distinctions of rank are not confused : when the people behave with propriety, the Government of the Commonwealth proceeds of itself.

5. Ceasing from gluttony and abandoning covetous desires, deal impartially with the suits which are submitted to you. Of complaints brought by the people there are a thousand in one day. If in one day there are so many, how many will there be in a series of years ? If the man who is to decide suits at law makes gain his ordinary motive, and hears causes with a view to receiving bribes, then will the suits of the rich man be like a stone flung into water,[2] while the plaints of the poor will resemble water cast upon a stone. Under these circumstances the poor man will not know whither to betake himself. Here too there is

---

[1]. The Chinese li, decorum, courtesy, proper behaviour, ceremony, gentlemanly conduct as we should say.—A.

[2]. i. e. they meet with no resistance.—A.

a deficiency in the duty of the Minister.

6. Chastise that which is evil and encourage that which is good. This was the excellent rule of antiquity. Conceal not, therefore, the good qualities of others, and fail not to correct that which is wrong when you see it. Flatterers and deceivers are a sharp weapon for the overthrow of the State, and a pointed sword for the destruction of the people. Sycophants are also fond, when they meet, of dilating to their superiors on the errors of their inferiors; to their inferiors, they censure the faults of their superiors. Men of this kind are all wanting in fidelity to their lord, and in benevolence towards the people. From such an origin great civil disturbances arise.

7. Let every man have his own charge, and let not the spheres of duty be confused. When wise men are entrusted with office, the sound of praise arises. If unprincipled men hold office, disasters and tumults are multiplied. In this world, few are born with knowledge; wisdom is the product of earnest meditation. In all things, whether great or small, find the right man, and they will surely be well managed: on all occasions, be they urgent or the reverse, meet but with a wise man, and they will of themselves be amenable. In this way will the State be lasting and the Temples of the Earth and of Grain will be free from danger. Therefore did the wise sovereigns of antiquity seek the man to fill the office, and not the office for the sake of the man.

8. Let the Ministers and functionaries attend the Court early in the morning, and retire late. The business of the State does not admit of remissness, and the whole day is hardly enough for its accomplishments. If, therefore, the attendance at Court is late, emergencies cannot be met: if officials retire soon, the work cannot be completed.

APPENDIX I

9. Good faith is the foundation of right. In everything let there be good faith, for in it there surely consists the good and bad, success and failure. If the lord and the vassal observe good faith one with another, what is there which cannot be accomplished? If the lord and the vassal do not observe good faith towards one another, everything without exception ends in failure.

10. Let us cease from wrath, and refrain from angry looks. Nor let us be resentful when others differ from us. For all men have hearts, and each heart has its own leanings, their right is our wrong, and our right is their wrong. We are not unquestionably sages, nor are they unquestionably fools. Both of us are simply ordinary men. How can any one lay down a rule by which to distinguish right from wrong? For we are all, one with another, wise and foolish, like a ring which has no end. Therefore, although others give way to anger, let us on the contrary dread our own faults, and though we alone may be in the right, let us follow the multitude and act like them.

11. Give clear appreciation to merit and demerit, and deal out to each its sure reward or punishment. In these days, reward does not attend upon merit, nor punishment upon crime. Ye high functionaries who have charge of public affairs, let it be your task to make clear rewards and punishments.

12. Let not the provincial authorities[1] or the Kuni no Miyakko levy exactions on the people. In a country there are not two lords; the people have not two masters. The sovereign is the master of the people of the whole country.

---

1. The Interlinear Kana has Mikoto mochi. The Kuni no Miyakko were the old local nobles, whose power was at this time giving way to that of the Central Government, represented in the provinces by the Kokushi, or local Governors.—A.

The officials to whom he gives charge are all his vassals. How can they, as well as the Government, presume to levy taxes on the people?

13. Let all persons entrusted with office attend equally to their functions. Owing to their illness or to their being sent on missions, their work may sometimes be neglected. But whenever they become able to attend business, let them be as accommodating as if they had had cognizance of it from before, and not hinder public affairs on the score of their not having had to do with them.

14. Ye Ministers and functionaries! Be not envious. For if we envy others, they in turn will envy us. The evils of envy know no limit. If others excel us in intelligence, it gives us no pleasure; if they surpass us in ability, we are envious. Therefore it is not until after a lapse of five hundred years that we at last meet with a wise man, and even in a thousand years we hardly obtain one sage. But if we do not find wise men and sages, wherewithal shall the country be governed?

15. To turn away from that which is private, and to set our faces towards that which is public—this is the path of the Minister. Now if a man is influenced by private motives, he will assuredly feel resentments, and if he is influenced by resentful feelings, he will assuredly fail to act harmoniously with others. If he fails to act harmoniously with others, he will assuredly sacrifice the public interest to his private feelings. When resentment arises, it interferes with order, and is subversive of law. Therefore in the first clause it was said, that superiors and inferiors should agree together. The purport is the same as this.

16. Let the people be employed (in forced labour) at seasonable times. This is an ancient and excellent rule. Let them be employed, therefore, in the winter months,

APPENDIX I

when they are at leisure. But from Spring to Autumn, when they are engaged in agriculture or with the mulberry trees, the people should not be so employed. For if they do not attend to agriculture, what will they have to eat? If they do not attend to the mulberry trees, what will they do for clothing?

17. Decisions on important matters should not be made by one person alone. They should be discussed with many. But small matters are of less consequence. It is unnecessary to consult a number of people. It is only in the case of the discussion of weighty affairs, when there is a suspicion that they may miscarry, that one should arrange matters in concert with others, so as to arrive at the right conclusion.

From: Aston's Nihongi Vol. II. pp. 128–133.

II.

The Taikwa Reform

1. An Edict Against Unlawful Appropriations

[A. D. 645]

Taikwa, first year, Autumn, 9th month, 19th day. Commissioners were sent to all the provinces to take a record of the total numbers of the people. The Emperor on this occasion made an edict, as follows:—

" In the times of all the Emperors, from antiquity downwards, subjects have been set apart for the purpose of making notable their reigns and handing down their names to posterity.[1] Now the Omi and Muraji, the Tomo no Miyakko and the Kuni no Miyakko, have each one set apart their own vassals, whom they compel to labour at their arbitrary pleasure. Moreover they cut off the hills and seas, the woods and plains, the ponds and rice-fields belonging to the provinces and districts, and appropriate them to themselves. Their contests are never-ceasing. Some engross to themselves many tens of thousands of shiro[2] of rice-land, while others possess in all patches of ground too small to stick a needle into. When the time comes for the payment of taxes, the Omi, the Muraji, and the Tomo no Miyakko, first collect them for themselves and then hand over a share. In the case of repairs to palaces or the construction of misasagi, they each bring their own vassals, and do the work according to circumstances. The Book of Changes says:—" Diminish that

---

1. The reference is to the institution of Be with names commemorative of the reign.—A.
2. A land measure of 15.13 acres.—A.

which is above : increase that which is below : if measures are framed according to the regulations, the resources (of the State) suffer no injury, and the people receive no hurt."[1]

"At the present time, the people are still few. And yet the powerful cut off portions of land and water[2] and converting them into private ground, sell it to the people, demanding the price yearly. From this time forward the sale[3] of land is not allowed. Let no man without due authority make himself a landlord, engrossing to himself that which belongs to the helpless."

The people were greatly rejoiced.

From : Aston's Nihongi Vol. II. pp. 204-205.

2. The Great Edict of 646 A. D.

[A. D. 646.]

Second year, Spring, 1st month, 1st day. As soon as the ceremonies of the new year's congratulations were over, the Emperor (Kōtoku Tennō) promulgated an edict of reforms, as follows :—

I. "Let the people established by the ancient Emperors, etc., as representatives of children be abolished, also the Miyake of various places and the people owned as serfs by the Wake,[4] the Omi, the Muraji, the Tomo no Miyakko, the Kuni no Miyakko and the Mura no Obito.[5] Let the farmsteads[6] in various places be abolished." Consequently

---

1. Vide Legge's "Yih-King," pp. 247 and 262.—A.
2. i. e. rice ground and other cultivated land.—A.
3. By sale is evidently meant letting. An early example of a "Land Act."—A.
4. According to the Nihongi (Aston Vol. I. p. 192) : "descendants of separated (wakare) Princes."
5. Chief men of villages.—A.
6. Of serfs.—A.

fiefs were granted for their sustenance[1] to those of the rank of Daibu[2] and upwards on a descending scale.[3] Presents of cloth and silk stuffs were given to the officials and people, varying in value.

Further We say: It is the business of the Daibu to govern the people. If they discharge this duty thoroughly, the people have trust in them, and an increase of their revenue is therefore for the good of the people.

II. The capital is for the first time to be regulated, and Governors appointed for the Home provinces and districts. Let barriers, outposts, guards, and post-horses, both special and ordinary, be provided, bell-tokens[4] made, and mountains and rivers regulated.[5]

For each ward in the capital let there be appointed one alderman,[6] and for four wards one chief alderman,[7] who shall be charged with the superintendence of the population, and the examination of criminal matters. For appointment as chief aldermen of wards let men be taken belonging to the wards, of unblemished character, firm and upright, so that they may fitly sustain the duties of the time. For appointments as aldermen, whether of rural townships or of city wards, let ordinary subjects be taken belonging to

1. Instead of the serfs taken from them.—A.
2. A general name for high officials.—A.
3. The "Roku-rei" gives a scale of sustenance-fiefs at a later period. A Prime Minister had 3000 houses, a Junior Prime Minister 2000, a Dainagon 800, etc., These fiefs were hereditary.—A.
4. I was at first disposed to regard the bells and tokens as different objects, but now agree with Dr. Florenz that they are the same. They were small globular bells, sometimes single, sometimes in groups as in the illustration, and indicated by their shape and number how many horses the bearer was entitled to. This institution was borrowed from China.—A.
5. By the regulation of mountains and rivers is meant the provision of guards at ferries and mountain passes which serve as boundaries between different provinces.—A.
6. The interlinear gloss is wosa, chief.—A.
7. The interlinear gloss is unagashi, one who demands.—A.

APPENDIX II

the township or ward, of good character and solid capacity. If such men are not to be found in the township or ward in question, it is permitted to select and employ men of the adjoining township or ward.

The Home provinces shall include the region from the River Yokogaha at Nabari[1] on the east, from Mount Senoyama in Kii on the south, from Kushibuchi in Akashi on the west, and from Mount Afusake-yama in Sasanami in Afumi on the north. Districts of forty townships[2] are constituted Greater Districts, of from thirty to four townships are constituted Middle Districts, and of three or fewer townships are constituted Lesser Districts. For the district authorities, of whatever class, let there be taken Kuni no Miyakko of unblemished character, such as may fitly sustain the duties of the time, and be made Tairei and Shorei.[3] Let men of solid capacity and intelligence who are skilled in writing and arithmetic be appointed assistants and clerks.

The number of special or ordinary post-horses given shall in all cases follow the number of marks on the posting bell-tokens. When bell-tokens are given to (officials of) the provinces and barriers, let them be held in both cases by the chief official, or in his absence by the assistant official.

III. Let there now be provided for the first time registers of population, books of account and a system of the receipt and re-granting of distribution-land.[4]

1. In Iga.—A.
2. A ri or sato consisted of 50 houses.—A.
3. Greater and Lesser Governors. These terms are rendered Kori no Miyakko and Suke no Miyakko in the interlinear glosses. But I have little doubt that the Chinese words are intended, and that these are mere translations, and not the real titles of these officials.—A.
4. The Denryō (Land Regulations) says, " In granting Kō-bun-den (land shared in proportion to population) men shall have two tan, women a third less, and children under five years of age none. Lands are granted for a term of six years." This seems to point to a general redistribution of lands once in six years, something after the manner still practised in Russia. —A. (1896)

THE TAIKWA REFORM

Let every fifty houses be reckoned a township, and in every township let there be one alderman who shall be charged with the superintendence of the population,[1] the direction of the sowing of crops and the cultivation of mulberry trees, the prevention and examination of offences, and the enforcement of the payment of taxes and of forced labour.

For rice-land, thirty paces in length by twelve paces in breadth shall be reckoned a tan.[2] Ten tan make one chō. For each tan the tax is two sheaves and two bundles (such as can be grasped in the hand) of rice; for each chō the tax is twenty-two sheaves of rice. On mountains or in valleys where the land is precipitous, or in remote places where the population is scanty, such arrangements are to be made as may be convenient.[3]

IV. The old taxes and forced labour are abolished, and a system of commuted taxes instituted. These shall consist of fine silks, coarse silks, raw silk, and floss silk,[4] all in accordance with what is produced in the locality. For each chō of rice-land the rate is one rod[5] of fine silk, or for four chō one piece forty feet in length by two and a half feet in width. For coarse silk the rate is two rods (per chō), or one piece for every two chō of the same length

---

1. i. e. of the registers of population.—A.
2. Allowing five feet to the pace, this would make the tan 9000 square feet. The Japanese foot is not very different from our own. The present tan is 10,800 square feet. The interlinear gloss of dan is kida, but I am strongly inclined to think that the Chinese word tan is here intended.—A.
3. The "Shūkai" editor brings in this last sentence at the end of the previous paragraph. It would then apply to the appointment of rural aldermen. The old reading is better.—A.
4. The "Shūkai" adds 布 or cloth, by which is meant fabrics of hemp or of the fibre of the inner bark of the paper mulberry. Textiles served the purpose of currency in this period, so that this commutation was in the nature of a substitution of payment in money for payment in rice.—A.
5. Ten feet.—A.

APPENDIX II

and width as the fine silk. For cloth the rate is four rods of the same dimensions as the fine and coarse silk, i. e. one tan[1] for each chō. [No rates of weight are given anywhere for silk or floss silk.][2] Let there be levied separately a commuted house tax.[3] All houses shall pay each one rod and two feet of cloth. The extra articles of this tax, as well as salt offerings,[4] will depend on what is produced in the locality. For horses for the public service, let every hundred houses contribute one horse of medium quality. Or if the horse is of superior quality, let one be contributed by every two hundred houses. If the horses have to be purchased, the price shall be made up by a payment from each house of one rod and two feet of cloth. As to weapons, each person shall contribute a sword, armour, bow and arrows, a flag, and a drum. For coolies, the old system, by which one coolie was provided by every thirty houses, is altered, and one coolie is to be furnished from every fifty houses [one is for employment as a menial servant] for allotment to the various functionaries. Fifty houses shall be allotted to provide rations for one coolie, and one house shall contribute two rods and two feet of cloth and five masu[5] of rice in lieu of service.

For waiting-women in the Palace[6] let there be furnished the sisters or daughters of district officials of the rank of

---

1. There are two tan to the hiki or piece, which now measures about 21½ yards.—A.
2. Passages in square brackets are part of the text, taken from the "old commentary" or quotations from other books. See Aston's Nihongi Vol. I., p. XXI.—Ed.
3. The Chinese is 調, rendered in Japanese by mitsugi, or tribute. Here it seems to exclude the rice-tax, but to include various miscellaneous taxes.—A.
4. Or "salted articles of food for the Emperor's table."—A.
5. Or shō 109 cubic inches.—A.
6. Uneme.—A.

Shōrei or upwards—good-looking women [with one male and two female servants to attend on them], and let 100 houses be allotted to provide rations for one waiting-woman. The cloth and rice supplied in lieu of service shall, in every case, follow the same rule as for coolies.[1]

From: Aston's Nihongi Vol. II. pp. 206–209.

3. Miscellaneous Regulations
(From Edicts of Kōtoku Tennō)

[A. D. 646]

SECOND year, Spring, 3rd month, 22nd day. When a man dies, there have been cases of people sacrificing themselves by strangulation, or of strangling others by ways of sacrifice, or of compelling the dead man's horse to be sacrificed, or of burying valuables in the grave in honour of the dead, or of cutting off the hair, and stabbing the thighs and pronouncing an eulogy on the dead (while in this condition). Let all such old customs be entirely discontinued.

[A certain book says :—" No gold or silver, no silk brocades, and no coloured stuffs are to be buried." Again it is said :—" From the Ministers of all ranks down to the common people, it is not allowed to use gold or silver."]

Should there be any cases of this decree being disregarded and these prohibitions infringed, the relations shall surely receive punishment.

Again, there are many cases of persons who, having seen, say that they have not seen, or who, having not seen, say that they have seen, or who, having heard, say that they

1. The serious student of Japanese social history ought to consult Professor Asakawa's book: The Early Institutional Life of Japan, Tokyo 1903. A fresh competent translation of the legal texts is highly desirable. —Ed.

APPENDIX II

have not heard, or who, having not heard, say that they have heard, being deliberate liars, and devoid of truth in words and in sight.

Again, there have been many cases in which slaves, both male and female, false to their masters in their poverty, betake themselves of their own accord to influential houses in quest of a livelihood, which influential houses forcibly detain and purchase them, and do not send them to their original owners.

Again, there have been very many cases in which wives or concubines, when dismissed by their husbands, have, after the lapse of years, married other husbands, as ordinary morality allows. Then their former husbands, after three or four years, have made greedy demands on the second husband's property, seeking their own gain.

Again, there have been very many cases in which men, relying on their power, have rudely demanded people's daughters in marriage. In the interval, however, before going to his house, the girl has, of her own accord, married another, and the rude suitor has angrily made demands of the property of both families for his own gain.

Again, there have been numerous cases of this kind. Sometimes a wife who has lost her husband married another man after a lapse of ten or twenty years and becomes his spouse, or an unmarried girl is married for the first time. Upon this, people, out of envy of the married pair, have made them perform purgation.[1]

---

[1]. Harahi, clearing away, purgation, is properly a religious ceremony. The Oho-harahi, or "Great Purgation," was performed every year by the Nakatomi as a general purification of the sins of the people. The ritual used on this occasion has come down to us, and is perhaps the most interesting of the Norito. When harahi was performed in the case of individual offences the necessary offerings to the Gods were provided by the guilty person. From this to a penalty the transition is easy, and has parallels in other countries. In the present passage the harahi was evidently what we

Again, there are cases in which women, who have become men's wives and who, being put away owing to their husbands' dislike of them, have, in their mortification at this injury, compelled themselves to become blemished[2] slaves.

Again, there are cases in which the husband, having frequent occasion to be jealous of his wife's illicit intercourse with others, voluntarily appeals to the authorities to decide the matter. Let such persons not lay their information until they have obtained, let us say, three credible witnesses to join with them in making a declaration. Why should they bring forward ill-considered plaints?

Again, there have been cases of men employed on forced labour in border lands who, when the work was over and they were returning to their village, have fallen suddenly ill and laid down to die by the roadside. Upon this the (inmates of the) houses by the roadside say :—" Why should people be allowed to die on our road?" And they have accordingly detained the companions of the deceased and compelled them to do purgation. For this reason it often happens that even if an elder brother lies down and dies on the road, his younger brother will refuse to take up his body (for burial).

---

should now call a "squeeze." The "Tsusho" commentator quotes here a statement by one Kurokaha, to the following effect :—" During the first month of the year following the marriage of a newly-united couple, their friends assemble at the house bearing pails of water, with which they souse the husband liberally. This is called harahi." It may not be out of place to point out that marriage is in many uncivilized countries considered as an infringement of the rights of the community which calls for some sort of compensation.—A.

2. The meaning of this term—rendered kotosaka in the "Original Commentary "—is not very clear. It perhaps applies to persons who were made slaves on account of some offence or vice. Dr. Florenz and some Japanese scholars whom he consulted take this view of this paragraph. I am not sure, however, that the real meaning is not that the husband, mortified that his wife has left him from dislike, sells her as a slave.—A.

APPENDIX II

Again, there are cases of peasants being drowned in a river. The bystanders say:—" Why should we be made to have anything to do with drowned men?" They accordingly detain the drowned man's companions and compel them to do purgation. For this reason it often happens that even when an elder brother is drowned in a river his younger brother will not render assistance.

Again, there are cases when people have applied to others for the loan of pots in which to boil their rice, and the pots have knocked against something and have been upset. Upon this the owner of the pot compels purgation to be made.

All such practices are habitual among the unenlightened vulgar. Let them now be discontinued without exception, and not permitted again.

Again, there are cases in which peasants, when they are about to proceed to the capital, apprehensive lest their riding horses should be worn out and unable to go, give two fathoms of cloth[1] and two bundles of hemp to men of the two provinces of Mikaha or Wohari, to hire them to feed their horses. After they have been to the capital and are on their way home, they make them a present of a spade, and then find that the men of Mikaha, etc., have not only failed to feed their horses properly, but have allowed them to die of starvation. In the case of horses of a superior class, they conceive covetous desires, and invent lying tales of their having been stolen, while in the case of mares which become pregnant in their house, they cause purgation to be made, and in the end make a plunder of the beast.

Such things having coming to our ears, We therefore now establish the following regulation:—

Whenever horses are left at livery in any of the provinces

1. Cloth was evidently used as money.—A.

along the highway, let the owner take with him the man whom he engages for this purpose, and make a full statement to the village elder, handing over (to the latter) at the same time the articles given as remuneration. It is unnecessary for him to cause any further payment when he returns home. If he has caused the horse to suffer harm, he should get nothing.

If anyone disobeys this edict, a severe penalty shall be imposed.

The dues payable to Market Commissioners,[1] for main roads and to ferrymen, are abolished and lands are granted instead.

Beginning with the Home provinces, and embracing the provinces in all four quarters, during the agricultural months,[2] let everyone apply himself early to the cultivation of the rice-land. It is not meet at such a time to let them eat dainty food or drink sake. Let faithful messengers be appointed to intimate this to the Home provinces. And let the Kuni no Miyakko of the provinces in every quarter choose good messengers to urge (the peasants to work) in accordance with the edict.

Autumn, 8th month, 14th day. An edict was issued, saying :—

Going back to the origin of things, we find that it is Heaven and Earth with the male and female principles of nature,[3] which guard the four seasons from mutual con-

---

1. The "Shoku-un-ryō" says the Market Commissioner shall have superintendence of the currency, commerce, the genuineness of wares, the justness of weights and measures, buying and selling prices, and prohibitions and offences (relating thereto.)—A.
2. i. e. of getting in the crops.—A.
3. The Yin and Yang of Chinese philosophy. The interlinear gloss has samuku-atataka, i. e. " cold and warm," a most inadequate rendering.—A.

APPENDIX II

fusion. We find, moreover, that it is this Heaven and Earth[1] which produces the ten thousand things. Amongst these ten thousand things Man is the most miraculously gifted. Among the most miraculously gifted beings, the sage takes the position of ruler. Therefore the Sage Rulers, viz. the Emperors, take Heaven as their examplar in ruling the World, and never for a moment dismiss from their breasts the thought of how men shall gain their fit place.

Now as to names of the early Princes, the Omi, Muraji, Tomo no Miyakko and Kuni no Miyakko have divided their various Be[2] and allotted them severally to their various titles (or surnames). They afterwards took the various Be of the people, and made them reside in the provinces and districts, one mixed up with another. The consequence has been to make father and child to bear different surnames, and brothers to be reckoned of distinct families, while husbands and wives have names[3] different from one another. One family is divided into five or split up into six, and both Court and country are therefore filled with contentious suits. No settlement has been come to, and the mutual confusions grows worse and worse. Let the various Be, therefore, beginning with those of the reigning Emperor and including those in the possession of the Omi, Muraji, etc., be, without exception, abolished, and let them become subjects of the State. Those who have become Tomo no Miyakko by borrowing the names of princes, and those who have become Omi or Muraji on the strength of the

---

1. i. e. Nature.—A.
2. Instituted in commemoration of Princes and bearing their names, or names intended to recall their memory.—A.
3. Na or Names must here apply to surnames, or rather Be names. The Japanese at this time had no proper surnames, and the Chinese characters for the two kinds of names are not always rightly distinguished.—A.

names of ancestors,[1] may not fully apprehend our purport, and might think, if they heard this announcement without warning, that the names borrowed by their ancestors would become extinct. We therefore make this announcement beforehand, so that they may understand what are our intentions.

The children of rulers succeed one another in the government of the Empire, and it is well known that the names of the actual Emperor and of his Imperial ancestors will not be forgotten by the world. But the names of sovereigns are lightly given to rivers and plains,[2] or common people are called by them. This is a truly fearful state of things. The appellations of sovereigns, like the sun and moon, will float afar : the names of those of the Imperial line[3] will last for ever, like unto Heaven and Earth. Such being our opinion, we announce as follows :—

Do ye all, from those of the Imperial line down to the Ministers, the Daibu, Omi, Muraji, and Tomo no Miyakko, who do Us service, (in short) all persons of whatever Uji[4] [One book has 'royal subjects of whatever name'], give ear to what We say. With regard to the form of your service, We now abolish the former offices and constitute

---

2. The "Shukai" quotes here the instances of Kibitsuhiko no Mikoto, whose descendants were called Kibi no Omi, and Achiki, whose descendants were styled Achiki no Fubito.—A.

2. The "Shukai" editor instances Annei Tennō, whose name of Shikitsuhiko is borne by the plain of Shiki in Yamato, and Yūriaku Tennō, whose name of Ohohatsuse is applied to the River Hatsuse-gawa. But it is more likely that the facts are the other way, and that the names of places were given to the Emperors. The "Shoʰu-ni-hon-go-ki" (a continuation of the Nihongi) records an edict which directed the alteration of names of persons, villages, mountains, or rivers, which coincided with the names (imina) of Emperors.—A.

3. lit. ancestors and children. But I strongly suspect that the former ideogram is a mistake for one denoting : imperial.—A.

4. House of nobles.—A.

APPENDIX II

afresh the hundred bureaus. We shall, moreover, grant grades of rank and confer official dignities.[1]

Let the local Governors who are now being despatched, and also the Kuni no Miyakko of the same provinces, give ear to what we say. In regard to the method of administration notified last year to the Court Assembly,[2] let the previous arrangement be followed, and let the rice-lands which are received and measured be granted equally to the people, without distinction of persons. In granting rice-lands the peasants' houses should adjoin the land. Those whose houses lie near the lands must therefore have the preference. In this sense receive Our injunctions.

In regard to commuted taxes, they should be collected from males (only).

Labourers should be supplied at the rate of one for every fifty houses. The boundaries of the provinces should be examined and a description or map prepared, which should be brought here and produced for Our inspection. The names of the provinces and districts will be settled when you come.

With respect to the places where embankments are to be constructed, or canals dug, and the extent of rice-land to be brought under cultivation, in the various provinces, uniform provision will be made for causing such work to be executed.

Give ear to and understand these injunctions.

From: Aston's Nihongi Vol. II. pp. 220–226.

1. This edict seems intended as a final severance of titles of various kinds from the offices they nominally represent. Official rank and grade of office do not invariably correspond, though they do in a general way. A Daijin, for example, is not necessarily first rank, though he will doubtless hold high rank, second or third at least.—A.

2. Chōshū. See Aston's Nihongi Vol. II, p. 213: "They seem to have been officials who reported on the conduct of local officials."

III

Laws Concerning Monks and Nuns
(From the Yōrō Code A. D. 757)

(The T'ang codes did not contain a chapter on this subject, but the Kyaku of the Chêng-kwan era (A. D. 627–649) included the Dōsō Kyaku, which were issued in 636 and, as the name shows, dealt not only with Buddhist monks but also with priests of other religions, viz Taoists.
There is evidence to show that these T'ang Kyaku formed the basis of the Japanese ryō dealing with monks and nuns; but it is not clear to what extent the latter contained new material especially adapted to conditions in Japan. Article 27, for instance, seems to have been inspired by actual conditions; and several other articles are evidently framed so as to fit the social and administrative system then prescribed.—G. B. S.)

This law comprises 27 articles of which the gist is as follows :—

1. Monks and nuns who are guilty of any of the following offences shall be punished by the civil authorities in accordance with the law :—

> By false reading of omens predicting disasters or making treasonable statements and leading astray the people.
> Studying military treatises.
> Committing murder and robbery.
> Falsely pretending to have attained holiness (i. e., according to the commentaries, to have passed through the four stages and become an Arhat).

2. Monks and nuns who practise fortune-telling, or pretend to cure illness by exorcism or magic shall be expelled from holy orders : but this shall not apply to the cure of

APPENDIX III

sickness by the recitation of spells (mantra) in accordance with Buddhism.

3. Monks and nuns voluntarily reverting to lay status shall inform their superiors who shall make the necessary record, and report to the proper authority. Failure to report shall be punished by hard labour.

4. Monks or nuns who bribe officials with church property; or form disorderly gatherings; or insult the heads of the church; or slander their elders and superiors, shall be punished by hard labour. But this shall not apply to assemblies where matters are reasonably and properly discussed.

5. Monks or nuns who, not residing in a monastery or temple, set up (unauthorized) religious establishments and preach to congregations of the people,
or falsely expound good and evil,
or assault their elders and superiors,
shall be expelled from holy orders. Officials of provinces and districts who being aware of such conduct do not prohibit it shall be punished in accordance with law.
Persons desiring to beg for food must make an application supported by the joint seals of their superiors through the provincial or district offices. The authorities grant permission after satisfying themselves that true ascetic practice is intended. In the capital application shall be considered by the Genba-ryō (q. v. Pt. I. p. 86). Begging must be done before noon, by presenting the mendicant's bowl, and nothing but food must be asked for.

(This interesting article is designed to prevent the abuse of ecclesiastical privilege for private ends. The first clause is against preaching heresy and quarrelling with teachers of the orthodox sects. The second is to ensure that only genuine " mendicants " shall beg for food, in

LAWS CONCERNING MONKS AND NUNS

accordance with Buddhist tradition.—G. B. S.)

6. A monk may take from his home as a disciple a young boy who is a close relative, but he must be returned to his home on reaching the age of seventeen.

A nun may take a female who is willing (irrespective of her age).

7. Monks and nuns may not drink wine or eat flesh or consume the five pungent things (i. e. garlic, scallions, onions of different kind, ginger) under penalty of thirty days hard labour. If they are needed as medicines they shall be supplied by the superiors for a limited period.

Those guilty of disorderly conduct through drunkeness or of brawling shall be expelled from holy orders.

8. Monks and nuns who in respect of disputes as to their private affairs instead of going through the proper official channel present direct memorials to the government or who importune the households of officials with improper petitions shall be punished by hard labour for fifty days and if the offence is repeated for one hundred days.

(Note. For " private affairs " some commentaries give " temple affairs."

The " proper channel " would be from the monk to his superior in the monastery, then to the head officials of the sect, then to the Gembaryō, then to the competent minister (in this case Jibushō) and so to the Council of State if necessary.—G. B. S.)

This shall not apply to the bona fide statement of a case where through an unfair decision of the ecclesiastical or civil authorities justice has been denied or delayed.

9. Monks and nuns shall not perform music or play games of chance under penalty of one hundred days hard labour. But this does not include the harp[1] or the game

1. " Koto ".

of go.

10. Monks and nuns may wear robes of brown, green, black, yellow, earth-colour etc., but they may not wear other colours nor may they wear robes of figured or embroidered stuffs.

Each offence shall be punished by ten days' hard labour. Wearing lay garments shall be punished by one hundred days' hard labour.

(Note. The permitted colours are apparently: a yellowish red, green, black, yellow, earth-colour, but the commentaries are not very illuminating in explaining what the shades are. The general intention seems to be to forbid extravagance in colour and pattern.—G. B. S.)

11. A monk may not allow a female to stay in his dwelling place.

A nun may not allow a male to stay in her dwelling place.

If a stay of one night or more is made, the offender (i.e. the monk or nun) shall be punished by ten days' hard labour. For five days or more, thirty days' hard labour. For ten days or more, one hundred days' hard labour. If the superiors of the monastery or nunnery are aware of the offence and permit it, they shall be punishable in the same way as the offender.

(Note. A visit during the day time is permitted.)

12. A monk may not enter a nunnery and a nun may not enter a monastery, except to be received by a superior or for a visit on account of death or sickness or for the purpose of religious ceremony or observance or instruction.

13. When monks or nuns for the purpose of religious meditation wish to purify their minds by solitude and fasting in a mountain retreat they shall make application through the proper channels with the approval of their Superiors.

LAWS CONCERNING MONKS AND NUNS

The local authorities must be kept informed of their movements.

17. Monks and nuns bringing private suits before the civil authorities must appear temporarily in their lay capacity.

(This means that they must state their lay names and domicile, as well as their religious appellation and the institution to which they belong. As members of a religious order they cannot acquire private property beyond the minimum necessary for their own use; but they can, it seems, be confirmed in rights which they possessed before entering the order. The commentaries give as an example suits for confirmation of rights of ownership in serfs or servants. Vide the next Article.—G. B. S.)

18. Monks and nuns may not accumulate for themselves land, buildings and other forms of wealth nor may they buy and sell for profit or lend at interest.

(The commentaries explain that ' accumulate ' here means the acquisition of property not necessary for personal consumption or use. Thus a monk might acquire necessary clothing, utensils, etc., and he might have one or two servants and a horse to ride. Similarly he might exchange goods or lend goods or money so long as he did not make a profit out of the transaction. Property acquired in contravention of this article was confiscated by the church. Property acquired before entering holy orders could be distributed at the discretion of the owner.)

24. When private or public slaves or servants have entered religion and subsequently have reverted to the laity either as punishment for an offence or voluntarily, they shall be restored to their former masters and resume their original status.

25. Monks or nuns who have been three times punished by hard labour for one hundred days shall for the third

APPENDIX III

period be sent to monasteries or nunneries in the " outer " provinces, but not the home provinces.

26. On the occasion of religious festivals (saie) offerings may not be made of slaves, horses, oxen, or weapons, nor may these be accepted by monks and nuns.

27. Monks and nuns shall not mutilate themselves or take their own lives.

(The article appears to refer to a practice of self-mutilation by burning or cutting which mendicant monks adopted in order to impress the populace. The Shoku Nihongi contains (under the date Yōrō I, 4th month) an edict dealing with offences by monks in which this practice is mentioned: " forming bands, cutting and burning hands and arms, preaching false doctrine from house to house, begging by threats " etc.—G. B. S.)

From: Early Japanese Law and Administration, by G. B. Sansom, Part II, Transactions of the Asiatic Society of Japan, New Series Vol. XI., December 1934.

IV

THE HŌJŌ-CODE OF JUDICATURE
("Jōyei-Code," A. D. 1232)

1.—The Shrines of the gods must be kept in repair; and their worship performed with the greatest attention.

The majesty of the gods is augmented by the veneration of men, and the fortunes of men are fulfilled by the virtue of the gods. Therefore the established sacrifices to them must not be allowed to deteriorate; and there must be no remissness in paying ceremonial honours to them as if they were present.[1] Accordingly throughout the provinces of the Kwanto Dominion[2] and likewise in the Manors,[3] the Land Reeves,[4] the Kannushi (Shinto priests) and others concerned must each bear this in mind, and carefully carry out this duty. Moreover, in the case of shrines which have been enfeoffed[5] (endowed with benefices) the deed of grant must be confirmed each generation, and minor repairs executed from time to time as prescribed

---

1. There is a reference here to the Confucian Discourses, Bk. III c. 7. "He (Confucius) sacrificed (to his ancestors) as if they were present... He sacrificed to the gods as if the gods were present."—H.
2. Kwantō go bun no kuni-guni, i. e. the provinces constituting the share or dominion of the Minamoto House in the region East of the Hakone Barrier. These were the eight provinces of Sagami, Musashi, Kodzuke, Shimotsuke, Hitachi, Shimosa, Kazusa and Awa. Sometimes the word Kwantō is used to designate these eight provinces only; but its more general use is to denote all the country East of Hakone barrier.—H.
3. Shō yen; literally farm-steads and gardens. These were estates of good arable land, with serfs attached, granted by the Emperors to their favourites in full ownership, free from all imposts and exempt from the jurisdiction of the Provincial Authorities.—H.
4. Ji-tō; literally, 'Land-heads'. There were revenue and commissariat officers first appointed throughout the provinces and districts by Yoritomo in 1186 to collect the newly imposed military tax.—H.
5. Yū-hō no yashiro.

therein. If serious damage should happen to a shrine a full report of the circumstances is to be made, and such directions will be given (from Kamakura) as the exigencies of the case may require.

2.—(Buddhist) Temples and pagodas must be kept in repair and the Buddhist services diligently celebrated.

Although (Buddhist) temples are different from (Shintō) shrines, both are alike as regards worship and veneration. Therefore the merit of maintaining them both in good order and the duty of keeping up the established services, as provided in the foregoing article is the same in both cases. Let no one bring trouble on himself through negligence herein.

In case the incumbent does what he pleases with the income of the temple benefice or covetously misappropriates it, or if the duties of the clergy be not diligently fulfilled by him, the offender shall be promptly dismissed, and another incumbent appointed.

3.—Of the duties devolving on Protectors in the Provinces.

In the time of the August Right General's[1] House it was settled that those duties should be the calling out and despatching of the Grand Guard for service at the capital, the suppression of conspiracies and rebellion and the punishment of murder and violence (which included night attacks on houses, robbery, dacoity and piracy). Of late years, however, Official Substitutes (Daikwan) have been taken on and distributed over the countries and townships and these have been imposing public burdens (corvée) on the villages. Not being Governors of the provinces[2] they

---

1. U-Dai-sho ; General of the Right, the Military rank by which Yoritomo was generally designated. The higher offices military as well as civil, were duplicate, Right and Left, the Left being the superior of the two.—H.

2. Koku-shi Kunitsukasa : The highest representative of the imperial authority in each of the 66 kuni or provinces.—H.

THE HŌJŌ-CODE OF JUDICATURE

yet hinder the (Agricultural) work of the province : not being Land-Reeves they are yet greedy of the profits of the land. Such proceedings and schemes are utterly unprincipled.

Be it noted that no person, even if his family were for generations vassals of the August House (of the Minamoto) is competent to impress[1] for military service unless he has an investiture[2] of the present date.

On the other hand again, it is reported that inferior managers and village officials in various places make use of the name of vassals of the August House as a pretext of opposing the orders of the Governor of the provinces or of the lord of the Manor.[3] Such persons, even if they are desirous of being taken into the service of the Protectors, must not under any circumstances be included in the enrolment for service in the Guards. In short, conformably to the precedents of the time of the August General's House, the Protectors must cease altogether from giving directions in matters outside of the hurrying-up of the Grand Guards and the suppression of plots, rebellion, murder and violence.

In the event of a Protector disobeying this article and intermeddling in other affairs than those herein named, if a complaint is instituted against him by the Governor of the Province or the lord of a Manor, or if the Land-Reeve or the folk aggrieved petition for redress, his downright lawlessness being thus brought to light, he shall be divested of his office and a person of gentle character

1. Kari-moyosu ; to hunt up or call together as for a hunting party.
2. Shotai ; What one is begirt or equipped with, what one carries, or possesses.—H.
3. Ryō-ko ; These were the owners of the Shō-yen, mostly Court Nobles (Kuge) : They were exempt from taxation, central or provincial and from military duty or imposts.—H.

APPENDIX IV

appointed in his stead. Again, as regards Delegates (Daikwan)[1] not more than one is to be appointed by a Protector.

4.—Of Protectors omitting to report cases of crime and confiscating the successions to fiefs, on account of offences.

When persons are found committing serious offences, the Protectors should make a detailed report of the case (to Kamakura) and follow such directions as may be given them in relation thereto; yet there are some who, without ascertaining the truth of falsehood of an accusation, or investigating whether the offence committed was serious or trifling, arbitrarily pronounce the escheat of the criminal's hereditaments, and selfishly cause them to be confiscated. Such unjust judgments are a nefarious artifice for the indulgence of license. Let a report be promptly made to us of the circumstances of each case and our decision upon the matter be respectfully asked for, any further persistence in transgressions of this kind will be dealt with criminally.

In the next place, with regard to a culprit's rice-fields and other fields, his dwelling-house, his wife and children, his utensils and other articles of property. In serious cases, the offenders are to be taken in charge by the Protector's office; but it is not necessary to take in charge their farms, houses, wives, children and miscellaneous gear along with them.

Furthermore, even if the criminal should in his statement implicate others as being accomplices or accessories, such are not to be included in the scope of the Protector's judgment, unless they are found in possession of the booty (or other substantial evidence of guilt be forthcoming).

5.—Of Land-Reeves in the provinces detaining a part of

---

1. These must not be confounded with the Daikwan of the Tokugawa time, who were far inferior in rank and importance.—H.

the assessed amounts of the rice-tax.[1]

If a plaint is instituted by the lord of the Manor alleging that a Land Reeve is withholding the land-tax payable to him, a statement of account will be at once taken, and the plaintiff shall receive a certificate of the balance that may be found to be due to him. If the Land-Reeve be adjudged to be in default, and has no valid plea to urge in justification, he will be required to make compensation in full. If the amount is small, judgment will be given for immediate payment. If the amount be greater than he is able to pay at once, he will be allowed three years within which to completely discharge his liability. Any Land-Reeve who, after such delay granted, shall make further delays and difficulties, contrary to the intention of this article, shall be deprived of his post.

6.—Governors of provinces and Manorial Houses may exercise their normal jurisdiction without referring to the Kwantō (authorities).

In cases where jurisdiction has heretofore been exercised by the Governor's Yamens,[2] by lords of Manors,[3] by Shintō Shrines or by Buddhist Temples on the footing of lords of Manors, it will not be necessary for us now to introduce interference. Even if they wish to refer a matter to us for advice, they are not permitted to do so.

In the next place, as regards the bringing of suits before

---

1. Nen-gu; The annual land-tax paid in rice (or equivalent produce) out of which the expenses of the Central Government at Kyōto and of the respective provincial governments were defrayed.—H.

2. Koku-ga; The head office of each province, corresponding somewhat to the yamen of a Chinese province governor.—H.

3. Ryō-ke: The Noble Houses mentioned in article 2. They thus enjoyed twofold privilege, being independent of the local civil authority viz. the Governor of the Province; and exempt from interference on the part of the new feudal-military official the Shugō or Protector of the Province.—H.

APPENDIX IV

us direct, without producing a letter of recommendation from the local tribunal.

The proper procedure in bringing a suit is for the parties to come provided with letters of recommendation from their own tribunal, whether it be that of a Provincial Governor, a manor, a shrine, or a temple. Hence persons who come unprovided with such letters have already committed a breach of propriety and henceforth their suits will not be received in judicature.

7.—Whether the fiefs which have been granted since the time of Yoritomo by the successive Shōguns[1] and by Her Ladyship the Dowager (Masako) are to be revoked or exchanged in consequence of suits being brought by the original owners.

Such fiefs having been granted as rewards for distinguished merit in the field, or for valuable services in official employment, have not been acquired without just title. And if judgment were to be given in favour of some one who alleged that such was originally the fief of his ancestors, though the one face might beam with joy, the many comrades could assuredly feel no sense of security. A

1. The three Shōguns of the Minamoto line were Yoritomo (1192 –1199), and his two sons Yori-iye (1199–1203) and Sanetomo (1204–1219). Yori-iye was deposed and soon after assassinated by his grandfather Hōjō Tokimasa, the first Shikken or Power-holder. Sanetomo was assassinated by his nephew, son of Yori-iye, instigated by Hōjō Yoshitoki, the second Shikken, Tokimasa's son. Both Tokimasa and Yoshitoki, however, had to share the power with Yoritomo's widow, Masako, daughter of Tokimasa. After the death of her second son Sanetomo, she procured the appointment of Shōgun for her infant grandson by a daughter, wife of a Fujiwara noble, she herself at the same time being nominated guardian of this infant commander-in-chief. At all periods of crisis during the stormy 25 years after her husband's death she had the controlling voice, aided by the advice of her trusty counsellor Oye Hiromoto, president of the council of government (Hyōjō-shū). Each crisis involved the extermination of one or more of the greater vassal's families and the confiscation and re-distribution of their fiefs.—H.

stop must be put to persons bringing such unsettling suits

In case, however, one of the grantees of the present epoch should commit a crime, and the original owner, watching his opportunity should thereupon bring a suit for recovery of possession, he cannot well be prohibited from doing so.[1]

In the next place, as regards attempt that may be made to disturb tenures by occasion of the Shōgun's judicature having through failure of heirs come to an end.

Whereas some persons who, in consequence of not having right on their side, were formerly non-suited, are found scheming, after allowing an interval of years to elapse, to bring suit a second time, the mere framing of such an intention is an offence of no light criminality. Henceforward should any persons, disregarding the adjudications of the Shōgun and his successors, wantonly institute suits of disturbance, in every such case the grounds of the invalidity of the claim are to be endorsed at full length upon the title-deeds in his possession.

8.—Of fiefs which, though deeds of investiture are held, have not been had in possession through a series of years.

With respect to the above, if more than twenty years have elapsed since the present holder was in possession, his title is not to be enquired into and no change can be made: following herein the precedent of the time of the Yoritomo house.[2] And if any one falsely alleging himself to be in possession, obtains by deceit a deed of grant, even though he may have the document in his possession, it is

---

1. On the ground, probably, that the feoffee's title by merit which availed against the previous owner having now been extinguished by guilt, the latter's right revives.—H.

2. The office of Shōgun had, on the failure of Yoritomo's heirs, been bestowed on a Fujiwara noble.—H.

APPENDIX IV

not to be recognized as having validity.

9.—Of plotters of treason.

The purport of the provision relating to such persons cannot well be settled beforehand. In some cases, precedent is to be followed; in others, such action should be taken as the particular circumstances may require.

10.—Of the crimes of killing, maiming and wounding : furthermore, whether parents and children are to be held mutually responsible for each other's guilt.

A person who is guilty of killing or maiming, unless he acted without premeditation, as in a chance altercation or in the intoxication of a festive party, shall be punished in his own person by death or else by banishment or by confiscation of his investiture; but his father, or his son, unless they have actually been accomplices, shall not be held responsible.

Next, the offence of cutting or wounding must be dealt with in the same way, the culprit alone being responsible.

Next, in case a son or a grandson slays the enemy of his father or grand-father, the father or grand-father, even if they were not privy to the offence, are nevertheless to be punished for it. The reason is that the gratification of the father's or grand-father's rage was the motive prompting to the sudden execution of a cherished purpose.

Next, in case a man's son, without his knowledge, is guilty of killing or maiming another, or attempting to do so, for the purpose of appropriating that other's post or seizing his property or valuables, if the fact of the father's non-connivance is clearly proven by the evidence, he is not to be held responsible.

11. Whether in consequence of a husband's crime the estate of the wife is to be confiscated or not.

In cases of serious crime, treason, murder and maiming,

also dacoity,[1] piracy, night-attacks, robbery and the like, the guilt of the husband extends to the wife also.[2] In cases of murder and maiming, cutting and wounding, arising out of a sudden dispute, however, she is not to be held responsible.

12.—Of abusive language.

Quarrels and murders have their origin in abusive and insulting language. In grave cases the offender shall be sent into banishment, in minor cases, ordered into confinement. If during the course of a judicial hearing one of the parties gives vent to abuse or insults, the matter in dispute shall be decided in favour of the other party. If the other party however has not right on his side, some other fief of the offender shall be confiscated. If he has no fief, he shall be punished by being sent into banishment.

13.—Of the offence of striking (or beating) a person.

In such cases the person who receives the beating is sure to want to kill or maim the other in order to wipe out the insult; so the offence of beating a person is by no means a trivial one. Accordingly, if the offender be a Samurai, his fief shall be confiscated; if he has no fief he shall be sent into banishment: persons of lower rank, servants, pages and under, shall be placed in confinement.

14.—When a crime or offence is committed by Deputies, whether the principals are responsible.

When a Deputy[3] is guilty of murder or any lesser one of the serious crimes, if his principal arrests and sends

---

1. San-zoku, mountain bandits, as opposed to Kai-zoku, sea bandits. Both denote concerted action of numbers, as opposed to robbery by individual violence, gitō.—H.
2. Because these crimes involve premeditations, repetition or a long course of wrong-doing, the wife must have been cognisant of them.—H.
3. The Daikwan appointed by a Protector of a Province is here intended.—H.

him on for trial, the master shall not be held responsible. But if the master in order to shield the Deputy reports that the latter is not to blame, and the truth is afterwards found out, incriminating him, the former cannot escape responsibility and accordingly his fief shall be confiscated. In such cases the Deputy shall be imprisoned (in order to be tried and dealt with).

Again, if a Deputy[1] either detains the rice-tax payable to the lord of the Manor or contravenes the laws and precedents even though the action is that of the Deputy alone, his principal[2] shall nevertheless be responsible.

Moreover, whenever, either in consequence of a suit instituted by the lord of a Manor, or in connection with matters of fact alleged in a plaintiff's petition, a Deputy receives a summons from the Kwanto or is sent for from Rokuhara, and instead of making up his mind to come at once, shilly-shallies and delays, his principal's investiture shall in like manner be revoked. Extenuating circumstances may, however, be taken into consideration.

15.—Of the crime of forgery.

If a Samurai commits the above, his fief shall be confiscated ; if he has no investiture he shall be sent into exile. If one of the lower class commits it, he shall be branded in the face by burning. The amanuensis shall receive the same punishment.

Next, in suits if it is persistently alleged that the title-deed in the defendant's possession is a forgery and when the document is opened and inspected, if it is found to be indeed a forgery then the punishment shall be as above

---

1. Here the Daikwan meant is one appointed by a Jitō, or Land-Reev to collect the military impost.—H.
2. Shu-nin, Master of Superior; the Protector in the one case, the Land-Reeve in the other.—H.

provided; but if it be found to be without flaw, then a fine proportionate to his position shall be inflicted on the false accuser, to be paid into the fund for the repairing of Shrines and temples. If he have not means wherewith to pay the fine he shall be deported.

16. Of the lands which were confiscated at the time of the military disturbance of Shokyu (1219–1221).

In the case of some whose tenements were confiscated in consequence of their having been reported to us as having taken part against us in the battle at the Capital, it is now averred that they were innocent of such misdoing. Where the proof in support of this plea is full and clear, other lands will be assigned to the present grantees of the confiscated estates, which will be restored to the original holders. By the term present grantees is meant those of them who have performed meritorious services.

In the next place, amongst those who took part against us in the battle at the Capital were some who had received the bounty of the Kwanto (i. e. had received grants of land from the Shogun). Their guilt was specially aggravated. Accordingly they were themselves put to death and their holdings were confiscated definitively. Of late years, however, it has come to our knowledge that some fellows of that class have, through force of circumstances, had the luck to escape punishment. Seeing that the time for severity has now gone by, in their case the utmost generosity will be exercised, and a slice only of their estates, amounting to one fifth, is to be confiscated. However, as regards Sub-Controllers and village officials, unless they were vassals of the Shogun's own House, it is to be understood that it is not now practicable to call them to account, even if it should come to be found out that they were guilty of siding with the Capital. The case of these men was discussed in the Council last year and settled in this sense ; consequently no different principle is applicable.

Next as regards lands confiscated on the same occasion in respect of which suits may be brought by persons claiming to be owners. It was in consequence of the guilt of the then holders that those lands were confiscated, and were definitively assigned to those who rendered meritorious service. Although those who then held them were unworthy holders, there are many persons we hear who now petition that in accordance with the principle of heredity the lands may be allowed to revert to them by grant. But all the tenures that were confiscated at that time stand irreversibly disposed of. Is it possible for us to put aside the present holders and undertake to make enquiry into claims of a past age ? Henceforth a stop must be put to disorderly expectations.

17.—As regards the guilt of those who took part in the battle on the same occasion, a distinction is to be made between fathers and sons.

As regards cases in which although the father took the side of the Capital the son nevertheless took service with the Kwanto and likewise those in which although the son took the side of the Capital the father took service with the Kwanto, the question of reward or punishment has been decided already by the difference of treatment. Why should one generation be confounded with the other as regards guilt ?

As regards cases of this kind occuring amongst residents[1] in the Western provinces, if one went to the Capital, whether he was the father or the son, then the son or the father who remained at home in the province cannot be

1. Military gentry (Bushi) living in the Kwansai, or provinces West of Hakone Barrier. In the Kwanto they would have been feudal barons.

held blameless. Although he may not have accompanied his guilty kinsman he was his accomplice at heart. Nevertheless in cases where owing to their being separated by long distances or boundaries it was impossible for them to have had communication with one another or to be cognizant of the circumstances, they are not to be regarded as reciprocally involved in each other's guilt.

18.—Whether, after transferring a fief to a daughter, parents may or may not revoke the transfer on account of a subsequent estrangement.

A set of doctrinaires avers that though the two sexes are distinct as regards denomination, there is no difference between them as regards parental benefactions and that therefore a gift to a daughter is as irrevocable as one to a son. If, however, the deed of assignment to a daughter were held to be irrevocable she would be able to rely upon it, and would have no scruples about entering upon an undutiful and reprehensible course of conduct. And fathers and mothers, on the other hand, forecasting the probability of conflicts of opinion arising, must beware of assigning a fief to a daughter. Once a beginning is made of severing the relation of parent and child the foundation is laid for disobedience and insubordination. In case a daughter shows any unsteadiness of behaviour, the parents ought to be able to exercise their own discretion accordingly. When the question is understood to rest on this foundation the daughter, induced by the hope of the deed of assignment being confirmed, will be on her best behaviour and punctilious in the discharge of her filial duty; and the parents, impelled by the desire of completing their fostering care, will find the course of their affection uniform and even throughout.

Note. The commentator, Takai Ranzan remarks :—

APPENDIX IV

" At this period it was allowed to divide a fief granted by the lord and assign a portion of it to a daughter upon application to the Authorities. Hence there were " female tenures". And it was not without reason that these were asserted to be irrevocable. So far as the parents minds were concerned, the sons and the daughters were alike their children. The sons, by meritorious services, were able to obtain large emoluments. The daughters had no such opportunities; for they were during their whole lifetime dependent upon others and were liable also to be divorced. During the lifetime of the parents that would not so much matter; but they looked ahead and foresaw that when the succession devolved to the brothers the sisters' position would be in many ways embarrassing: hence the practice of dower was the outcome of deep affection; and that the brother, after succeeding (to the headship of the house) should be debarred from interfering with a tenure apportioned to the daughter by his parent was no more than was necessary to give effect to the parents' affection.

In after generations, farmers and merchants granted fields and urban building-sites as portions to their daughters; but the military families (buke) did not apportion tenures (chigyo) to their daughters. Since a daughter's duty was implicit obedience (jun-jo) before everything else, if she had the wealth of a tenure of her own her filialty towards her father-in-law and mother-in-law would have been impaired, even the husband would have been contemned, and the path of implicit obedience would have been lost. Hence it was by keeping her without income that her life-long submission was secured. As times and manners change together, government has to be adapted to the customs prevailing at the time."

19.—Of kinsmen, whether near or distant, who having been reared and supported, afterwards turn their backs on the descendants of their original masters.

Of persons who were dependent on a kinsman for their upbringing some were treated on a footing of affectionate intimacy as if they were sons; and where that was not so (owing to their belonging to a lower rank in life) they were maintained as if they were vassals. When persons so circumstanced rendered some loyal service to their masters, the latter, in their abounding appreciation of the spirit so displayed have in some cases handed them an allocation-note and in other cases have granted them a deed of enfeoffment. Yet they pretend that those grants were merely free-will gifts and take a view of things opposite to that taken by the sons or grandsons of their first master, with the result that the tenor of the relations to each other becomes very different from what it ought to be. For a time they act coquettishly, and those who were on the footing of sonship keep it up whilst the others observe the etiquette proper to vassalship; and then after a period of shilly-shallying some of them avail themselves of (literally, borrow) the badge of somebody who is not related to them, whilst the others go the length of taking up the opposite way of thinking. When such persons forgo all at once the predecessor's benefaction and act in opposition to his son or grandson the fiefs which were so assigned to them are to be taken from them and given back to the descendant of the original holder.

20.—Of the succession to a fief when the child, after getting the deed of assignment, predeceases the parents.

Even when the child is alive, what is to hinder the parents from revoking the assignment? How much more, then, are they free to dispose of the fief after the child has died;

APPENDIX IV

the thing must be left entirely to the discretion of the father or grandfather.

21.—Whether when a wife or concubine, after getting an assignment from the husband, has been divorced, she can retain the tenure of the fief or not.

If the wife in question has been repudiated in consequence of having committed some serious transgression, even if she holds a written promise of the by-gone days she may not hold the fief of her former husband. On the other hand, if the wife in question had a virtuous record and was innocent of any fault and was discarded by reason of the husband's preference for novelty, the fief which had been assigned to her cannot be revoked.

22.—Of parents who when making a disposition of their fief pass over a grown-up son whose relationship has not been severed.

When parents have brought up their son to man's estate and he has shown himself to be diligent and deserving then, either in consequence of a stepmother's slanders or out of favouritism to the son of a concubine although the son's relationship has not been severed, suddenly to leave him out and without rhyme or reason make no grant to him, would be the very extreme of arbitrariness. Accordingly, for the wife's son who has now arrived at manhood one fifth of the fief must be cut off and assigned as his share to any older brother who is without sufficient means. However this grant should be made to depend upon proofs given, no matter whether the recipient be the son of the wife or the son of a concubine, and however small the amount of the share may be. Even if he be the son of the wife but has no service to show he does not come within the scope of the rule; neither, on the other hand, do persons who have been unfilial (even though they have

THE HŌJŌ-CODE OF JUDICATURE

rendered service).

23.—Of the adoption of heirs by women.[1]

Although the spirit of the (ancient) laws does not allow of adoption by females, yet since the time of the General of the Right (Yoritomo) down to the present day it has been the invariable rule to allow women who had no children of their own to adopt an heir and transmit the fief to him. And not only that, but all over the country, in the capital as well as in the rural districts there are abundant evidences of the existence of the same practice. It is needless to enumerate the cases. Besides, after full consideration and discussion, its validity has been recognized, and it is hereby confirmed.

24.—Whether a widow who has succeeded to her husband's fief and who marries again should continue to hold it.

Widows who have succeeded to the fief of their deceased husband should give up everything else and devote themselves to their husbands' welfare in the after-world and those who disregard that observance cannot be held blameless. Hence if any such, soon forgetting their conjugal constancy marry again, the fief held by their late husband is to be granted to the husband's son. If the deceased husband had no son, the fief should be disposed of in some other way.[2]

25.—Of vassals in the Kwanto who married their daughters to Court nobles and assigned fiefs to them, thereby diminishing the sufficiency of the public services.

As regards such fiefs, although they were assigned to

---

1. In antiquity women (i. e. widows) were not allowed to adopt children as heirs to the fief. It was Yoritomo who first allowed the privilege of transmitting the inheritance through females to adopted children.—H.

2. Such as, for instance, by specially instituting an heir, or granting the fief to a temple or monastery.—H.

daughters and thus became alienated, nevertheless the assessment for public services must be imposed thereon in accordance with the holders' rank and standing. Even although when the father was alive the son-in-law's fief may have been, as a matter of favour, exempted, after his death, service must be insisted on. If, presuming on the dignity of his position, the holder of such a fief omits to perform personal service, the said fief must be for long withheld from him. In general, there must be no obstinacy as regards public services, which are equally required of all in the Kwanto even to the Ladies-in-waiting in the Palace.[1] After this, if any one still makes difficulties, he is not to have the tenure of the fief.[2]

26.—Of revoking an assignment to one son, after a Government patent of assurance[3] has been granted and then making the assignment to another son.

That matters of this kind are to be left to the discretion of the parents has been already practically laid down in a preceding section. Hence even when a Government writ of quiet possession of title has been granted to the heir first instituted, yet if the father changes his mind and decides to assign the fief to another son, it is the subsequent decision which is to take effect, and must be confirmed by an adjudication.

27.—Of fiefs the successions to which have not yet been dealt with.

These should be distributed when suitable occasions offer, due regard being had in each case to the extent of

1. The Shōgun's palace at Kamakura.—H.
2. It was an established principle that Court Nobles (Kuge) were exempt from military service and from assessment or contributions towards it. Hence alienations of their estates by vassals tended to diminish the resources of the feudal governing power.—H.
3. Ando no on Kudashi-bumi.—H.

THE HŌJŌ-CODE OF JUDICATURE

service rendered and after testing the abilities (of the several claimants).

28.—Of trumping up false statements and instituting slanderous suits.

That those who with smooth faces and artful innuendoes prejudice their lord's mind in order to ruin others are guilty of a very heinous sin is stated in the Scriptures.[1] For the sake of the world and for the sake of individuals, they must be rebuked.

If a slanderous accusation is made in the expectation of getting a fief, the fief of the slanderer must be given to the person slandered. If the slanderer has no investiture he must be sent into banishment. If, on the other hand, the slander has been concocted in order to mar another's official career, the offender must be disqualified from ever being employed again.

29.—Of passing over the proper magistrate and having recourse to different persons in order to trump up a law suit.

In such cases, when the proper magistrate is disregarded and a suit is concocted by one who has changed his allegiance and attached himself to a different patron, occasion is afforded for a clashing of judgments even when nothing of the kind is intended. Therefore in such cases the plaintiff must be debarred for a time from bringing his action. As regards his patron there must be a Government injunction issued (restraining him from maintaining the suit).

If when a suit is brought before him, a magistrate is neglectful and allows twenty days to pass without his taking any action in the matter, the parties may make an application to the Courthouse (at the Shōgun's Palace).

---

1. Mon-jaku, i. e. the Confucian scriptures or Chinese classics, not the Buddhist scriptures or Sutras.—H.

30.—Of a party to a pending suit who, instead of awaiting the judgment, sends in a letter from a person high in authority.

In such cases the successful party exults in winning the case by the strength of his powerful connection, whilst the losing side grieves over the influence wielded by those high in office and position. Hence one vaunts his obligation to his powerful patronage, whilst the other distrusts the judgments of the established legal tribunals. It is mainly in this way that the course of government administration is polluted. Therefore this practice must henceforth be peremptorily put an end to. Suitors must either have recourse to the magistrate or the case must be referred direct to the Court-House.[1]

31.—Of persons who, not having justice on their side and therefore failing in their suits, accuse the Magistrate of partiality.

When a person, who not being in the right fails to get leave to institute a suit, then trumps up a charge of partiality against the Magistrate, such conduct is extremely reckless and reprehensible. Henceforth if any such person, after making false allegation, trumps up a groundless accusation of that kind, he shall be punished by the confiscation of one-third of his fief. If the offender has no investiture he is to be expelled from the locality. If, again, the Magistrate has been guilty of some mistake in the matter, he is to be disqualified from ever again holding office.[2]

32.—Of harbouring brigands and bands of evil-doers within a fief.

It is rumoured that there are cases of such persons being

---

1. Tei-chu, the Court-yard of the Council of Government at Kamakura. —H.
2. The accuser being punished none the less.—H.

THE HŌJŌ-CODE OF JUDICATURE

harboured; but inasmuch as they have not actually been discovered it is impossible to punish the culprits, and no open rebuke has been administered to those suspected of harbouring them. However, when the people of the county point out the places of hiding, if the brigands are arrested then that county passes as being quiet: If they continue at large, then that county is deemed to be infested, etc., etc.[1]

In like manner if the malefactors have located themselves on the borderland between two counties, it must be put to the proof which of the two they are in, and the suppressive measures taken accordingly. Again, if Land-Reeves are found allowing gangs of brigands to find refuge in their districts, they will be held to be equally guilty. First of all, when the information received gives ground for suspicion, the Land-Reeve will be summoned to Kamakura and detained; and is not to be granted leave of absence so long as that country remains in a disturbed state. Again, as regards those localities into which a Protector's Delegate[2] is prohibited from entering, whenever, in like manner, such gangs of evil-minded persons are found to have located themselves therein, they must be arrested without delay and handed over to the Protector's office. In case any sympathy is shown to the culprits, the Protector's Delegate will be authorised to enter into the domain, and the Land-Reeve's Deputy[3] must likewise be changed. If the Deputy

---

1. There is a lacuna in the text here. The lost portion doubtless contained directions as to the procedure to be followed in making the arrests, etc.—H.

2. Shu-go shi: the Shōyen or Manors of the Court Nobles are here meant. In ordinary times not even the Provincial Governors could interfere in their affairs, much less the upstart Protectors of the Shōgun's administration.—H.

3. Daikwan.—H.

is not changed the post of the Land-Reeve will be extinguished and the Protector's Delegate will receive authority to enter.

33.—Of robbing and theft; also of incendiaries. For the two kinds of stealing[1] the punishment (death) is already established by precedents. Can there be hesitation or reconsideration on that point? Next as regards the man who sets on fire (a house, etc.) he is to be regarded in the same light as a brigand and it is right that he should be outlawed.

34.—Of illicit intercourse with another person's wife.

Whoever embraces another person's wife is to be deprived of half of his fief, and to be inhibited from rendering service any more, regardless of whether it was a case of rape or adultery. If he have no investiture he must be sent into banishment. A woman who commits adultery shall in like manner be deprived of her fief, and if she have none she must also be sent into banishment.

35.—Of persons not coming up (to Kamakura) after being repeatedly summoned in a suit.

When a plaint has been instituted and the defendant has been thrice served with a summons to appear and plead, if he does not come and abide judgment, the plaintiff, if he has right on his side, shall forthwith obtain judgment in his favour; if he has not right on his side the property in dispute shall be awarded to some third party (who may have the next best claim to it).

When the subject-matter of the suit is dependent persons, horses, cattle or miscellaneous things,[2] they shall be restored, after investigation, to such third party according to the

---

1. These were gōtō, robbing with violence, and settō, thieving covertly. —H.
2. But not land: the omission is significant.—H.

inventory or description furnished by him. Otherwise they shall be appropriated for the repair of the temples and shrines.

36.—Of altering ancient land-marks and so engendering disputes.

There are persons who transgressing the ancient boundaries of their fiefs, trump up some new pretext of rival claim and others who disregarding the precedents of late years established, bring forward some old document and found a claim on it; and inasmuch as they suffer no particular loss even when they are unsuccessful in their claims, such nefarious fellows lightly concoct and institute law-suit to the no small infliction of unnecessary trouble on the judiciary.

For the future, when suits of this kind are brought, a surveyor must be sent to the locality in question to investigate accurately the boundaries and proofs; and if the claim of the plaintiff is found to be baseless, the extent of the land which he wrongfully sought to obtain by his suit shall be carefully measured, and a portion of like extent shall be subtracted from his fief and added to that of the defendant.

37.—Of vassals of the Kwanto applying to Kyoto for side offices[1] and for the superintendentships of estates.

This practice was strictly forbidden in the time of the Minamoto House. Of late years however, some persons, following the bent of their own ambitions, have not only disregarded the prohibition, but have entered into competition with others seeking to obtain the same appointment. Henceforth anyone found indulging in such ill-regulated ambition shall be punished by the escheating of the whole of his fief.

1. The appointment of Deputy (Daikwan) is here meant.—H.

APPENDIX IV

38.—Of Land-Reeves hindering the functions of the village Headmen within the limits of their charge.

When one who has been placed in general charge of a district as Land-Reeve endeavours under the pretext of their being within the district under his charge, to encroach upon villages which are distinct and separate there-from, he cannot escape blame. In such case, an Instruction will be issued to him stating that, even in the case of so low a post as that of village Headman, if the Land-Reeve of the whole district taking advantage of the weakness or illness of the village Headman, and transgressing the limits of his Instructions, forms unlawful designs against him and places unjustifiable hindrances in the way of his doing his work, an Instruction will be issued to the village Headman empowering him to pay the taxes to the Government direct (i. e. passing over the Land-Reeve altogether).

On the other hand, if a village Headman plays fast and loose and disregards established precedents in disobedience to the Land-Reeve, his post of Headman will be taken away.

39.—That those desirous of obtaining office or rank must have a written recommendation from the Kwanto.

That those who have performed a meritorious service and are desirous of being raised in rank therefore should be recommended (by us to the Emperor) is an established and impartial mode of proceeding ; and there is consequently no need to prescribe regulations about it.

As to applications for recommendations by persons who merely desire their own advancement they are strictly prohibited altogether, whether from high or low.

However, those who have been invested (by the Emperor) with the office of Kebishi (Metropolitan Police Magistrate) do not require a letter of recommendation (from Kamakura). If they be so fortunate as to receive the Imperial permission they may be appointed to Office or Rank direct.

Again those who are newly promoted to higher rank, and who after the lapse of the due length of years still enjoy (literally, bathe in) favour at the Court are not included in the above restriction.

40.—Of Buddhist clergy within the Kamakura Domain striving at their own option to obtain ecclesiastical positions and rank.

Inasmuch as it leads to the deranging of the due subordination in the hierarchy, the practice of applying at will (to Kyoto) for preferment is in itself a source of confusion and furthermore entails undue multiplication of the higher ecclesiastical dignities: for clerics of mature age and ripe intelligence are overpassed by younger men of slight ability; whereby the formers' labour and expenses in following their calling are made of no avail and the principles of religion are at the same time contravened.

Henceforth if any one should in future apply for preferment without first having received our permission he shall, if he be the incumbent of a temple or shrine, be deprived of his benefice. Even if he belong to the clergy specially attached to the chaplaincies of the Shōgun he shall nevertheless be dismissed.

Should, however, one of the Zen Sect make such an application, an influential member of the same sect will be directed to administer a gentle admonition.

41.—Of Slaves and unclassed persons.

(In cases of dispute respecting the ownership of such persons) the precedent established by the late Shōgun's House must be adhered to; that is to say, if more than ten years have elapsed without the former owner having asserted his claim, there shall be no discussion as to the merits of the case and the possession of the present owner

APPENDIX IV

is not to be interfered with.

42.—Of inflicting loss and ruin on absconding farmers under the pretext of smashing runaways.

When people living in the provinces run away and escape, the lord of the fief and others,[1] proclaiming that runaways must be smashed up, detain their wives and children, and confiscate their property. Such a mode of procedure is quite the reverse of benevolent government. Henceforth such must be referred (to Kamakura) for adjudication, and if it is found that the farmer is in arrear as regards payment of his land tax and levies, he shall be compelled to make good the deficiency. If he is found not to be so in arrear, the property seized from him shall be forthwith restored to him. And it shall be entirely at the option of the farmer himself whether he shall continue to live in the fief or go elsewhere.[2]

43.—Of persons falsely pretending that another's fief is within their tenure, and greedily appropriating the produce thereof.

To covertly get possession of a fief under false pretext of title must, as those Regulations come into operation, be deemed an offence. Therefore the produce which has been wrongfully appropriated in that way must be promptly accounted for and restored. If the aggressor be the holder of a fief it shall be escheated. If he has no fief he must be sent into banishment.

Again, as regards the practice of obtaining a deed of feoffment in respect of a fief which the applicant is actually holding, without there being any special ground for making

---

1. i. e. the Jito, or Jito Daikwan, etc.—H.
2. This liberal enactment was disregarded by the Tokugawa; who severely punished any attempt on the part of the farmers to leave their holdings.—H.

such application, it is open to the suspicion that some sinister motive underlies it. Henceforth the practice must be stopped.

44.—Of eager rivalries when a companion has incurred guilt and others covet his investiture before his case has been decided.

That those who have piled up meritorious services should make plans for realizing their hopes is an ordinary matter of course. But that, when a rumour is started of an offence having been committed, and before the degree of guilt has been ascertained, the hope of getting the fief in question should engender the desire to condemn the man is not what can be deemed a righteous mode of proceeding. And when after due investigation, a decision has been given, slanders as from the mouths of tigers follow one another without end like bees in a swarm. Even if it be only a case of claiming a redress of fortune, rival hopes that have been cherished for days together shall not have effect given to them.[1]

45.—When a report is made of some offence having been committed, of relieving a man of his post without investigating the matter.

If adjudicative action is taken in such cases without the matter being fully enquired into, the result is to leave a feeling of grievance and resentment, whether the offence were committed or not. Consequently there must be prompt and thorough investigation in such cases before deciding one way or the other.

46.—Of the respective limits of judicature of the incoming and outgoing Govenor of a province on the occasion of an exchange of fiefs.

---

1. Nihon Kodai Hoten adds :—Cases in which the place has been made vacant do not come within the rule.—H.

APPENDIX IV

In such cases the new Governor shall have adjudication as regards the annual rice-tax revenue; as regards his (the old Governor's—Ed.) own serfs and miscellaneous gear and also the horses and cattle of his train, the new Governor need not detain them; much more, then if any slight be offered to the previous Governor shall it be doomed a specially reprehensible remissness.

Things, however, which were confiscated (by the previous Governor) on account of serious offences are not included within the scope of this provision (i. e. the outgoing Governor may not take them with him).

47.—Of making a present to another person of documents of a fief not in one's possession: Furthermore; of village headmen making presents to influential Houses without the cognizance of the lord.

Henceforth those who make such presents shall be sent away bodily; those who receive them shall be fined for the benefit of the Shrines and temples repair fund.

In the next place, as regards headmen who without the cognizance of the lord of the manor make presents of the emoluments of their posts. Of course this practice goes on. Such a fellow shall be deprived of his emolument as headman, which shall be added to the Land-Reeve's share. In places where there is no Land-Reeve it shall be added to the lord's share.

48.—Of buying and selling fiefs.

That those who have inherited a private estate from their ancestors may under stress of necessity dispose of it by sale is a settled law. But as for those persons who either in consequence of accumulated merit or on account of their personal exertions have been made the recipients of special favours from the Government—for them to buy and sell such at their own pleasure is a proceeding that is by no means blameless. Henceforth it certainly must be stopped.[1] If, nevertheless, any persons, in disregard of the prohibition dispose of a fief by sale both the sellers and the buyers shall be equally dealt with as guilty.

49.—Of holding a formal trial in a suit when it is quite clear on the face of the documents that one of the parties has no case.

When the documents sent in by both sides disclose with perfect clearness the right or wrong of a claim, adjudication may be given at once without confronting the parties at a formal hearing.

50.—Of persons who, when a disorderly incident occurs, proceed to the scene of the affray without knowing the particulars.

As regards those who, in such cases, rush in to land their help as partizans, it is needless to make nice distinctions. As regards the gravity of their offence it is impossible to lay down a rule beforehand. The circumstances of each case must be taken into consideration. As regards those who, desirous of ascertaining the facts, and not being privy to the cause proceed to the scene of an affray it is not necessary to regard them as culpable.

51.—Of disorderly behaviour by persons holding a writ of summons or a Decree in a suit.

---

1. At this period the selling of hereditary possessions above referred to was that on the part of the farming folk, who had mortgaged their field and the selling of fiefs in the same manner is here forbidden. In after ages the practice of selling fiefs was utterly unknown. It was an altogether different matter, however, if one of the farmer folk committed an offence and his share of the land was taken away from him by the Land-Reeve, or if the Land-Reeve bought from the farmer folk their agricultural fields, wet or dry or their forest lands, paying them a money price for them. That was quite allowable. But the selling and buying of fiefs which had been granted by one's lord was not allowed at all. The two cases were widely different.—H.

APPENDIX IV

That when a plaint[1] is instituted a writ of enquiry (i. e. a Summons to the other party) should be issued is the established practice. But if the writ is made use of as a ground for disorderly behaviour, such malicious truculence must be held to involve culpability. If the contents of plaints show quite clearly that the claims are unreasonable or pettifogging, the granting of writs of Enquiry will be altogether stopped.

Solemn Oath

That questions of right or wrong shall be decided at meetings of the Council[2] (in accordance with these institutes).

Whereas a simple individual is liable to make mistakes through defect of judgment, even when the mind is unbiassed; and besides that, is led, out of prejudice or partiality, whilst intending to do right, to pronounce a wrong judgment; or again, in cases where there is no clue, considers that proof exists; or being cognizant of the facts and unwilling that another's shortcomings should be exposed, refrains from pronouncing a judgment one way or the other; so that intention and fact are in disaccord and catastrophes afterwards ensue.

Therefore: in general, at meetings of Council, whenever questions of right or wrong are concerned there shall be no regard for ties of relationship, there shall be no giving-in to likes or dislikes, but in whatever direction reason pushes and as the inmost thought of the mind leads, without re-

---

1. "Sojo (plaint) is the same as meyasu (i. e. eye case). Monjo (writ of Enquiry) is the sashigami (i. e. issue paper) of the present (Tokugawa) days."—H.
2. Hyōjōshu; the Cabinet or Supreme Council of the Shōgunate at Kamakura.—H.

gard for companions or fear of powerful Houses, we shall speak out. Matters of adjudication shall be clearly decided and whilst not conflicting with justice the sentence shall be a statute of the whole Council in session. If a mistake is made in the matter, it shall be the error of the whole Council acting as one. Even when a decision given in a case is perfectly just it shall be a constitution of the whole Council in session. If a mistake is made and action taken without good grounds, it shall be the error of the whole council acting as one. Henceforward therefore as towards litigants and their supporters we shall never say " Although I personally took the right view of the matter some or such a one amongst my colleagues of the Council dissented and so caused confusion, etc." Should utterance be given to any such reports the solidarity of the Council would be gone, and we should incur the derision of men in after times.

Furthermore, again when suitors having no colour of right on their side fail to obtain a trial of their claim from the Court of the Council and then make an appeal to one of its members, if a writ of endorsement is granted by him it is tantamount to saying that all the rest of the members are wrong. Like as if we were one man shall we maintain judgment. Such are the reasons for these articles. If even in a single instance we swerve from them either to bend or to break them may the gods Ben-Ten, Taishaku, the four great Kings of the Sky, and all the gods great and little, celestial and terrestrial of the sixty odd provinces of Nippon, and especially the two Gongen of Idzu and Hakone, Mishima Daimyōjin, Hachiman Daibosatsu and Temman Dai Jizai Tenjin punish us and all our tribe, connexions and belongings with the punishments of the gods and the punishments of the Buddhas ; so may it be.

APPENDIX IV

Accordingly we swear a solemn oath as above. Teiyei, 1st year 7th month, 10th day.

(Signed by)

    Saito Hyo-yei Niu-do Shami Jo-yen.
    Sato Sagami no Daijo Fujiwara Naritoki.
    Ota Gemba no Jo Miyoshi Yasutsura.
    Goto Sayemon no Shoi Fujiwara no Ason Mototsuna.
    Nikaido Mimbu Tai-yu Shami Gyonen.
    Yano Geki Tai-yu Sani Miyoshi Ason Tomoshige.
    ——Kaga no Kami Miyoshi Ason Yasunaga.
    Nikaido Oki Niudo Shami Gyo-sei.
    Chiujo Saki no Dewa no Kami Fujiwara no Ason Iyenaga.
    Miura Saki no Suruga no Kami Taira Ason Yoshimura.
    Hojo Settsu no Kami Nakahara Ason Morokazu.
    Hojo Musashi no Kami Taira Ason Yasutoki.
    Hojo Sagami no Kami Taira Ason Tokifusa.

*   *   *

From the Introductory Notes of the late Mr. John Carey Hall:

" Even a cursory reading of the Code discloses the fact that this feudal law was superimposed on the existing customary law; and was not intended to supersede the latter. As a fact, however, the feudal law grew at the expense of the Imperial law and ultimately superseded it. Another point worthy of remark in the Code is the high position of women. They were allowed to hold fiefs; and the wife could hold separately from the husband. The comparatively high position of women at the opening, as compared with the close of the Tokugawa period has already been noticed by Professor Chamberlain. In the Hojo times it was higher still.

" The Code is written in Chinese, not Japanese, and the style is clumsy and unpolished. It was intended only for the use of the High Court at Kamakura (the Monjusho) and the Bugyo or feudal Magistrates who exercised jurisdiction over the vassals of the suzerain Shōgun in the

THE HŌJŌ-CODE OF JUDICATURE

remoter provinces; hence the circumstance that it was written in a learned script, which very few of the warriors of that time understood. It was not till the Tokugawa times that it came to be printed. From at least as early as the middle of the eighteenth century it was used as an elementary manual of the Chinese ideographs, which were printed large, in the sosho or abbreviated script, as models for copying." (p. 15)

From: Japanese Feudal Law: The Institutes of Judicature: being a translation of "Go Seibai Shikimoku"; the Magisterial Code of the Hōjō Power-Holder, by John Carey Hall. In: Transactions of the Asiatic Society of Japan, Vol. 34, 1906.

V

THE ASHIKAGA CODE

("Kemmu Shikimoku", A. D. 1336)

WHETHER THE ARMY HEADQUARTERS SHOULD BE AT KAMAKURA AS HERETOFORE OR AT SOME OTHER PLACE

In antiquity, both in China and our own country, there have been frequent shiftings and changes in society, more than there is time to enumerate. When we come down to later times, we find affairs become much more complicated and troublesome, so that such transitions were probably not so easy to effect. Especially remarkable as regards local changes is the case of the district of Kamakura, where in the year-term of Bunji (A. D. 1185-1189) His Highness the Right Commander-in-Chief (Yoritomo) for the first time established a Military Office. In the Shokiu year-term (1219-1221), Yoshitoki, in rank a second-class Court noble (Ason) swallowed the empire. Must it not be called a lucky place for the Baronial Houses (Buke)! Their incomes were ample and their power great. They became, however, luxurious and avaricious, and did not reform accumulated evils; and at last (i. e. in Takatoki's case) brought upon themselves extinction. Even though their seat were to be shifted to somewhere else, if they do not mend their ways and abandon the rut that upset the cart, can there be any doubt that they will totter and be imperilled? Both the Chow and Tsin (Dynasties of China) were within the Yao-Han barrier; yet the Tsin were overthrown in the second generation, whereas the Chow maintained their line 800 years. The Dzui and the Tang dynasties both lived in Changan. The Dzui were overthrown in the second generation, whereas the Tang lasted for 300 years. Therefore the duration of a locality of power must depend on the goodness or badness of the system of government. It is not the badness of the locality but the badness of the men that counts. If any one desires to shift the locality of government, must he not follow the direction of public opinion?

THE QUESTION OF THE SYSTEM OF GOVERNMENT

As regards this subject, seeing that we have to ponder the circumstances of the time and frame administrative arrangements to suit, we have Japan and China to choose between; and the problem is, which methods of each should we adopt?

On the whole, succeeding as we do to the inheritance of an age in which the Baronial Houses securely flourished shall we, following in their footsteps, dispense good government? If so, we have Senators of ripe experience, the Counsellors of the Hyōjō Shu (council of Government at Kamakura), and public servants of all grades in abundance. If we make our appeal to the realities of the old Kamakura régime, is there anything in which it can be said to have been wanting? In the ancient (Chinese) Statutes it is said :—" Virtue means exercising good government, and government consists in making the lives of the folk endurable and easy, etc." Shall we promptly put an end to the distress of the myriads and at once issue our authoritative directions to them? The most important points are, in the main, as follows :—

1. Economy must be universally practised.

APPENDIX V

Under the designation of " basara "[1] (the fashion or chic) there prevails a love of eccentricity or originality, figured brocades and embroidered silks, of elaborately mounted swords, and a hunting after fashions, and of everything calculated to strike the eye. The age may almost be said to have become demented. Those who are rich become more and more filled with pride; and the less wealthy are ashamed of not being able to keep up with them. Nothing could be more injurious to the cause of good manners. This must be strictly kept within bounds.

2. Drinking parties and wanton frolics must be suppressed.

It is particularly important that excesses of this nature should be put down. Much more when, through infatuation for their mistresses, men have recourse to gambling. Besides these misdoings, under the pretext of holding tea parties or under the disguise of poetical competitions, meetings are held for the purpose of laying gambling bets. Is not the waste caused by this course of conduct incalculable?

3. Crimes of violence and outrage must be quelled.

Robberies from houses in the open daylight, armed burglaries, murders and massacres occur frequently, and highway robberies take place at all the crossways, and the cries of distress from the victims never cease. For the prevention of such conduct imperative instructions must surely be issued?

4. The practice of entering the private dwellings of the people and making inquisition into their affairs must be given up.

---

1. I conjecture that this word is Basra (or Bussorah), the river port where the manufactures of Bagdad were transhipped from river boats into sea-going vessels.—J. C. H.

When a person exerts himself to improve his condition in life and has a new or a bigger house built, he is immediately subjected to an inquisition (by his superiors) as to his means and so forth, and the house taken from him. Consequently he has no place wherein to hide himself, and he becomes a waif, and at last loses his means of livelihood. It is a most pitiable state of things.

5. In the present state of affairs, more than half the area of the capital has been reduced to vacant spaces (i. e. burnt down). Are they to be restored to their original owners and the rebuilding of their dwellings permitted?

The talk of the streets is to the effect that all who took part in the Imperial departure to the top of the mountain (Hiyeizan) are to be condemned, high and low without execption; and—without investigation as to the truth or falsity of the allegation—to have their properties confiscated, and so forth. Applying the provisions of the law to the matter, is there (not) a distinction to be made between the principals in turbulence and sedition and those who are only accomplices or merely their dependants and subordinates? Should (not) scrupulous investigations be made into each case, and the treatment be made different accordingly? Did an immense number of such confiscations (not) take place in the sequel of the Shokiu disturbance? If we are again now to take away the whole of their properties, will the Ducal Houses (Kuge) and the holders of Court offices (not) be reduced to cruel destitution?

6. Co-operative building clubs for the erection of substantial fire-proof houses to be promoted.

Whether we regard the immense contributions both in money and gratuitous labour that have been levied on the people, or the prevalence of the practice of breaking into their houses for booty, it is to be feared that the erection of houses will come to an end entirely, and so the commodities which all, both high and low, stand in need of will cease to be supplied, and the poor become unable to make a living for themselves. If the plan of having (substantial fire-proof) dwellings erected (by voluntary Co-operative clubs) be carried out, will it (not) become a basis for giving a sense of security to all the people?

7. Men of special ability for government work must be chosen for the posts of Protectors of the provinces.

In a time such as the present are we (not) to call upon faithful warriors and assign to them the office of the Protectorship in the provinces; and for those who have merited rewards are we (not) to procure the grant of Manors (Shōyen)? The provincial Protector is an ancient military functionary; the tranquility or disturbance of the whole county depends entirely on that office. If men of unquestionable capacity and such only be chosen to fill it, will (not) the minds of the folk be set at rest?

8. A stop must be put to the practice of influential nobles and women of all sorts and Buddhist (Zen) ecclesiastics making their interested recommendations (to the Sovereign).

9. Persons holding public posts must be liable to reprimand for negligence and idleness; moreover, they should be subject to the principle of careful selection for their posts.

The above two provisions have been settled principles of government for generations; they are not at all in the nature of new-fangled changes.

10. Bribery must be firmly put down.

Although this principle also (like the two preceding) is by no means now enunciated for the first time, a special injunction of more than ordinary stringency is required to deal with it. However subordinate his social position may be, were he worth only a hundred cash, the man who accepts a bribe must be excluded from all employment for an indefinitely long period ; and if the amount of the bribe accepted be inordinate, he must lose all official employment for the rest of his life.

11. Presents made from all quarters to those who are attached to the Palace, whether of the Inside or Outside Services, must be sent back.

Whatever those in authority may be fond of, their subordinates will likewise affect. A reform in the direction of purity and honesty must be carried out. Rarities and curiosities from China and such like must particularly be disallowed as presents or souvenirs.

12. Those who are to be in personal attendance on the rulers (Sovereign and Shōgun) must be selected for that duty.

It has been said : " If you want to know what sort the prince is, look at his ministers ; if you want to know what sort a man is, look at his companions." Hence, seeing that the goodness or the reverse of a sovereign is at once apparent by looking at the character of the ministers he has under him, must they (not) henceforth be chosen on the ground of their capabilities ? Again, when members of the ruler's entourage form cliques and in concert recommend or disparage some one, can anything be more calculated to engender quarrels and disorder ? In the histories of the Chinese royal families and in the history of our own we have numerous instances of this. Then again, there is a further source of abuses when, for the sake of affording amusement, artistic performers, by their skill or beautiful costumes, work their way into royal favour and regard. Such adventurers should not be admitted to

APPENDIX V

the royal entourage. Ought not this to be seriously considered (by the Sovereign)?

13. Ceremonial etiquette to be the predominant principle.

For regulating a state there is nothing that surpasses a regard for ceremonial formalities. For the prince, there should be a princely style of ceremonial; for the vassal (or minister) there should be a ministerial style. In all matters the distinction between higher and lower should be maintained; and both in speech and demeanour the observance of ceremoniousness should be deemed of cardinal importance.

14. Men noted for probity and their adherence to high principles should be rewarded by more than ordinary distinction.

That is the way to advance men of worth and to get rid of the bad. Directions should be issued by those having authority marking this distinction of character, by expressions of commendation or the reverse.

15. The petitions and complaints of the poor and lowly must be heard and redress granted.

In the administration of Yao and Shun this point was held to be of the first importance. In the Canon of History it is said: "What the ordinary man holds to be of small account the sage deems to be of high concern." This must be carefully borne in mind by those in power. Pity and commisseration find their appropriate object in the poorer classes. Their distressful petitions should be entertained and dealt with; and it is imperative that instructions in that sense should be issued.

16. The petition and claims of temples (Buddhist) and Shrines (Shinto) are to be dealt with on their merits, and are either to be approved, or, on the contrary, to be rejected

if they deserve to be rejected.

In some cases these make a display of their spiritual influence : in others they make a pretext of establishing or enlarging their religious edifices : or again they make a display of mysterious signs and wonders, or proclaim that it is for the purpose of offering up prayers ; and other such like motives are put forward as the ground of their petitions. The closest investigation should be made before sanctioning such requests.

17. There should be certain fixed days appointed for the rendering of decisions and issuance of government orders.

As a cause of distress to people in general nothing is more vexatious than remissness and neglect on the part of those in authority over them ; and on the other hand matters should not be hastily dismissed off hand without going to the root of the questions at issue. Definite decisions should be given for one side or the other. That there should be no grievances left for the people to complain of is the chief object of authoritative instructions.

Such, in effect, is the purport of the foregoing seventeen articles. Although I, Ze-yen, am a scion of the stock of Li Tsao, I have become an unintelligent rustic of the moors and wilds ; yet I have had the honour of being called in to advise respecting the principles of stable government ; and the above is the outcome of what I have gathered from the study of the history and institutions of China and Japan in ancient and modern times. At the present day throughout all the provinces there is no rest for the shield and spear. Ought we not indeed to stoop and pick one's steps warily ? The ancients had a saying :—" When living in safety, nevertheless take thought for danger." But we are now living in danger, and should we refrain from taking thought

APPENDIX V

for the dangers we are in? Now is just the time to be apprehensive: these are the days when it behoves us to be circumspect. Looking back to distant times, let us take example by the virtuous influence of the two sage Emperors of the Yengi and Ten-ryaku periods (Daigo, 898-930, and Murakami, 947-967); to nearer times, by the example of the practical activity of Yoshitoki and Yasutoki, father and son. Let these be our teachers for the modern time. Above all, if we can dispense a system of government such as the myriads of the people can look up to with respect, will not this be the foundation for complete and peaceful security within the four seas? Accordingly the above is, in general terms, the tenor of the suggestions which we have the honour to submit for consideration.

(Signed) Shin-yei
(″   ) Ze-yen.

Kemmu, 3rd year, 11th month, 7th day.
(A. D. 10th December, 1336.)

Present at the Council :—The ex-Minister of the Interior; Ze-yen (Lay name Dosho or Michitaka); Shin-yei (Bonze); Genyei Hoin (Bonze); Dazai Shoni; Akashi Mimbu Tai-yu; Ota Shichirozayemon no Jo; Fuse Hiko-Saburo Niudo (i. e. religieux); Eight persons as above.

From: Japanese Feudal Laws II.—The Ashikaga Code. By J. C. Hall.
In: Transactions of the Asiatic Society of Japan, Vol. 36, 1908.

VI

Feudal Law and Administration in South Kyūshū

1. Petition of a Local Official and Marginal Sanction of the Domanial Lord[1], 1147 A. D.

(Tomo Nobufusa, the author of this petition, was of the illustrious family that traced its ancestry back to a " heavenly deity " who is said to have accompanied Ninigi, the progenitor of the Imperial house, when he descended upon Japan in the mythical age. The successors of the former for a long period served the court as chiefs of guardsmen and councillors of state, but in the ninth century were ousted from their high place by the Fujiwara, who gradually gained control over nearly all the important posts in the central government. Members of the Tomo family then scattered in remote parts of the country, where they, like men of other old families from Kyōto, served as minor provincial officials. Their descendants multiplied in an increasing number of branch families, and maintained their local prominence with more or less success. Their presence on the basin of the lower Sendai is revealed in this document and many others following.

It will be seen that, at the time of his writing this petition, Tomo Nobufusa was an agent of a shō,[2] being its financial commissioner (ben-zai shi) for the lands it held in Iriki *in* and its administrative official (ji-tō) of its lands in neighboring districts in Satsuma and Taki kōri.[3] That shō was

---

1. The domanial lord was Fujiwara Tadamichi, regent for the Emperor, descendant in the fourth generation of the premier Yorimichi, the first lord of Shimadzu shō. Later, Yorimichi's successor, Motozane, assumed the family name Konoe.—A.
2. Private domain.—Ed.
3. The largest administrative territorial unit was the kuni (" province "), which was divided into kōri and in, these being subdivided into gō which consisted of several mura(hamlet).—Ed.

APPENDIX VI

Shimadzu, the origin and character of which were described in our Introduction. In the cadastral survey of the kuni of 1197 (No. 9), we note that the shō held yosegori, that is, districts the taxes from which were divided between itself and the kuni government, in both Iriki *in* and Satsuma kōri, and it is assumed that a similar condition existed fifty years before, at the time of this document. It was, then, in one of the yose-gōri in Satsuma kōri of Shimadzu shō that Nobufusa had been and now wished to continue to be the ji-tō.

It is one of the most important events in the institutional history of Japan that, early in 1186, Yoritomo, the first suzerain of Kamakura, was authorized to appoint from among his own vassals ji-tō in a majority of the districts, public and private, in Japan. It has, however, been known that before that date there had been occasional instances of agents in shō designated by this title; and, therefore, it is of special interest that we here meet a ji-tō forty years before Yoritomo, in a district in far Satsuma which was half public and half private in its financial status. His function as a local agent probably consisted largely in receiving and forwarding the taxes that were due to the domanial lord of the shō.

As ji-tō of Yamada mura, Nobufusa was responsible to the domanial lord of the shō, who was at Kyōtō; as be-zai shi of Iriki *in*, he was presumably accountable to the kuni government of Satsuma, whose offices were located half a mile northwest of the Niita temple. Another district, Kuruma-uchi in Taki kōri, over which also he had been granted jitō-ship was, however, administered at present by the deputy of the domanial lord. Such diversity of control was not unnatural, when we consider that a yose-gōri was, in its financial obligation, neither wholly public as part of the kuni nor wholly private as part of the shō.

It will be noted that for his jitō-ship Nobufusa owed to the domanial lord a " fee for appointment." K. A.)

" Tomo Nobufusa, bettō,[1] the ben-zai shi of Iriki *in*,

---

1. Bettō, a term of Sinico-Buddhist origin, was usually a title for the chief of an office; its usage, however, had become irregular. Here its

petitions, appealing for decision by the man-dokoro[1] of the shō.[2]

"That, in accordance with the repeated orders, a renewed marginal sanction[3] be granted him, concerning [the office of] jitō of Yamada mura, of Satsuma Kōri.

"On respectfully examining the records,[4] [it is found that] Nobufusa, though personally poor and incapable, has, with utmost effort and to the fullest capacity, rendered to Kyōto his fees for appointment,[5] and received orders appointing him ji-tō of Yamada mura and Kuruma-uchi. As for Kuruma-uchi, it is at present controlled by the deputy, and is therefore beyond (Nobufusa's) power. It is petitioned that, as regards Yamada mura, a marginal sanction that [his ji-tō office thereof] is assured, be granted him, so that [the document] may be preserved as testimony for all time. Thus does he respectfully petition.

"Kyu-an 3 y. 2 m. 9 d. [12 March 1147]. Tomo Nobufusa, petitioning."

[Marginal order]:[6]

"Following precedents, [the petitioner] shall be (the holder of) the jitō shiki,[7] so ordered.

connotation is not clear, but the bettō probably was, if one may infer from Nos. 4 and 12 C, an official connected with the central administration of the shō.—A.

1. Executive office of the domanial lord.
2. Shimadzu shō.
3. Ge-dai (literally, marginal heading), marginal order, a sample of which is found in this No. This was an informal procedure, which world hardly be used at the first appointment.—A.
4. A conventional beginning of formal statements.—A.
5. A fee was paid to the domanial lord at appointment and reappointment.
6. The marginal sanction by the domanial lord, like most ge-dai from whatever source, is written usually on the first margin—i.e., on the right-hand side of the paper, as Japanese writing proceeds from right to left,—instead of at the end, as is done for convenience in this translation.—A.
7. Shiki, literally, office, but usually meaning the income incident upon the office.—A.

APPENDIX VI

" Nakahara,[1] *u e-mon no zho*,[2] (monogram[3])."

From: K. Asakawa, Documents of Iriki pp. 91-93.

2. REPUDIATION OF SONS, ABOUT 1277 A. D.

(THIS short letter presents several points of capital importance. In the first place, the document shows the origin of serious family dissensions which led to a series of judicial processes before the shō-gun's court, revealing the character of feudal justice as administered under the Hōjō regency at the height of its power....

The document further shows how the real meaning of the term go ke-nin[4] had changed. The shō-gun at Kamakura, after the assassination of the last of the Minamoto lords in 1219, was a mere figurehead, the actual power of his feudal government having fallen into the hands of the Hōjō, the family of the regent. The shō-gun's direct vassals no longer saw in him the object of his personal devotion; without relinquishing his nominal allegiance to the suzerain, therefore, and without discarding the title go ke-nin, the vassal had now chosen as his personal lord one of the Hōjō—in this instance, the regent himself.

Still more interesting is the nature of feudal contract which obtained in this period. Homage, strong as was the bond of fidelity it involved, required for its inception no definite form of ceremonial act, and was, so far as formality was concerned, easily made: a father would promise the faith of his sons to his own lord, and nevertheless a son would readily attach himself to another lord. It is true that the former act merely put into effect the principle of hereditary following, and constituted no real difference from the successive allegiance which was often promised in written letters of homage used in European feudalism

1. An official of the domanial lord's man-dokoro.—A.
2. An official title, originally in the Imperial palace guard but now nominal.—A.
3. Monograms originally grew out of signatures; personal names were at first done in cursive form into single abridged characters, and then more or less purely fanciful monograms were devised.—A.
4. "Lower grade vassals to the feudal government" (Honjō).—Ed.

in the later stages of its evolution. But the free choice of a lord by a son without serious reason which he could urge against his father's lord would seem extraordinay. Nor did the lord inflict any measure of sanction upon the faithless son or his father. Was this because the son had not yet personally done homage to the lord, and also because the new lord was his kin? Did the father's lord consider that the son's offense lay between himself and the father, and between father and son, rather than between himself and the son? K. A.)

"I have the honor to inform you that, despite the fact that I had said to my lord,[1] as you are aware, that my three sons would serve[2] him, Yōichi Shigekazu and Shichiro Yorishige have disobeyed my command and gone to another lord,[3] and that, [for that offense], I have forever repudiated[4] them, so that henceforth we are no longer parent and children. I report this in order that [my lord] may understand it. I beg you to announce it to the lord at an opportune moment. Respectfully reported.

4th month 5th day.[5]   Jō-Butsu,[6] *monogram*.

"To Suwa nyū-dō[7] *dono*."

From: K. Asakawa, Documents of Iriki pp. 154-155.

1. From the next document it would appear that the lord was Hōjō Tokimune, the regent.—A.
2. Hō-kō, service.—A.
3. In Nos. 27 and 39 this lord is seen to have been Yoshimasa, of a collateral branch of the Hōjō.—A.
4. Fu-kyō, literally, failing in filial duty, but used often in the sense of disinheriting an unfilial child.—A.
5. No year is given, but the letter is apparently of the same year as the next document. The date is, then, 8 May 1277.—A.
6. The Buddhist name of Shigetsune, Jō-Shin's son, and the first lord of the Terao branch of the Iriki-in family.—A.
7. An attendant on the lord regent. An indirect address to the lord, out of respect for him.—A.

APPENDIX VI

3. Judgment of the Shō-gun's Court, 1280 A.D.

"In regard to Zhitchō North mura, in Kawae gō, of Mimasaka kuni, and to Tō-no-hara, in Iriki *in*, of Satsuma kuni, in dispute (so-ron) between the nun Myō-Ren, widow of Shibuya Goro-shirō Shigetsune hō-shi, Buddhist name Jō-Butsu, his son Iya-shirō Shigemichi, and [the latter's] daughter Taketsuru, [on the one side], and Yo-ichi Tameshige, original name Shigekazu, [on the other side].

"Although the points raised in the accusations and refutations [in the aforesaid case] are many, [the facts] in brief are [as follow]. Jō-Butsu's domains were devised to Shigemichi and the others in the 3d year of Ken-chi [1277]. As for Tameshige, that he was repudiated is evident in Jō-Butsu's autographic letters. Yet [for Tameshige] to have invaded Zhitchō North mura and Tō-no-hara and committed outrages, was exceedingly unreasonable. Now, although Tameshige claims that, whereas he held both the homestead at Shibuya and the other domains in accordance with Jō-Butsu's autographic letter of devise, Myō-Ren and the others seized the Shibuya homestead while Tameshige was away in his domain in Minasaka, Shigemichi and others replied that the said devise was a letter written before the repudiation, and that they dealt with [the domains] in accordance with the subsequent letters and [the shō-gun's] orders; and Tameshige had no word of refutation.

"Also the extreme want of reason on Tameshige's part is apparent in the fact that, whereas, if he possessed a letter of devise, he should [first] accuse Shigemichi and the others, he referred to it in his letter of refutation [only so late as] when they accused him; and then, though he came up [to Kamakura] after receiving frequent summonses, he did not undergo questions and answers, but fled to Mutsu[1].

"Next, although Tameshige says that it was wicked duplicity on the part of Shigemichi and the others to have caused the summons of Kō-an 1st year 5th month 19th day to be given [to Tameshige], and, on the 6th month 3d day of the same year, to have secured on a false pretense the order of investiture; when Shigemichi and the others reply that [the investiture] was applied for through the commissioner Ise nyū-dō Gyō-Gwan during Jō-Butsu's lifetime, and was granted after official examination, Tameshige does not refute it.

"Then Shigemichi and the others shall, according to Jō-Butsu's letters of devise and the orders of investiture, hold (ryō-shō) the aforesaid domains (sho-ryō).

"Next, although Shigemichi and the others say that Tameshige should be punished for not having obeyed the summons when he was urged from Rokuhara [to appear], but having on the contrary destroyed the order, and beaten and wounded a messenger and broken his right and left fingers, Tameshige has disputed the matter, and no report has been received from Rokuhara; and, therefore, the matter will not be adjudged (sa-da) for the present.

"Next: Tameshige petitions that Kageyasu, the proxy of Myō-Ren and the others, be punished for his abusive calumny, since he stated in his letter of accusation that, while night-attacks, robbery, dacoity, and piracy, were regular offences for which penalties had been defined, Tameshiges's acts were unparalleled wickednesses. But since Tameshige invaded domains of Shigemichi and the others and wantonly obstructed [their enjoyment of them], the words referred to cannot be dealt with as calumny, and therefore will not be

---

1. Ō-shu (the extreme northern kuni Mutsu) may be a miscopy of Sas-shu, i.e., Satsuma.

APPENDIX VI

taken cognizance of (sa-da).

" In pursuance of the command of the Lord of Kamakura, it is decreed thus.

" Ko-an 2 y. 12 m. 22 d. [24 January 1280].

Sagami-no-kami Taira no Ason,[1] *monogram.*"

From: K. Asakawa, Documents of Iriki pp. 167–168.

4. RECORDS OF SERVICE AT ARMS, 1339 A.D.

(WHEN a service in arms was rendered at a battle, the warrior drew up a careful account of his exploit, describing his feats, his encounters with the enemy, and the injuries he inflicted upon him and those he and his followers sustained, and citing the names of trustworthy eye-witnesses. The letter was also called an ikken zhō, for the commanding general certified the report with the usual phrase in three characters, ikken shi owannu, " [I] have seen [the report]," over his monogram. Sometimes, as in the following examples, the phrase ran (in only two characters): uketamawari owannu, " [I] do recognize [the statement]."[2] The report was then forwarded by him to the shō-gun, and on its strength the latter would reward the service of the warrior. K. A.)

a. Report

" [HIS] loyal services at arms reported by Saburo-zhirō Toshimasa, the proxy and son of Gon-Shūin Ryo-Sen,

1. Hōjō Tokimune, the regent. The successive Hōjō regents (shikken) were ex officio chiefs of the executive (man-dokoro) and military (samurai dokoro) offices of the shō-gun's government at Kamakura. In fact, the shō-gun was the nominal head, and the shikken the real ruler of feudal Japan.—A.

2. The ikken zhō was, therefore, an extremely abridged form of the vidimus or inspeximus, the confirmation meaning, however, that of the truth of the statement, not the authenticity, of the document it certified.—A.

part holder (ryō-shu) of Miyasato gō, Satsuma Kuni.

"Since there was a rumor on the 6th month 18th day of this year [25 July 1339] that the southern insurgents of this kuni would come, [Toshimasa] on that day betook himself into the fortress of Ikari-yama, and, being given charge of the turret by the river, guarded it. On the 19th day [26 July], when forces were despatched to chastize the enemy, Shikibu Tozaburo, Toshimasa went forth in person, and burned up Tozaburo's lodging. On the 20th of the same month, as the insurgents came and attacked the fortress of Ikari-yama, Toshimasa rendered service at arms [at the turret] by the river. When, on the 22nd day [29 July], the southern insurgents, together with Shibuya Mago-zhiro,[1] the same [family] Ko-shiro nyū-dō, the same [family] Heizhi-goro,[2] and others, besieged the fortress and fought strenuously, Toshimasa fought [at the turret] by the river; but hearing, on the same day, at the hour of tori,[3] that the enemy had broken down the main entrance of the fortress, [Toshimasa] hastened to the main entrance and did service, and repulsed the enemy. These acts were witnessed at the same place by Sakawa Hyō-ē Shirō and Taki Hiko-roku.[4] At the night-battle of the 25th day [1 August], when the enemy tried to break down the ent-

1. Terao Shigehiro.—A.
2. The fifth Iriki lord, Shigekatsu.—A.
3. Six o'clock in the afternoon.—A.
4. An interesting incident of this day is reported by Sakawa Hisakage to the Shimadzu lord thus: "When on the 6th month 22nd day [29th July] the enemy of southern Satsuma and men of the Shibuya attacked the fortress of Ikari-yama and a fierce battle was fought, and when the enemy had already broken down the fences on the rampart and invaded [the ground of the fortress], there issued from the sacred mount of the Nita temple two or three whistling arrows (kaburaya) and shot into the ranks of the enemy. As if [inspired by this manifestation of] divine will our forces were encouraged, and fought for victory, and the insurgents were defeated and retired."—A.

APPENDIX VI

rance [facing] the river, and our forces issued from the little gate [facing] the river with a view to dispersing the enemy, Toshimasa as [a leader of] these forces went out of the fortress and repulsed the enemy, as was witnessed by the present commander.[1] When, on the 29th day [5 August], the enemy retired from the fortress of Ikari-yama, and entrenched himself in the fortress of Fuji-no-ue, Iriki *in*, [Toshimasa] wished immediately to hasten to that field of battle and fight; but since he was commanded, as men were deficient in the fortress [of Ikari-yama], to guard [the latter], he did the guard [service]. Therefore, in order that at once, in accordance with the facts of his service at arms, [his merits] be reported,[2] and also that he be granted a certifying seal, he presents a brief statement thus.

"Ryaku-ō 2 y. 7 m.—d. [August 1339]."

"Sakawa Hisashige's '[I] do recognize' and monogram."

b. Reward

"Since it was excellent that you, as our ally,[3] guarded the fortress of Ikari-yama and rendered service at arms, the vacated land,[4] [namely,] the rice-land and land formerly held by Miyasato Rokuro-zhirō nyū-dō, of Satsuma kuni, are given to you in custody.[5] You shall hold them. We shall at the same time report the circumstances to Kyōto. Therefore, a statement is made thus.

"Ryaku-ō 2 y. 6 m. 23 d. (30 July 1339).

1. Sakawa Hisashige.—A.
2. To Takauji, in Kyōto.—A.
3. Mitaka, Supporter.
4. Kessho.—A.
5. Adzuke-oku, to give in trust, as though temporarily.—A

Hisakage,[1] *monogram*.
Michiaki,[2] *monogram*.
" Gon-Shuin Saburo-zhiro *dono*."

From: K. Asakawa, Documents of Iriki pp. 239–241.

5. FEUDAL OATH AND PLEDGE, 1481 A.D.

(WHEN the eleven-year old Shimadzu Takehisa, later Tadamasa, later Takamasa, succeeded his father Haruhisa, in 1474, the three kuni were still torn with strife and rebellion, and an arduous, tragic life awaited the youthful lord. It was probably on his attainment to majority that the following oaths were exchanged between him and Iriki-in Shigetoyo. Two months later, Takehisa and Shigetoyo's son Shigetsuna mutually swore oaths in nearly identical terms, which are omitted here. (K. A.)

A

" Oath.[3]

" That whatever changes may occur in the three kuni, I will, as heretofore, serve the lord with single [devotion] and without a second thought;

" That my mind has several times been expressed to Murata dono, and that there remains naught else; and

" That if a calumny or an evil report should [arise], I beg that [the lord] deign to tell me of it and I be permitted to utter my thought.

1. Hisakage also gave " in custody " to a Nobutoki pieces of land in Satsuma Kori.—A.
2. Possibly a miscopy of Naoaki; the character Nao and Michi are somewhat similar in cursive form.—A.
3. Ki-sho mon. In the original copy, the word ki is omitted. By this error the genealogist of the family was misled to think that the document was a responsive letter posterior to B (the two characters shomon of the mutilated word being the same as those of uke-bumi, for which see No. 22). That this is wrong may be inferred from the texts of the two documents. B was a response to A, not A to B.—A.

APPENDIX VI

" If these statements be false, [... (The names of deities) ...]¹

" Bun-mei 13 y, kanoto ushi,² 6 m. 23 d. [19 July 1481].

      Shimotsuke no kami, Shigetoyo.

" Respectfully presented to Murata Hizen no kami dono."³

B

" Pledge.⁴

" That I acknowledge [your oath] that whatever changes may occur in the three kuni you will entertain (kokorozasu) toward me single [devotion] ; and that I, too, will, whatever may happen in the world, consult you with single [faith] ;

" That I acknowledge [your statement] that you will be ever more loyal toward me ; and that since you are of that mind, I will regard your important affairs as my own, and we will mutually rely and be relied upon ; and

" That if, despite this understanding, a calumny or an evil report should arise, we would mutually explain ourselves with complete frankness.

" If these statements be false, the punishments of the
 the Ten-sho Dai-zhin Gu, of Ise,
 the Gon-gen of the three places of Kumano,
 the Great Bodhisattva Sho Hachiman.
 the Ten-man Ten-zhin, and
 the Great Myo-zhin Upper and Lower Suwa,
would be visited [upon me].

" Ten-myo 13 y., kanoto ushi, 6 m. 23 d. [19 July 1481].

---

1. The copyist omitted the conventional ending of the oath.—A.
2. The 38th of the sexagenary cycle.—A.
3. Murata Tsuneyasu, a chief councillor of Takehisa.—A.
4. Kei zho.—A.

FEUDAL LAW AND ADMINISTRATION IN SOUTH KYŪSHŪ

Takehisa, *monogram.*
" Iriki-in *dono.*"

From: K. Asakawa, Documents of Iriki pp. 295–296.

6. MILITARY SERVICE, 1576 AND C a. 1578 A. D.

A

" Apportionment of men (shu mori) at the time of the attack upon the fortress of Taka-baru, Ten-sho 4th year (1576).

" Assignment (of service) for the expedition :

" Those (holding) one chō[1] of ta : one man per cho, [meaning] two men, master and follower; providing their own rice for food. Besides, one attendant laborer (tsumefu) shall be provided by the churches and temples; 3 draught horses shall be assessed upon churches and temples.

" Next, the implements to be carried :
" 1 te-kabushi,[2] height 3,5 shaku, width 2,5 shaku; 1 log, 6 shaku long;

1 hoe (kuwa);	1 broad-axe (yoki);	1 sickle (kama);
1 saw (noko);	1 chisel (nomi);	1 adze (nada);
1 dirt-carrier (mokko);[3]		1 coil of rope.

" Those [holding more than] 2 chō : one man per chō, [meaning] three men, master and followers; providing their own rice food. 2 draught horses shall be assessed upon churches and temples, as well as widows.

" The aforesaid implements for work (fu-shin) shall be

1. Meaning more than one chō and less than two.—A. ta are wet rice fields. 1 chō at that time equal to 2.9408 acres, or 1.19016 ha. 1 koku equal to about 5 bushels, or 1.8 hl.—Ed.
2. Not clear; literally, " hand cover."—A.
3. Small rope-net with loops at the ends through which a pole may be thrust in for carrying on two men's shoulders. See E. S. Morse, Japan day by day, 1917. I, 117.—A.

APPENDIX VI

carried into the camps at the rate stated above for each chō of ta.

"Up to 100 chō and 1,000 chō, the assessments shall be [the proportionate multiples of that for] one chō of ta.

"Those who have no land (mu-ashi shu) shall provide between two of them one attendant laborer (tsume-fu)[1] being assessed (also ?) upon churches and temples, and widows; rice for food to be their own provision. Three draught horses shall be provided likewise by churches and temples.

"For thirty days during the expedition the rice for food shall be self-support; beyond thirty days, it will be provided by the authorities. Those (holding ta) between five and nine tan shall provide their own rice for food; those between one and four tan shall receive rice for food from the authorities.

"Ten-sho 4 y. 8 m. 1 d. (24 August 1576)."

(Notes in red added during the Tokugawa period quote opinions estimating the equivalents of a chō in terms of koku of rice: two say that the average of one chō of all grades of ta would be 35 koku, another gives 25 koku, and still another says) :—

"The taka of 8,000 chō was 240,000 koku. At this rate, 1,000 chō were 30,000 koku; 100 chō, 3,000 koku; 10 chō, 3000 koku; 1 chō, 30 koku. According to the record office, the assessment of taka followed from former times was as stated above; that is, at those times one chō was computed at 30 koku....."

From: K. Asakawa, Documents of Iriki, Yale University Press, 1928. pp. 315–316.

[1]. This would remind one of Charlemagne's capitularies ordering the poorer subjects to combine themselves in groups, so that each group should be able to equip and send one of the men "in hostem."—A.

VII

Some Notes on Early Japanese Marriage Institutions

by Kurt Singer

The quest for prehistoric beginnings and folk-lore survivals lies outside the scope of this book. But since no other Japanese institutions seem to have undergone greater changes since the Dawn of History than those concerned with the relations between the two sexes, it may be appropriate to devote this short Appendix to some of those ancient texts which point to the existence of modes of social life widely divergent from the legal and moral conceptions of later Japan, but perhaps still lingering on in some form or other, beneath the institutional surface even of modern Japan, by virtue of that enigmatic " retentive power " which, in spite of violent changes and the urge to modernize continues to characterize, more than any other trait, the social texture of this country.

This problem never seems to have been treated systematically by foreign writers. The views most widely held by Westerners are based on the sweeping statements of Prof. B. H. Chamberlain who observed some decades ago in his Introduction to the translation of the " Kojiki ":—" We are nowhere told of any wedding ceremonies except the giving of presents by the bride or her father, the probable reason being that no such ceremonies existed. Indeed late on into the Middle Ages cohabitation alone constituted matrimony—cohabitation often secret at first, but afterwards acknowledged, when, instead of going round under cover of night to visit his mistress, the young man brought her back publicly to his

APPENDIX VII

parent's house. Mistress, wife, and concubine were thus terms which were not distinguished, and the woman could naturally be discarded at any moment. She was indeed expected to remain faithful to the man with whom she had had more than a passing intimacy, but no reciprocal obligation bound him to her."[1] No reader of ancient Japanese literature will deny that some aspects of early and medieval social life are portrayed in these sentences with a fair degree of precision; but they do not contain the whole truth. If the student seeks for ceremonies similiar to the Christian marriage sacrament, and for legal restraints arising out of contractual obligations, he will indeed be disappointed. But if he begins to realize that outside the familiar framework of rites and standards which characterize modern Western civilization, it is possible to have more than arbitrariness, licence and disorder, he will be able to discover religious and moral conceptions of a different kind at the roots of customs that have contributed to create and to maintain social structures of immense stability.

* * *

Some parts of Japan must have been known by the Chinese of the Han period. But the first detailed account of conditions and customs of what was called by them the " country of the Wa," is contained in the Weichi, annals of the Wei dynasty written at the end of the third century A. D. The passages concerning the Wa seem to have been compiled from reports of official missions sent some decades before to Himiko, or Pimiko, queen of the Wa. This queen was formerly often identified with the Empress

---

[1]. Translation of " Ko-ji-ki," by B. H. Chamberlain, Second Edition, Kobe 1932, p. XLV.

Jingō who ruled according to official chronology at that time but to which recent historians have assigned a later reign.[1] It seems to be still an open question whether the country Great Yabadai over which Queen Himiko ruled, was situated in South Kyūshū and inhabited by Kumaso (Hayabito), probably of Indonesian origin, or identical with the Yamato region of central Japan, the cradle of the historical Japanese Empire. The latter thesis is upheld by some archaeologists. As, however, many of the customs recorded by the Weichi are not different from those of later Japanese and as on the other hand, the Imperial House had settled, according to the Sacred Books of Japan, first in South Kyūshū and was closely related to ruling clans living there, this difference of interpretation does not matter here.

On the family institutions of the country of the Wa, the Weichi says : " All men of high rank have four or five wives ; others two or three. The women are faithful and not jealous. The wives and children of those who break the laws, are confiscated, and for grave crimes the offender's families are exstirpated."[2] This is clearly the picture of a society based on the strictest of patriarchal principles, but a picture which perhaps is shaped, as in the case of Tacitus' Germania, by preconceptions and ideals of the foreign observer.

" The country was originally under the rule of kings, but in the course of seventy years under the control of these kings, the country became disorderly and civil wars

---

1. A. Wedemeyer : Japanische Frühgeschichte, Supplement der Mitteilungen der Deutschen Gesellschaft für Natur-und Völkerkunde Ostasiens Tokio 1930, pp. 24-55, 169-232.
2. Translation taken from Sansom, A Short Cultural History of Japan, p. 29.

APPENDIX VII

ensued. Amid the disturbance a woman was chosen to ascend the throne, who was entitled Himiko. The queen enchanted the people into submission by means of witchery. Though fairly advanced in age, she was unmarried. At the outset, she was able to govern the country successfully with the aid of her brother, but later, when she ascended to the throne, she could achieve nothing particularly notable. She had one thousand maids to wait upon her and only one man about her who humbly served her with food and drink."[1] After her death " a great mound was raised over her, more than a hundred paces in diameter, and over a thousand of her male and female attendants followed her in death. Then a king was raised to the throne, but the people would not obey him, and civil war broke out, not less than one thousand persons being slain. A girl of thirteen, relative of Himiko (or Pimiko) named Iyo (or Ichiyo), was then made queen and order was restored."[2]

Apparently there was no hereditary succession of kings, and the queens mentioned here were chosen not upon matriarchal principles, but because certain magical rites were in the possession of female " witches " or priestesses, and probably priestess-families. Even in later Japan government was called matsuri-goto, religious ceremony; mi-ko, priestesses or mediums were attached to a shrine, and preceded probably in many cases male priests (compare the story of the sacrificial festival of Jimmu Tennō when Michi no Omi no Mikoto is appointed by him Ruler of the Festival and granted the title of Idzu-hime, Dread Princess; Aston's Nihongi Vol. I, 1. 122). Princess Okinaga-tarashi,

---

1. Translation taken from Takekoshi, Economic Aspects of the Civilization of Japan, London 1930, pp.1-3.
2. Sansom's translation. A complete, carefully annotated German version is given by Professor Wedemeyer, l.c. pp. 171-185.

later Queen Jingō, then consort of Chuai Tennō herself was at times "divinely possessed" and delivered oracles at the playing of a flute by the Emperor (Chamberlain's Kojiki, pp. 277-8.) This is not the place to discuss Corean and the especially important Riu-Kiu parallels; but it may be mentioned that the art of "calling gods" into the soul of a medium is even now not extinct, but grows beneath the surface of town and village life wherever the police does not interfere. The astronomer Professor Percival Lowell has described such practices minutely in his "Occult Japan."

As not only the noble class of the Wa, but also commoners seem to have practised polygamy, in varying degrees, the problem arises how this state of affairs is compatible with a normal distribution of male and female births. The most probable solution appears to be that this race was continuously sending out young warriors and adventurers to other regions in order to find land, women and treasures for themselves. Perhaps the custom, known from many instances recorded in the Nihongi, to have the youngest son succeed to rulership and the inheritance, has sprung up from similar conditions. In fact, there have been various waves of invasions of the Japanese mainland by different sub-clans of the "children of the sun" imposing their rule to the indigenous population or to their forerunners, and marrying their wives. The last of these conquerors coming from Kyūshū, is according to Japanese tradition Jimmu Tennō, first Emperor of Yamato.

* * *

Jimmu Tennō, whose Japanese name is Kamu-yamato-ihare-biko, although he was not born in Yamato and had never resided in the region of Ihare proper, married a

APPENDIX VII

Satsuma princess before proceeding to central Japan, but there is no indication that she followed him there. A son he had by her accompanied him and was after his death slain by a younger son from his second wife, the " Chief Empress " I-suke-yori-hime, a daughter of Oho-mono-nushi-no-kami (a deity generally identified with Oho-kuni-nushi, the Great God of Izumo) by a princess from Mishima. It is the tradition of the way in which this second wedding came about with which we are here concerned. According to the Kojiki (Chamberlain pp. 176-180) the daughter of the Izumo God had been pointed out to the Emperor by his Augustness Oho-kume, chief of a warrior-clan that had followed Jimmu Tennō from Kyūshū.

" Hereupon seven beauteous maidens were out playing on the moor of Takasazhi, and I-suke-yori-hime was among them. His Augustness Ohokume, seeing I-suke-yori-hime, spoke to the Heavenly Sovereign in a Song, saying:

" *Seven maidens on the moor of Takasazhi in Yamato—which shall be interlaced?* "

Then I-suke-yori-hime was standing first among the beauteous maidens. Forthwith the Heavenly Sovereign, having looked at the beauteous maidens, and knowing in his august heart that I-suke-yori-hime was standing in the very front, replied by a song, saying:

" Even (after nought but) a fragment (-ary glimpse) I will intertwine the lovely (one) standing in the very front."

Then His Augustness Oho-kume informed I-suke-yori-hime of the Heavenly Sovereign's decree, whereupon she, seeing the slit sharp eyes of His Augustness Oho-kume sang in her astonishment, saying:

SOME NOTES ON EARLY JAPANESE MARRIAGE INSTITUTIONS

"..[1]
Wherefore the slit sharp eyes?"

Then His Augustness Oho-kume replied by a song, saying:

"*My slit sharp eyes (are) in order to find the maiden immediately.*"

So the maiden said that she would respectfully serve (the Heavenly Sovereign).[2] Hereupon[3] the house of Her Augustness[4] I-suke-yori-hime was on (the bank of) the River Sawi. The Heavenly Sovereign made a progress to the abode of I-suke-yori-hime, and augustly slept (there) one night.[5] (The reason why that river was called the River Sawi was that on the River's banks the mountain-lily-plant grew in abundance....).[6] Afterwards, when I-suke-yori-hime came and entered into the palace, the Heavenly Sovereign sang augustly saying:

"*In a damp hut on the reed-moor
having spread layer upon layer
of sedge mats, we two slept!*"

The meeting of young men and women arranged in rows, on a spot far from their houses and fields, the exchange of jesting verses between them, and the final choice of a spouse, recall the spring festivals of earliest China and their ethnological parallels from different races of South Eastern

---

1. The first lines of this short poem are so hopelessly unintelligible that the commentators are not even agreed as to how the syllables composing them should be divided into words. Ch.
2. Q.d., as his wife. Ch.
3. This initial expression is meaningless. Ch.
4. Having become the Emperor's consort, this Honorific title is now prefixed for the first time to her name. Ch.
5. Literally, "one sojourn." Ch.
6. Later addition?

APPENDIX VII

Asia... customs the social significance of which has been for the first time but exhaustively treated by Professor Marcel Granet in his Festivals and Songs of Ancient China (English translation, London 1932). The custom was observed in historic Japan under the name of uta-gaki, "line of song," or kagai, "alternate songs" and has been described by Professor Karl Florenz as follows in a paper La Poésie archaïque du Japon (Compte Rendu Analytique of the First International Congress of Far-Eastern Studies, Hanoi, 1902): "Two groups gathered in the public square and drawn up facing each other, sang alternately; the choruses were punctuated with improvisations. One singer stepped forward and improvised a song to which a member of the opposite group extemporized a response in the same manner. The youths used this means of declaring their love or paying court to her whom they had choosen. She replied in song. Sometimes it amounted to a battle of songs between the rival sides : the most famous is that which the Nihongi chronicles in the year 498, which took place between the eldest son of the Emperor Ninken (later Buretsu Tennō) and a noble named Shiki for the hand of Kage-hime. The nobility abandoned the custom of uta-gaki under the influence of Chinese ideas, but it has survived in the country in the bon-odori, the dances at the Buddhist festival of the dead." (cited by Granet, l. c. pp. 259–60) The strophic and antistrophic short wooing songs exchanged by the god Izanagi, the "Inviting Male," and the goddess Izanami, the "Inviting Female," before uniting themselves in the act of marriage and creating thereby the gods and islands of Japan (Kojiki, pp. 20–22), may represent an archaic specimen of such uta-gaki songs; or symbolic representations of them on a sacral stage where the legends of gods and heroes were enacted in the form of a kagura.

SOME NOTES ON EARLY JAPANESE MARRIAGE INSTITUTIONS

There can be scarcely a doubt that uta-gaki and Chinese spring festivals belong to a common type, and have originated from similar customs and beliefs. But obviously, the tales of the moor of Takasazhi and the meeting at Tsubaki-ichi belong to a later stage of history. The Chinese festivals that have left their traces in the Shih-king, are affairs of early villagers living in strict exogamy and bound by the most exacting of taboos. Their function is " to bring together in a brief communion people who ordinarily live apart, who are usually filled with antipathy for one another." (Granet l. c. p. 225) There was no freedom of choice among the young people who were allowed to meet here. " It would appear that the contests in which love was generated, far from being occasions for individual preference and for licence, simply brought together young people who were intended for one another and were under the necessity of loving one another." (p.203) Their marriages formed the most stable of social relationships, the young girl on leaving her parental house, being considered as a kind of hostage who entered the life of an antagonistic group, guaranteeing thereby the continuity of peaceful relations between the two sections of an exogamous pair of families. Such relations were often spoken of as alliances. " A girl is wedded once and for all." (p.197)

Japan, which is supposed, by not too well informed writers, to have built its civilization entirely upon Chinese models, has never accepted the exogamic basis of Chinese society. Where a principle of matrimonial relationships can be discovered from literary texts, it is endogamy of the strictest kind, at least in the ruling families, with some very important exceptions. Marriages with sisters from the same father but different mothers, with former consorts of the late father, with aunts, are quite common even in historic times. Whether it is permissible to consider the mythical tales of gods marrying their sisters from the same mother as testimonies of a former actual practice of incest in the strictest sense, remains doubtful. Professor Chamberlain and Sir George Sansom have drawn such inference from the fact that in ancient Japan, a wife is called imo, "younger sister." But in primitive societies "sister" does not necessarily mean the same kind of relationship as with us. Very often all the young men of a tribe belonging to the same age-group are called brother, all the young girls sister, and a similar custom prevailed also in ancient China from which early Japan has taken most of its family terminology. There, all cousins, of however distant relationship, were once called brothers (Granet, La Civilisation Chinoise, Paris 1929, p.185), and the father was terminologically not distinguished from paternal uncles. "Sister" would therefore be the appropriate name for all the young girls of a generation or group which were eligible for marriage. It is quite possible that in Japan, as in other families claiming to be Children of the Sun, incestuous marriage of the Egyptian type was practised, in order to preserve the purity of solar blood. The traditions however, that have been handed down to us do not warrant this belief. The marriage between Izanagi no Mikoto and Izanami no Mikoto proves neither more nor less than that between Zeus and his sister Hera. The earliest rulers of Yamato appear to marry, as will be shown elsewhere, into another family of Heavenly Deities, and the myth of the creation of children by Amaterasu Oho-Mikami and her brother Susanowo no Mikoto, extant in so many divergent versions that there is some presumption of a loss of its original signification, even resembles, in its intention, those exogamous marriages that were entered in order to establish peaceful relationships. . . . Is it pure chance that the marriage of Jimmu Tennō, descendant of Amaterasu Oho-Mikami, with a daughter of the Great God of Izumo, descendant of Susanowo no Mikoto, sounds like an earthly, and political, echo of that matrimonial Prologue in Heaven?

How all these questions may ever be answered, it is certain that the song-contests in the Kojiki and Nihongi are very remote from the rustic modes of life and sentiment that have crystallized in the Shih-king songs. Brides are here not pre-ordained, and marriages no alliances, dictated by communal traditions. The spirit of a court society, noticed already by Granet (Festivals etc. p.218) in the tale of Tsubaki-ichi, may be felt also in that of Takasazhi moor: it is the individual girl that is sought and conquered " in a kind of court of love." Young men and women are not homogeneous representatives of eligible companions, but definite individuals the personal characteristics of which appear in the songs of the Kojiki while the Shih-king songs move in the sphere of strict impersonality.

If it should be true that the Bon-odori of later Japan have sprung from the Uta-gaki, they must have preserved a pre-feudal pattern of rustic song-contests allied to primitive fertility cults, and often degenerating into licence and promiscuity after the decay of the social order in which they originated.[1]

*　　*　　*

---

1. Speaking of the uta-gaki, Mr. E. R. Kellogg, Spring and Autumn Fires in Japan, TASJ, XLVI, p.36 n.2., states: " Intimacy was promiscuous at these gatherings," citing Kata Totsudo, Nihon Fuzoku Shi, 1917, for his authority. Professor Granet seems to be disposed to consider such licentious forms of the festivals under review as signs of decay, and there is much to be said for this thesis.

APPENDIX VII

Another trait of the Jimmu Tennō legend that finds no parallels in Chinese spring festivals, is I-suke-yori-hime's living in a hut on the banks of a river known for its abundant flowers, apparently far from the house of her parents. It is here that the Emperor is united to her "for one sojourn" and that sons are procreated the names of whom are distinctly related to the element of water: their significant components are wi, well, and nuna-kawa, lagoon-river (or river-mouth ?). In China too, the spring festivals take place more often than not on the banks of rivers, and the hunting for wild flowers that grow there, is an ever-recurring theme of the corresponding songs. But we never hear of such solitary huts, and it would be indeed quite irrational to expect the stern villagers of those exogamous societies to allow their young daughters to dwell for some time far from the eye of their mothers. These are evidently manners of an aristocratic class. In fact we are told that in feudal China a young girl of one of the great families at the age of fifteen, at which she becomes marriagable and engaged, withdraws for a sojourn of three months to the Shrine of the Ancestors or, in the case of princely families, to the Temple of the Great Ancestress, in profound retirement (Granet, Civilisation Chinoise, p.407f). Such girls living in ritual seclusion are termed "pure maidens," and they are thought of as being given to perfect chastity. But the scholar to whom we are, in this field, deeper endebted than to any other sinologue, has observed that this term is found also in songs in which an assignment is made, and as other forms of pre-nuptial intercourse of the type of a trial-marriage are recorded on good authority, (Se-ma-ts'ien, tr. by Chavannes IV.282, 284–5), Granet ventures to think that the identification of "purity" and "chastity" was an invention of later ritualists and that at an earlier date the girl in retirement, guided by an experienced duegna or some other member of her family, was acting in the same way as those Chinese family daughters who were offered to a young man sent to the family of his mother in order to find a bride, according to the custom of primitive exogamy where the son of a certain mother has to marry the daughter of one of her sisters (or some of them) : it was hoped that " se tenant près de lui a titre de servante, elle fixerait son coeur." This may sound a rather hardy hypothesis, based not on texts or ritual, but on constructive analogy and on the principle of continuity only. But if the fairy tales of young princesses confined to a steep tower where no ray of sun is allowed to enter, but who conceive there in a miraculous way have had any foundation in the actual customs of an earlier age, such ritual retirements may have contributed to form those tales.

In Japanese literature allusions to temporary abodes of a quaint rustic charm, like that " damp hut on the reed-moor " of which Jimmu Tennō sings, are abundant. One of the first poems of the Manyōshū (I. 7) ascribed to Princess Nukada,[1] says :

I remember so well
The temporary lodge of Uji
Where once we stayed.
It had the roof thatched with grass
Mown in the autumn's field.

This may be the recollection of a romantic episode from the furtive beginnings of a great love, but it is equally possible that a hut of seclusion is meant (or alluded to), similar to that of the banks of the River Sawi. And if the Chinese analogy is valid, the " hereupon " of the Kojiki-

1. Translation by Tetsuzō Okada, Three Hundred Poems from the Manyōshū, Tokyo, Seikanzō, 1935, p. 3.

text, which Chamberlain considered as meaningless, would gain a very definite significance : it is after her engagement that the bride-to-be retires to a pure and purifying abode.

The reasons for undergoing a series of purification rites before entering the life of a married woman, are not far to seek, if we start from religious notions common to many early societies. Every transition from one mode of life to another, is held perilous and calls for rites by which the dangers of crossing the threshold of the still unknown are to be averted. This principle applies a fortiori to the consummation of marriage which is generally conceived as the entering into the female body of superhuman powers of demonic or divine origin, uncontrollable and perilous to the uninitiated and unprepared : antecedent purification, therefore, becomes necessary, not primarily in the later ritualistic meaning of cleansing, but of consecration, dedication, or " Weihung." The Kojiki and Nihongi furnish no text in proof of the thesis held by some English authors (Aston, Sansom) that the consummation of marriage was considered by the ancient Japanese as involving pollution. Such a " puritan " view which seems even to go further than biblical legislation (3 M. 15) must have been quite unintelligible to nations that practised sexual union in order to give fertility to the soil, and which scarcely thought of associating the consummation of marriage with occurrences implying ritual impurity (kegare). Phallic deities are, in Japan as elsewhere in the ancient world, identified with gods averting all kinds of evils (Sae no kami). The ancient Japanese built special huts for childbirth and for funerals, and they burnt them after the act implying impurity was over. If there had been in fact for similar reasons nuptial huts, as Aston inferred from the nuptial song of Susanowo no Mikoto and similar texts, we ought to hear of their being burnt after they had been used. But no text affords even a glimpse of such a custom, and where, as in the sacred island of Miyajima, childbirth and death are not tolerated by the stern Goddesses of the Shrine, we hear of no taboo prohibiting the consummation of marriage.

The house built by Izanagi no Mikoto and Izanami no Mikoto round the Heavenly Spear, according to the Kojiki, and the Many-fenced House built by Susanowo no Mikoto for his Bride of Suga, may have been originally nothing else than the future mansions of the newly married, necessarily new constructions like the new sacred Hall of Weaving erected for Amaterasu Oho-Mikami's celebration of the Festival of the First Fruits. It is the beginning of a new phase of life that demands the construction of a fresh abode, and the song of the Izumo god of marriage leaves no doubt that the function of the many fences is not to protect the country from pollution but rather to protect the bride from profane looks and rival aggression. But as gods and rulers, and palaces and shrines are designated by the same words (kami, miya), it is quite possible that in later times the houses built by kings of an earlier age and containing their wedding chamber (kumido, if Aston's hypothesis: Nihongi, Vo.. I p.54 n. 1 is correct), have become shrines connected with the ceremony of marriage or of initiation.

It is to the Temple of Ancestors or of the Great Ancestress that the Chinese bride-to-be of noble descent retires in order to be purified, and perhaps in order to be initiated; and as in Japan most ancient shrines are built near a river or pool, the " temporary huts " may have been near or within the shrine precincts. We know nothing about the rites performed in ancient China at these occasions. But it is perhaps not too fanciful to connect the Japanese legends of the impregnation of princesses by a " red arrow " or by a "serpent" with reminiscences of rites of initiation and sacral defloration by the priest as the representative of the god, rites later perverted into a ius primae noctis of the feudal lord, or symbolically surviving in the custom of putting the emblem of the god on the bed of the bride. It is by a red arrow that the Yamato consort of Jimmu Tennō is procreated; it is by showing a special kind of arrow that one of his former enemies Nigihayabi no Mikoto, is recognized by him as descendant of the Heavenly Deities: and it is from the family which worships Nigihayabi as ancestor, that the first consorts of Jimmu Tennō's next descendants are taken. According to an old Japanese tradition, to which Professor Kochi Doi has drawn my attention, in later times as well a new Emperor before acceding to the Throne was purified by a girl-priestess representing in this rite a Daughter of the Sea-God, like that to which the grandfather and father of Jimmu Tennō had been married. Such girls from noble families, among which the Nakatomi were the most important, lived for some time in sacral seclusion, near a river or a well, weaving garments that had to be used in the ceremony of clothing the new ruler. They alone knew the secret of tying and untying the inner girdle of his costume with a magical knot, and we may surmise that a kind of hieros gamos was enacted during this nocturnal cermony. It was by virtue of such rites that one of the descendants of the Heavenly Grandson, not necessarily the first-born, attained the status of a Living God, creating life and well-being: the accession to the throne coincided with the presentation of the First Fruits, born from the union of Sky and Earth, Fire and Water, Sun-Prince and Dragon-Princess.

* * *

SOME NOTES ON EARLY JAPANESE MARRIAGE INSTITUTIONS

Much of what has been said in the preceding pages may appear as a fragile web made from dim traditions, scanty texts and doubtful analogies, yet they may be helpful in finding an interpretation for one of the most curious passages of the Kojiki. Emperor Suinin, son of Emperor Sūjin who may have been a contemporary of Queen Himiko of Yabadai, and whose son may have reigned in the second half of the third century A. D., had married Princess Sahaji, daughter of King Hiko-imasu who had been a half-brother of Emperor Sūjin. Sahaji-bime, or Saho-bime, was therefore a cousin of her husband Emperor Suinin. and through her father of Imperial lineage. " When this Heavenly Sovereign made Saho-bime his Empress, Her Augustness Saho-bime's elder brother, King Saho-biko, asked his younger sister, saying : 'Which is dearer (to thee), thine elder brother or thy husband ?' She replied, saying : 'My elder brother is dearer.' Then King Saho-biko conspired, saying : 'If I be truly dearer to thee, let me and thee rule the empire.' " Here indeed we have possibly a faint trace of joint rule of brother and sister, if not of incestuous marriages in ruling families, for Saho-biko and Saho-bime were of the same father and the same mother. Warned by a dream in which the Empress is symbolized by a serpent, the Emperor questions her. She confesses the plot, but decides to share the fate of her brother, flees to the bulwark where he is besieged, and is slain with him. In vain the Emperor " who could not restrain (his pity for) the Empress, who was pregnant and whom he had loved for now three years " tries to take her back by force. The Empress, deludes the messengers by a kind of witchery, but delivers the new-born child.

" Again did the Heavenly Sovereign cause the Empress to be told saying : ' A child's name must be given by the mother: by what august name shall this child be called?' And again he caused her to be asked: 'How shall he be reared?' She replied saying: 'He must be reared by taking an august mother and fixing on old bathing women and young bathing women.' So he was respectfully reared in accordance with the Empress's instructions. Again he asked the Empress, saying: 'Who shall loosen the fresh small pendant which thou didst make fast?' She replied, saying: 'It were proper that Ye-hime and Oto-hime, daughters of King Tatasu-michi-no-ushi prince of Taniha, should serve thee, for these two queens are of unsullied parentage.' So at last (the Heavenly Sovereign) slew King Saho-biko, and his younger sister followed him."" (Chamberlain's Kojiki, pp. 228-31)

Although there is something balladesque about this story, and though its vividness may be partly explained by the possibility that the account in the Kojiki was taken from a dramatic representation in a Kagura scene, there can be no doubt that it gives a true picture of customs totally different from those of the eighth century when the Kojiki was compiled. An Imperial Consort, even one involved in the most atrocious form of treason, has still the right to decide the name of the Emperor's child, and is consulted about her successors near the Emperor. These must be taken from a certain group women eligible, according to the text of Chamberlain's translation, because being " of unsullied parentage "; but the literal translation is, as he himself observes : " pure subjects "—which recalls the term denoting those Chinese young girls living in pre-nuptial retirement. They alone are entitled to tie and to loosen the " inner girdle," midzu no wo-himo, translated by " fresh small pendant " by Chamberlain. In later times lovers separated for some time used to promise each other that no one else would loosen this inner girdle. But it would seem that in the story of Saho-bime more than mere dispensation from this graceful obligation is asked for.

The text does not allow us to decide whether the group of eligible maidens was determined by the principle of endogamy. In fact, the new consorts taken according to the counsel of the first Empress, were descendants of the same Emperor (Kaikua) as Saho-bime and granddaughters of the same half-brother of Emperor Sūijin, Hiko-imasu, but from another wife named Okinaga-no-midzu-yori-hime. This was a daughter of the "Heavenly God of Mikage," a deity known only as being worshipped by a family of lower Shintō priests (hafuri) in Afumi, where also a place named Okinaga existed. King Hiko-imasu, father of Saho-bime and her successors, is a son of Oke-tsu-hime, from the family of the Wani no Omi, a name recalling the "crocodile" (wani) and therefore the legend of the grandmother of Jimmu Tennō showing her nature as daughter of the Sea-Dragon-King by appearing in the form of this mythical animal; provided that Wani is not derived from a Chinese family name Wang, as in the later case of Wani Kishi, ancestor of the Fumi no Obito, a descendant of Emperor Kao Ti, of the earlier Han dynasty who is said to have come from Korea during the reign of Emperor Ojin, 378 or 379 A.D., and introduced Chinese characters and literature to Japan. (Wedemeyer, l.c. p.57)

Among the descendants of Hiko-imasu and Okinaga-no-midzu-yori-hime, there are several remarkable personalities. His granddaughter Hibasu-hime, identical with Ye-hime in the text cited, is mother of Emperor Keiko and therefore grandmother of Yamato-dake, and also mother of Yamato-hime, famous priestess of Ise who assists her nephew by lending him her "garment and skirt" (Kojiki, p.249).

But the most illustrious member of this family is in a later generation, in paternal line, Princess Okinaga-tarashi, the later Jingō Kōgō, Warrior-Empress and Magician Priestess, who from her mother's side claims descent from the Corean ruler-deity Ama-no-hi-boko. Her son is the Emperor Ōjin, later identified with the war-god Hachiman, according to a legend of the Japanese middle-ages half man, half dragon, a god from Usa in North-Kyūshū, not appearing in Kojiki or Nihongi, and according to De Visser another form of the father or grandfather of Jimmu Tennō, and therefore husband or son, or both, of a Dragon Princess of the Sea.

Before we leave this illustrious family, we may point to some characteristic name-givings occurring in the story of Emperor Ōjin, whose Japanese name is Homuda Wake. According to the Kojiki, he had married three daughters of Homuda-no-ma-waka-no-mikoto. Homuda was a place-name in Kahachi, and the identity of name is certainly not fortuitous. The bearer of the name Homuda Wake whoever he may have been, must have been adopted into the family of his wives, provided he had not married his own sisters. The Nihongi has preserved another version according to which this prince bore a name that was not given him at his birth, but acquired later, by virtue of a kind of alliance. Here the father of Emperor Ōjin's wives is not mentioned, but he receives his name Homuda by way of exchange with the Great God of Ke-hi (according to the reading of Wedemeyer, Aston has Tsutsuhi) in Tsunoga in Koshi, a deity whom he, accompanied by the chancellor Take Uchi no Sukune, was sent to worship by his mother. According to Professor Wedemeyer, it is probable that Tsunuga had specially strong relations with the family of Jingö Kōgō, who started from here when she left central

Japan to join her husband in Kyūshū. The bay of Kehi was probably the place where Ama-no-hiboko and his followers originally landed. (l.c. p.155f) The former name of the prince is said to have been Izasa-wake. We never hear that the Great God of Kehi was later called Izasa, but we know that the long-sword belonging to the "divine treasures" brought over by Ama-no-hiboko, bore just this name. On the other hand it is interesting to learn that the Great Deity of Kehi was female. She is called Oho-ke-tsu Ohokami, a name identified by Professor Wedemeyer with Oho-ge-tsu-hime, Ukemochi no kami, Toyo-uke-bime, daughter of Izanagi and Izanami, and wife of Oho-toshi-no Kami, son of the Great God of Izumo according to later genealogies. To-day she is worshipped at the second of the Great Shrines of Ise (Gegū), and has become one of the chief goddesses of this country. We are not concerned here with the relationships between deities of the Japan sea facing Corea and those of Yamato—relationships which appear to be much closer and more intricate than the trisection introduced by Chamberlain into Kyūshū-, Izumo-, and Yamato-cults would indicate. Enough has been said to show that uterine and matrimonial connexions, symbolized or reinforced by cultic relations with female deities are granted a more important place in these traditions centering round a ruler of the second half of the fourth century, than should be expected in a strictly patriarchal family system. But it ought also not be forgotten that the family of Jingō Kōgō claims not only descent from the Heavenly grandson of the Sungoddess of Japan, but also from a Corean prince identified with a solar deity and through him from that half historical, half mythical, Tajimamori who was sent by Emperor Suinin westward, in order to bring him Fruits of Eternal Life. He returned

APPENDIX VII

after an absence of twelve years with what we, following Kochi Doi, may well suppose to have been a symbolic representation of the Tree of Life in the form used in Westasiatic cults: a spear garlanded with fruits and leaves; but he also appears in these legends as a late descendant of those solar heroes starting westwards like Gilgamesh and Herakles to fetch the Plant of Life. We are treading a soil on which myth and fact, legend and history are not yet separated by a hard and fast demarcation line: myth remains plastic, life itself full of divine meaning.

* * *

One of the most ancient Japanese poems, embedded in the Kojiki shows the God Yachihoko wooing Princess Nunakawa in the land of Koshi, under the cover of night. He asks to be admitted into her room, but has to return as the birds of dawn are crowing; it is only next night that he will be united to his mistress.[1] Yachihoko is one of the names of the Great God of Izumo; it may mean "Eight-Thousand Spears," but there is room for the doubt whether hoko, spear, does not stand here, as in other instances of mythical language, for a phallic symbol. Nunakawa is supposed to be a place name in Echigo, a province on the sea of Japan, northwards from Izumo, like Koshi. Yet it may be significant that the same word occurs in the name of a son of Jimmu Tennō; it denotes according to Chamberlain " lagoon river "—a kind of locality often connected with certain purification rites which seem to have taken place at the mouths of rivers where fresh-and saltwater are mingling.

A variant of this poetical dialogue is preserved in the Nihongi, as songs exchanged by the Imperial Prince Magari

1. Chamberlain's Kojiki, pp. 90–94.

no Ohine and the Imperial Princess Kasuga, daughter of Emperor Ninken, in the year A.D. 513.[1] The prince, says the Nihongi, " had in person betrothed himself to her," i.e. without an " intermediator "; he has passed the night in her room and if he has to blame the cock it is only because its crowing announces the hour of parting. The theme here resembles that of the " Taglieder " of the German minstrels, and the style of the song is called " elegant " by the compiler of the Records; whereas the Yachihoko songs of the Kojiki are classed as " divine words." We have left the sphere of myth and ritual for that of courtly romance, but the lovers of the early sixth century are still repeating the words of their divine models, and perhaps a faint echo of archaic customs may be heard lingering on in those lines that speak of " the august girdle of small pattern, girded on by our Great Lord who rules peacefully, hanging down in a knot." Aston thought that these words had been introduced there only for the sake of a literary kind of word-play—which would be farfetched indeed if those words did not contain an allusion to the " inner girdle," quite appropriate to this occasion. The mentioning of Mount Mimoro, closely connected with the Yamato cult of the Great God of Izumo, as well as the epithet " secluded " given to the name of the river Hatsuse may also have conveyed particular associations to those initiated into princely marriage rites.

The Manyōshū (Book XIII, part II) contains two more songs of this type—one in which the lover, after a wearisome journey, expresses his determination to enter the house of his mistress, though day is already dawning (No. 178, F.V. Dickins, Primitive & Mediaeval Japanese Texts, p.

---

1. Aston's Nihongi, Vol. II. pp. 9-11.

APPENDIX VII

201-2), and another where the girl describes her embarassing situation:

> *within our homeplace*
> *my mother sleepeth she*
>   *from doorway furthest,*
> *my father sleepeth he*
>   *to doorway nearest—*
> *and if my side he leaveth*
>   *my mother knoweth*
> *and if the house he leaveth*
>   *my father knoweth—*

(ib. No. 179, p. 203)

This second song at least leaves no doubt that the lover is secretly visiting his mistress at the house of her parents. This form of prenuptial intercourse is still practised by many tribes of Formosa, according to Florenz (Nihongi, 1901, p.264 n.30), but it is by no means restricted to primitive races. We learn from Plutarch (Lycurgus c.15) that in Sparta young men used to visit their wives only at night, sometimes for years, even after children had been born to them, and that they continued to dwell in the men's camp. The bride had been taken by force from the house of her parents, and was apparently living in a home of her own. Such customs correspond to a state of strife and conquest carried on by small bands of warrior invaders unable to marry according to the rules of endogamy or exogamy. The literary sources of Japan do not tell of marriage by rape nor of common dwelling places of warriors; but it is said that even to this day the young men of some Japanese villages (wakamono-kumiai) are living together for several years in a kind of "men's house."

If this should prove to be a relic of ancient customs, lasting on into times where marriage by rape was no more feasible, the nightly calls of lovers at the home of their mistresses could be easily explained, as a kind of compromise with the parents of the girl who must have been reluctant to forego the labour done by a daughter and could not be compensated by a kind of "Laban's marriage," as practised even now in some parts of Japan in rural communities where the future husband of a daughter has to serve for a certain period in the household of his father-in-law. In European villages "trial-nights" of prenuptial intercourse often precede marriage proper. The extension of such practices over an indefinite period in Japan may be due to several social circumstances, but also to the preference given by the Japanese to forms of social life that allow the fullest scope compatible with the ultimate interests of the nation, to the factors of plasticity and flexibility.

This tendency may also have been responsible for the curious fact that such customs which seem to belong to the sphere of archaic life or have been early restricted in other countries to rural areas, can be observed in the uppermost classes of the most refined epoch of Japanese civilization: the court society of the Heian epoch.

* * *

For the study of social relationships in that period, no other book seems to give ampler information than the Ochikubo Monogatari, a novel dealing with the fairy-tale theme of the wicked stepmother and the final triumph of the lovely, modest and all-forgiving girl. The book was probably written between A.D. 970 and 1000, but some detail of state administration indicates that the events of the narrative ought to be located in the ninth century, i.e. some decades after the

APPENDIX VII

transfer of the Capital from Nara to Heian, the later Kyōto.

The society depicted here is strongly centred around the Throne, whose favour or disfavour determines the rise and fall of individuals and families more than time-honoured claims of clans and estates. No rigid tie links office and rank to family and birth. Commoners beginning their career as bodyguard soldiers and personal attendants like the Tachihiki of this story, may if their former masters are gaining court influence, rise to the post of a Provincial Governor, a post held in other cases by sons of court nobles of high rank; and a former servant girl, like Emon, who has lived in a kind of marriage with this upstart since the days of his humbler service, may then find herself the wife of a high local official. If we may follow the very attractive hypothesis of Mr. Whitehouse to whom we owe an English version of this novel, the Ochikubo Monogatari has been written by a woman of this class. There are in fact many passages which point to female authorship while others make it quite improbable that a lady of noble birth should have written such a book. It may be added that the view of genteel life is taken from a point slightly below the social horizon, while the author appears to be quite at home and plainly enjoying herself in the servant's quarter, never tired in extolling the fidelity, resourcefulness and ability of this class in aiding their incomparably charming and well-meaning masters and mistresses, who would be quite unable to find by their own means a way out of their endless troubles in a world of fiendish intrigue and spiteful rivalries. The scene where Emon, promoted to the position of chief maid-servant of a grand house, meets her former colleagues who have now become her subordinates, looks like a typical day-dream of such a girl. The book although starting from the fairy-tale motive of the cruel stepmother is remarkable for its curious blend of uncanny directness, cheerful cynicim, vague sentimentality and crude joking. It should give some hint on the social origins of the Realistic Novel.

Here we are interested only in the matrimonial relationships as depicted by the unknown authoress. There are two ways in which such relationships may be entered into by men and women of the nobility : either by employing a middleman (nakōdo), as done in modern Japan by all classes, but a middleman at that time not necessarily of equal status, possibly only a quite plebeian fostermother ; or, after a preliminary exchange of letters for some time, by secretly invading the sleeping-room of the future bride in the house of her parents. The second way may be chosen even if the girl happens to be a daughter of a minister of state. In both cases it seems to be customary for the Lady to stay in the home of her parents until her Lord deigns to lead her to his own mansion. If he does not appear in the third night, the engagement even if it should have been formal, is considered as void. And afterwards also, even if there has been formal betrothal, the Lord is free to continue or discontinue his relations with the Lady. The ceremonial difference between the two modes seems to be little more than this, that the Lord is ushered in by the attendants of the Lady's house in the one case, but that he has to find his own way in unnoticed in the other. In both cases he is expected to leave the house before dawn at the first two visits. Only at the third morning he is expected to stay until broad daylight, and he is then handed a washing basin and given a meal of rice gruel. It is customary to exchange letters after he has left the Lady. There are thus surviving traces of pre-nuptial " trial-nights," and the demarcation line between a transitional love affair and a life-long marriage is less clearly drawn than in any other great civilization. But there are customary and ceremonial rules of the game, and whether the Lord is free to discontinue his calls depends obviously on the degree of his social influence and that of his family. In modern Japan similar dynamic conditions seem to decide the question if a husband is entitled to send the woman who has been his wife for a shorter or longer period, to the house of her parents, litigation in court being ruled out by custom in most of these cases. Thus far, gentilicial organization has retained its power.

Among the inferior classes or in the relations between noblemen and members of those classes, Chamberlain's formula " cohabitation alone constituted marriage " is applicable without reserve. The Lord of the story, after intruding rather rudely into the Lady's sleeping-room without her consent and conversing with her for the first time, seems to regret that he has treated her " as an ordinary woman." On the other hand, even attendants of the status of Emon and her lover begin their relations by exchanging letters for several years. Most of these letters contained poems, a custom recalling, once more, the uta-gaki of archaic times.

*　　*　　*

As a last but signal instance of that " retentive power " which according to the happy phrase of late Count Okuma, characterizes Japanese society and civilization, the " House Communities " or " Joint Undivided Families " of Hida, Gifu Prefecture, may be described here, from a Japanese report dated 1888:

" One of their most curious customs is that they live together in the same house. They do not care to separate from the family (kanai) and go to housekeeping for themselves as younger sons and daughters usually do. There are therefore, in each family many adults. The family of Mr. Yoheiji, in Kitani kuni, consists of thirty persons, that of Mr. Otsuka, of thirty-seven; and so on. Still, among so many persons, there are usually only two or three married couples. For, except in the case of the heir apparent (sōzoku-nin), no lawful marriages are made by the sons or the daughters; they have illicit relations with those of other families. One result is that the number of members of the family increases in proportion to the numbers of daughters it contains, for a child of such an illicit relation is brought up by the mother in her family. The head of the family supplies only the child's food; the mother must supply everything else; though if she cannot provide the father assists. Formerly when a birth occurred, and notice was sent, as required by law, to the Kōchō (head official of a mura under the Meiji Government), the child was represented to be that of the married son or daughter in whom the succession was vested (sōzoku-nin). But recently the Kōchō, beginning to think that the children of these couples were very numerous, discovered the truth. He then advised them to put an end to such customs and to contract lawful marriages, and to give up the practice of living together as one family and either establish separate homes or emigrate to other provinces. But these are their ancient customs, and in spite of the advice of the Kōchō, they have not changed them."[1]

We find here a very instructive combination of strong patriarchal authority and of forms of matrimonial rela-

[1]. Notes on Land Tenure and Local Institutions in Old Japan, edited from Posthumous Papers of Dr. D.B. Simmons by H. John Wigmore (published by the Asiatic Society of Japan, 1891), pp.217–220, based on an account by M. Fujimori in Tokyo Jinrui Gak-kwi Zasshi (Bulletin of the Tokyo

APPENDIX VII

tionships which one might be tempted wrongly to call " matriarchal " or " matrilinear." The custom of bringing up children in the home of the mother, is here correlative not with the absence of the idea of marriage proper, but of its realization in its strictest form (in the case of the heir), and not with general licentiousness but with the centralisation of the will and property of the family in one hand. It is interesting to note that the heir apparent is not necessarily a man, and that children of other members of the family are in this case represented as children of the female sōzoku-nin.

As " house-communities " of a similar kind, e.g. the Serbian " zadruga," have been often interpreted as survivals from an imaginary very primitive, sexually anarchic and economically communistic stage of civilization, it may be worth while noticing that, in Hida, the organization of work and the distribution of its products is far from being consonant with the ideas of egalitarian socialism.

" The head of the family once a year gives a suit of summer clothes, made of hemp and coloured with indigo, to each member of the family. There are certain days, however, when the latter work for themselves, keeping whatever they can earn. These are, in spring-time, one day in every seven, and in summertime, one in every five. So that a thrifty person can earn enough to provide for himself a great many things besides the clothes given by the head of the family. On the other hand, a thriftless person will earn very little more, and the result is that, among the members of the same family, some may be rich and others poor." (p. 219) Here, too, we are confronted with a

Anthropological Society), Vol. III, July 1888. The passages cited above are translations by Dr. Simmons and Mr. Wigmore of parts of Mr. Fujimori's paper.

singularly bold combination of opposite principles : social solidarity and individual responsibility, planned economy (for the necessaries), and personal initiative (for the conveniences of life). This must have been invented by men of great constructive abilities.

The present-day villagers of those Hida boroughs are said to spring from members of the Heike-clan which took refuge in these mountain wildernesses after their defeat at the hands of the Genji-warriors in the second half of the twelfth century. As the architect Professor Bruno Taut has observed recently, their houses differ widely from later Japanese buildings ; while their tectonical logic is the same as that of medieval European constructions. Whether these architectural and social peculiarities are due to the special hardships these fugitives had to encounter on the barren soil of their mountain asylums, or whether we may be allowed to take them for remainders of older forms of life tenaciously adhered to by these descendants of a clan of the greatest valour and distinction, are questions which the writer of these notes does not undertake to answer.

LIST OF PLATES

1. *Tamamushi House-altar.* Beginning of the 7th century. Probably of Corean origin; according to tradition used by Empress Suiko; now in the Hōryuji Temple, near Nara. Height 233 cm.
   (Hōryuji Ōkagami)

2. *Hokkedo (Sangatsudo),* of the Tōdaiji Temple in Nara. Built in 733 by Emperor Shōmu for the monk Rōben; belonging to the Tōdaiji Temple since 752. The Hall of Devotees was added in the Kamakura Period, the older portions being recognizable by a slight entasis of the columns and massive brackets. Dimensions 60.5 × 83.5 shaku (1 shaku about 1 ft.).
   (Tōdaiji Ōkagami)

3-4. *Enjoying dance, music and scenery.* Part of the Kako-genzai ingwakyō, Tempyō Era (725–794). This sūtra was written by a calligrapher of the Nara court; the painter is unknown; he probably followed a Chinese model perhaps showing traces of the style peculiar to the Era of the Six Dynasties. Owner H.I.H. Prince Kuni.
   (Original Photograph)

5. *Young girls playing Japanese chess and admiring a cherry-tree.* Part of the Genji Monogatari Scroll. Painter unknown; traditionally ascribed to Fujiwara (or Kasuga) Takayoshi. Middle of the 12th century. Owner Marquis Tokugawa.

   The scene is taken from the chapter " Bamboo-River " (Takegawa), the young girls being daughters of Prince Genji's adopted daughter Tamakatsura. Compare Mr. Arthur Waley's translation of the passage reproduced on pp. 121 sq. of this book.
   (Original Photograph)

6. *Nightly Visit.* From the same scroll. The scene is taken from the chapter " The Eastern House " (Azumaya); com-

LIST OF PLATES

pare Mr. Arthur Waley's translation in "The Lady of the Boat," The Tale of Genji Vol. VI pp. 108–9. Kaoru, passing as Prince Genji's son from Nyosan, but in reality her child from Genji's younger friend Kashiwagi, visits Ukifune, illegitimate daughter of Genji's half-brother Prince Hachi, in order to carry her off.

(Original Photograph)

7. *Common people at a well.* Part of the Fan-sutra. Painter unknown. Second half of the 12th century. Owned by the Shitennōji Temple in Osaka.

(Original Photograph)

8–10. *Scenes of Devotion.* Part of the Heike-sūtra, written between 1163 and 1167 by members of the Heike-clan. The scenes are chosen from ch. 1, 13 and 21 of the Lotos Sūtra. Owned by the Itsukushima Shrine, Miyajima.

(Yamato-e Dōko Kwai)

11. *Courtlady serving a meal.* Part of the Murasaki Shikibu Scroll, painted by Fujiwara Nobuzane (1167–1268), according to Professor Fukui before the year 1206. The scroll illustrates scenes from Murasaki Shikibu's diary. Owner H.I.H. Prince Takamatsu.

(Original Photograph)

12. *Empress Rinko with the young prince.* Part of the Murasaki Shikibu Scroll owned by Mr. T. Masuda; from the same painter.

(Original Photograph)

13. *The end of a banquet.* Part of the Murasaki Shikibu Scroll owned by Mr. T. Masuda. See pp. 129 sq. of this book.

(Original Photograph)

14. *Portrait of Kakino-moto-no Hitomaro* (about 662–710 A.D.) From the Sanjū-rokka-sen (Thirty-six poets); formerly ascribed to Nobuzane. First half of the 13th century. Owner Mr. K. Morikawa, Aichi Prefecture.

(Yamato-e Dōko Kwai)

LIST OF PLATES

15. *Scene of confusion following upon the burning of the Palace.* From the Heike Monogatari Scroll, traditionally ascribed to Keion. Second half of the 13th century. Owned by the Boston Museum of Fine Arts.
(Yamato-e Dōko Kwai)

16. *Triumphant warriors.* From the same scroll.
(Yamato-e Dōko Kwai)

17. *Saigyō, then samurai of medium rank, conversing with his wife in the night before leaving his house in order to become a hermit.* Part of the Saigyō Monogatari Scroll, by an unknown painter. Second half of the 13th century. Owner Prince Y. Tokugawa, Aichi Prefecture.
(Yamato-e Dōko Kwai)

18. *The monk Saigyō in meditation.* Part of the Saigyō Monogatari Scroll owned by Mr. M. Ohara. Okayama Prefecture.
(Yamato-e Dōko Kwai)

19. *Young monks and novices playing Japanese chess.* From the same scroll.
(Yamato-e Dōko Kwai)

20. *Banquet of a Chikuzen warrior.* Part of the Ippen Shōnin Eden, painted by En-i in 1299. Owner Kwan-ki-kōji Temple in Kyōto. From Vol. IV.
(Original Photograph)

21. *Market at Fukuoka in Bizen.* From the same scroll, Vol. IV.
(Original Photograph)

22. *Autumn fields in the Northern Provinces.* From the same scroll, Vol. VIII.
(Original Photograph)

23. *Festival given in honour of Shōnin at the Itsukushima Shrine, with Bugaku Dance.* From the same scroll, Vol. X.
(Original Photograph)

24. *Feeding the poor at Taemadera Temple in Yamato.* From the same scroll, Vol. VIII.
(Original Photograph)

LIST OF PLATES

25. *Pan-maker* (Imoji). Part of the Tōhoku-in Uta-awase, painted in the first half of the 15th century, probably by Emperor Hanazono. Owned formerly by the Manshuin, now by the Imperial Household Museum, Ueno, Tokyo.

(Yamato-e Dōkō Kwai)

26. *Blacksmith.* From the same scroll.

(Yamato-e Dōkō Kwai)

27. *The Empress receiving her younger sister.* Part of the Makura no Sōshi scroll, painted perhaps by Princess Shinko, daughter of Emperor Fushimi. First half of the 14th century. Owner Marquis Asano.

(Yamato-e Dōkō Kwai)

28. *Banquet after the service in honour of the last Regent* (Kwanpaku). From the same scroll.

(Yamato-e Dōkō Kwai)

29. *Kyōto street scenes.* Part of the Rakuchū-rakugai-dzu-byōbu, a screen with pictures from "In- and Outside Kyōto," painted by Kano Eitoku in 1574. Owner Count K. Uesugi. As the screen, according to Professor Fukui, was painted from memory, the scenes depicted may correspond to an earlier date.

(Original Photograph)

30. *The Kyōto residence of the Hosokawa Daimyō.* From the same screen.

(Original Photograph)

31. *Mansion, near the Kamo River, of the Great Minister of the Right* (Udaijin). From the Ise Monogatari Jo, painted by Sōtatsu in the Era Kahei (1624–1643). Owner Mr. T. Masuda.

(Original Photograph)

32. *Noblemen conversing at Sumiyoshi Shrine.* From the same album.

(Original Photograph)

33. *The Deserted House.* From the same album.

(Original Photograph)

LIST OF PLATES

Frontispiece: *Longing for the Capital while crossing the Sumida River.* From the same album.

NOTE

All data included in the above list are based on notes which Professor R. Fukui, of Tōhoku Imperial University, Sendai, has kindly put at the disposal of the Editor. For any mistakes in interpreting these notes, the Editor alone in responsible. He feels also greatly obliged to Professor Fukui for the permission to reproduce Nos. 3-7, 11-13, 20-24, 29-33 from orginal photographs in possession of the Seminary of Japanese Art History of Tōhoku Imperial University. Of these, the scenes from the Ippen Shōnin Scroll are here reproduced for the first time, while those of Sōtatsu's Ise Monogatari had been accessible only in a private print.

For reasons of his own, the Publisher of this book has replaced a number of these original photography by materials made available through the courtesy of the Imperial Art Research Institute in Tokyo.

K. S.

PLATE 1

PLATE 2

PLATE 3

PLATE 4

PLATE 5

PLATE 6

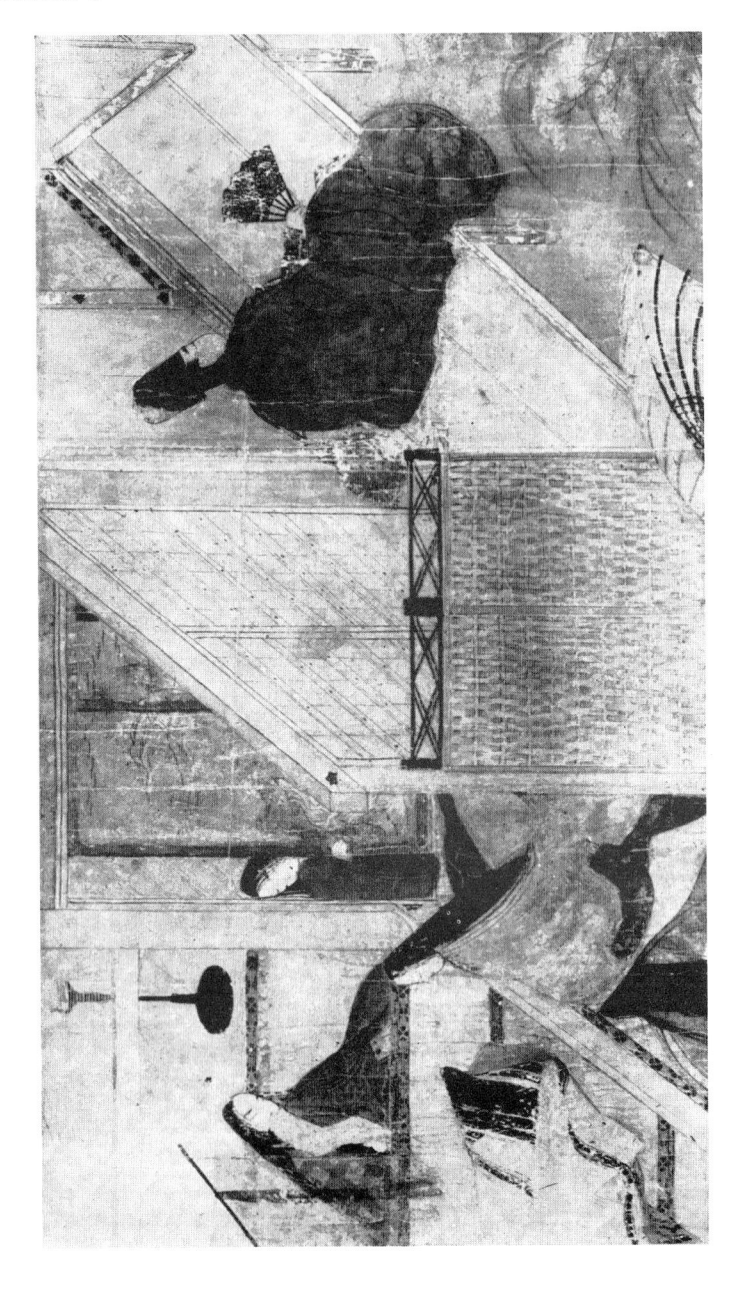

PLATE 7

PLATE 8

妙法蓮華經序品第一

如是我聞一時佛住
王舍城耆闍崛山中
與大比丘眾萬二千人俱
皆是阿羅漢諸漏已盡
⋯⋯
阿若憍陳如摩訶迦葉
⋯⋯迦葉那提迦葉舍利⋯⋯

PLATE 9

PLATE 10

PLATE 11

PLATE 12

PLATE 13

PLATE 14

PLATE 15

PLATE 16

PLATE 17

PLATE 18

PLATE 19

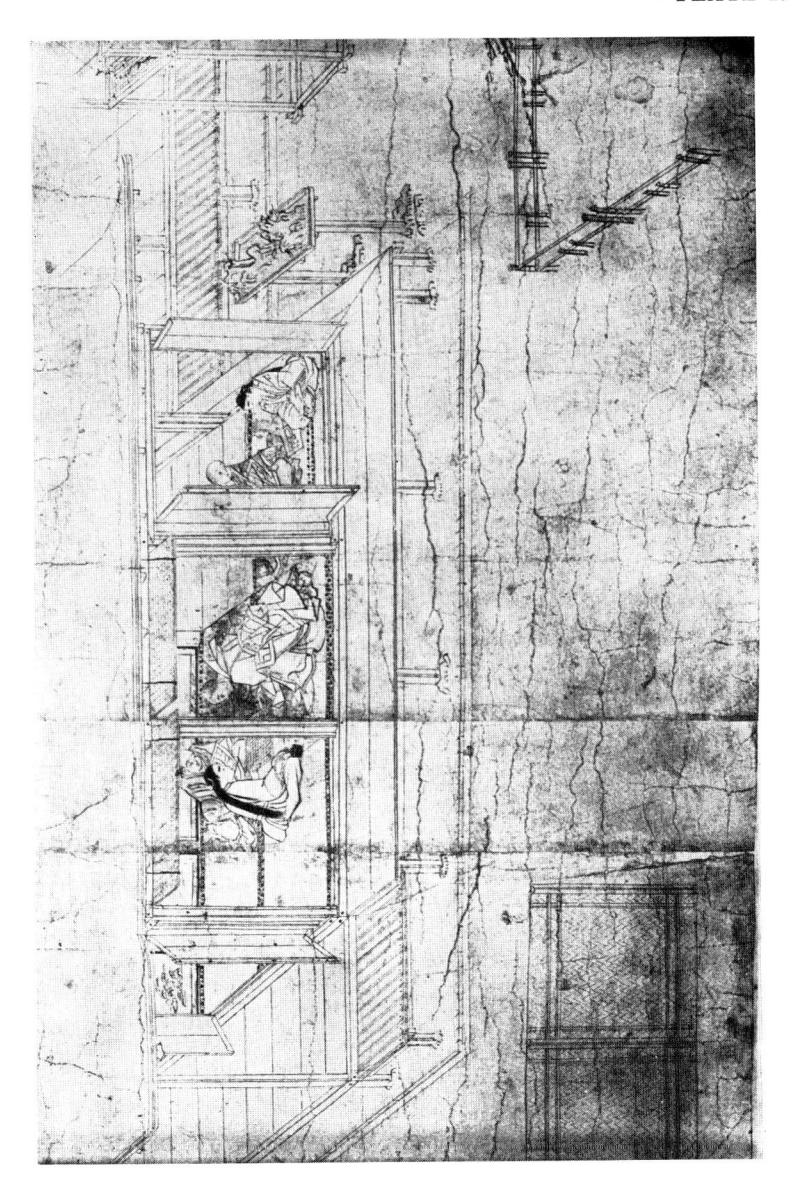

PLATE 20

PLATE 21

PLATE 22

PLATE 23

PLATE 24

PLATE 25

PLATE 26

PLATE 27

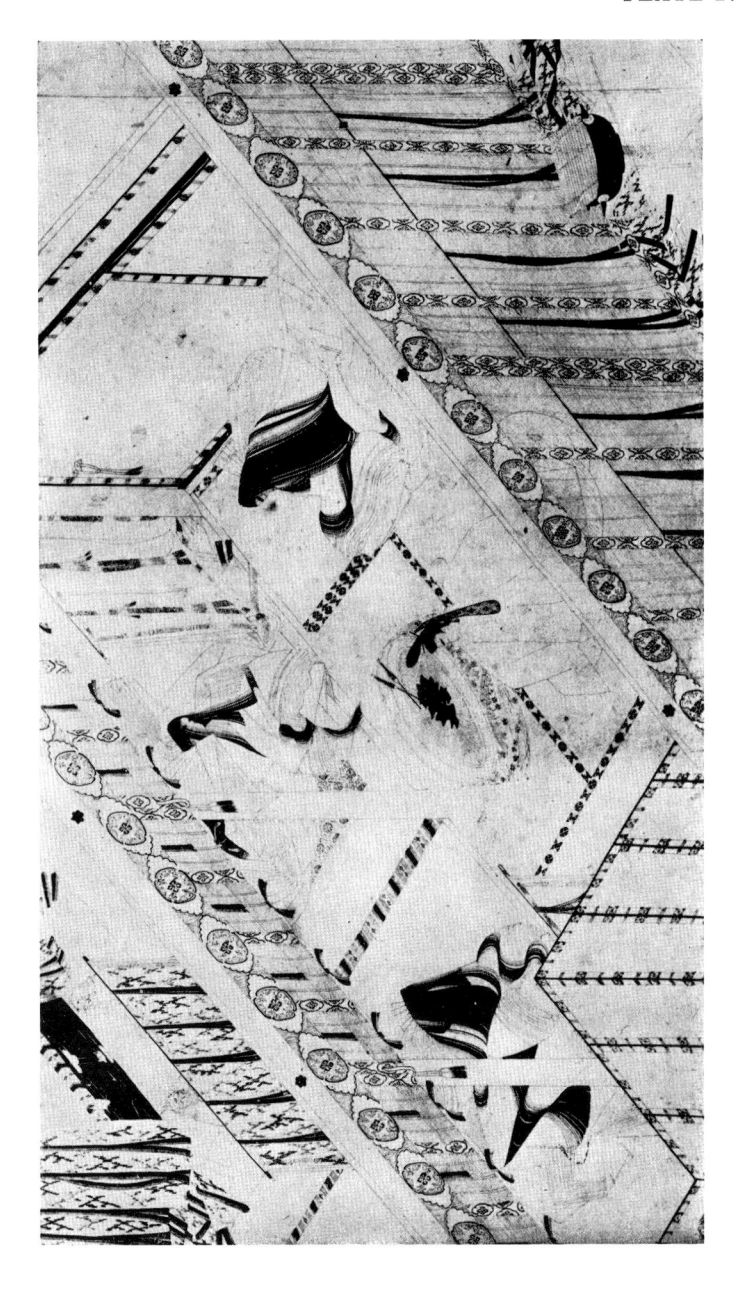

PLATE 28

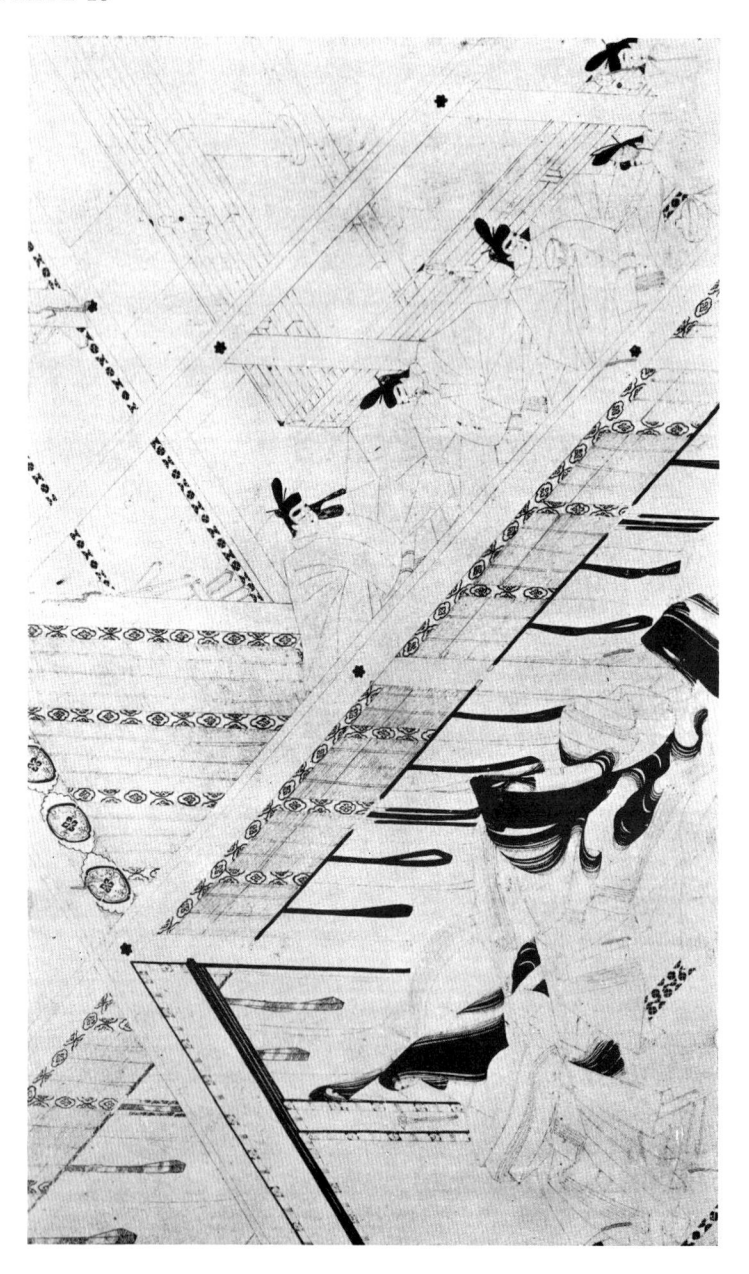

PLATE 29

PLATE 30

PLATE 31

PLATE 32

PLATE 33